D1154542

ALSO BY DOUG BRADLEY

DEROS Vietnam: Dispatches from the Air-Conditioned Jungle

With Craig Werner: *We Gotta Get Out of This Place: The Soundtrack of the Vietnam War*

Praise for *Who'll Stop the Rain*

"America's experience [in Vietnam] impacted its post-World War II global leadership in every way. And it taught us hard lessons about humility...Even more critically, the Vietnam experience forced America to reexamine the limitations of its great power. In *Who'll Stop the Rain: Respect, Remembrance, and Reconciliation in Post-Vietnam America*, Doug Bradley takes the reader into these coveys of shared national interests and public memory in very real, and very human, ways."
— Chuck and Tom Hagel, decorated Vietnam veterans

In a nation in danger of fracturing, Vietnam veteran Doug Bradley's latest book is a brave and invaluable attempt to bring us back together. Combining his personal experience, the music of the Vietnam era, and an eagerness to listen sympathetically to a broad spectrum of American voices, Bradley has produced a potent medicine for a sick nation.
— H. Bruce Franklin, author of *Vietnam and Other American Fantasies* and *Crash Course: From the Good War to the Forever War*

"For each Vietnam Veteran and their families there is a personal truth that sometimes clashes with the public truth about this divisive conflict. What Doug Bradley has done for the past decade-plus is use music as a way to bring together a population that can be so easily pulled apart. The popular music of the Vietnam Era acts as a glue, a shared common experience that veterans and others can use as a starting point to more meaningful discussions about their experiences and their personal place in the story of this war. The real world episodes in Bradley's book are powerful, and reminders that we are always much closer than we think."
— Jeff Kollath, Executive Director, Stax Museum of American Soul Music

"Doug Bradley once again reminds us why we should want to know more about the Vietnam War and its impact on our nation. *Who'll Stop the Rain* is a first-hand, compelling, important story by a very talented writer."
— U.S. Army General Martin Dempsey (retired), former Chairman of the Joint Chiefs of Staff

WHO'LL STOP THE RAIN

RESPECT, REMEMBRANCE, AND RECONCILIATION IN POST-VIETNAM AMERICA

by Doug Bradley

WARRIORS PUBLISHING GROUP
NORTH HILLS, CALIFORNIA

WHO'LL STOP THE RAIN

A Warriors Publishing Group book/published by arrangement with the author

PRINTING HISTORY
Warriors Publishing Group edition/December 2019

Warriors Publishing Group
16129 Tupper Street
North Hills, California 91343

Library of Congress Control Number: 2019953875
ISBN: 978-1-944353-28-5 (hardcover); 29-2 (paperback)
The name "Warriors Publishing Group" and the logo are
trademarks belonging to Warriors Publishing Group

10 9 8 7 6 5 4 3 2 1

Dedication

To the voices we still need to hear,
and the hearts we still need to heal

CONTENTS

PRELUDE

Memories are powerful reminders of our past that help shape and define our future. Fifty years ago, when the two of us arrived in the Republic of Vietnam, little did we know just how much our experiences there would affect our lives...and how we would come to see the world. Our service in Vietnam brought us together with many young, innocent Army privates from across America, none of us having any idea what awaited us in this far away, Southeast Asian land. It was no different for all the men and women who served in Vietnam—and for our nation and its future leaders as well. In a way, Vietnam imprinted all of us.

And it still does.

Our one constant in Vietnam was music. It was our relief and calm companion. The songs that blared from Armed Forces Radio—Otis Redding's "Dock of the Bay," Aretha Franklin's "Respect," and so many others—were our lifeline and stayed with us, not just for the twelve months of our tours in Vietnam, but, in many cases, for the rest of our lives. Like everyone who connects music with memories, when we Vietnam veterans hear those songs today, we are immediately transported back to that war. "Who'll Stop the Rain" by Creedence Clearwater Revival is another of those iconic songs, but in this book by fellow Vietnam veteran Doug Bradley, it's more than that.

Loneliness is a part of every war, and Vietnam was no different. Soldiers quickly become each other's families. This was particularly meaningful in Vietnam because it was the *only* war America fought in which we employed and replaced soldiers on an individual basis, *not* as part of a cohesive unit organized, trained, and deployed together *before, during, and after* their time in country. We left Vietnam the same way we came over—with a hundred-odd, uniformed strangers, guys whose departure dates simply matched ours. We learned later that this was not the best way to fight a war against a highly committed adversary.

Like all nations and individuals, we need to learn from these and other lessons, some very painful, and apply those lessons to building a better future. Vietnam is a good case in point. America's experience there impacted its post-World War II global leadership in every way. And it taught us hard lessons about humility, reminded the nation of the critical importance of its allies, and reinforced the centerpiece of the common interests of the post WWII world order. Even more critically, the Vietnam experience forced America to reexamine the limitations of its great power. In *Who'll Stop the Rain*, Doug Bradley takes the reader into these coveys of shared national interests and public memory in very real, and very human, ways.

In the end, the Vietnam War changed every institution in America. It also marked the first time the nation began to critically question its government and its leaders. The lies and deceit practiced during that volatile time also brought to light social injustice and an adverse system that had gone unchecked for too long, claiming the lives of more than 58,000 soldiers whose names are listed on the Vietnam War Memorial. The war drove two U.S. Presidents from office...and yet America survived.

But have we really learned the lessons of the war in Vietnam?

For us, one of the primary lessons gained during those years of war and national unrest is that we must always hold our leaders accountable. Character, honesty, and principles matter. They are not debatable virtues. If we fail to stay true to that governing North Star of leadership, as we did during the Vietnam War years, we will again fail our country. The men and women who gave their lives for their country in Vietnam, and in all our wars, deserve better. *Who'll Stop the Rain* helps remind us that we need to remain dedicated to this proposition.

— Chuck and Tom Hagel, Fall 2018

U.S. Army NCOs Tom and Chuck Hagel atop an M113 armored personnel carrier, Mekong Delta, Vietnam, 1968. (Photo courtesy Chuck Hagel)

Brothers Chuck and Tom Hagel served together in an Army rifle platoon in Vietnam in 1968. Both were wounded several times and saved each other's lives on numerous occasions. Chuck Hagel later served as a U.S. Senator from Nebraska (1997–2009) and as the 24th U.S. Secretary of Defense (2013–15). Tom Hagel is professor emeritus at the University of Dayton School of Law. He is Acting Judge for the Dayton Municipal Court; a commissioner on the Montgomery County, Ohio, Veterans' Service Commission; and a member of the American Bar Association's Committee on Training Trial Advocates.

OVERTURE
"Can I Get a Witness"

The stage was set, literally. After 26 months on the road and near-ly 100 presentations—all different, each special—Craig Werner, my co-author on *We Gotta Get Out of This Place: The Soundtrack of the Vietnam War*, and I were preparing to stand down. But not without a stirring sendoff over Veterans Day Weekend 2017, compliments of the talented folks at Twin Cities Public Television (TPT) in St. Paul, Minnesota.

So, there we stood, in front of 250 paying customers—veterans, family members, peace advocates, music lovers, baby boomers, and others. Behind us, an all-star band of 11 seasoned musicians led by pianist Dan Chouinard prepared a set comprising every-thing from a blistering Hendrix "Purple Haze" guitar solo to an angry "Eve of Destruction" and a haunting "Bridge Over Troubled Water." And there wasn't a dry eye in the room when Jerry Rau, a lo-cal Vietnam veteran and street musician who'd been away from the stage for five years, stepped up to the mic to play a moving acoustic version of "Leaving on a Jet Plane." Nineteen iconic songs in all, closing with The Animals' "We Gotta Get Out of This Place," a song that numerous 'Nam vets refer to as "the Vietnam veterans national anthem."

Alongside Craig and me were ten local vets prepared to give life to the powerful "solos" we'd included in *We Gotta Get Out of This Place*, special reminiscences from GIs in bunkers, helicopters, and hooches, triggered by tunes as varied as "The Letter," "For What It's Worth," and "Fortunate Son."

As vocalist Julius Collins mesmerized the audience with a Mar-vin Gaye-esque rendition of "What's Going On," I thought back to the story of Marvin and his Vietnam veteran brother Frankie Gaye and how Marvin wrote "What's Going On" for Frankie when he returned home to America. Momentarily, it's as if Julius and Marvin are singing a duet because the soothing sound of Marvin Gaye seems audible too, reminding me of the importance of having a witness.

And bearing witness.

Doug Bradley (gesturing) and Craig Werner in the classroom.
Madison, Wisconsin. Photo courtesy Emily Auerbach.

Knowing the Gaye brothers' Pentecostal upbringing, I have a deeper appreciation for the concept of witness, which has less to do with the lover's cry in Marvin's hit record, "Can I Get A Witness," than with Marvin and Frankie's lives growing up in black churches. Marvin's 1963 song brought the idea of *witnessing* to hundreds of thousands of listeners like me who'd never entered a black church. Like Marvin, all three members of the Holland-Dozier-Holland songwriting team shared a background in Gospel music. Lamont Dozier explained to *New Musical Express* magazine that "gospel music influenced myself and the Holland brothers because it was the thing you had to do every Sunday—go to church. Black gospel music was part of the lifestyle."

Hell, yes. When the preacher in a Black church asks, "Can I Get A Witness?" he's asking the congregation for affirmation. Often, a chorus of voices shouts back "Amen!" So too when a Vietnam veteran like Dan Naylor shares something private and powerful about his military service when he hears Brook Benton sing "Rainy Night in Georgia."

I've been seeking my own "Amen" of sorts for decades—from my Vietnam and post-Vietnam experiences to more than a decade of interviews with Vietnam veterans about their music-based memories for *We Gotta Get Out of This Place: The Soundtrack of the Vietnam War,* and more than two years of book presentations nationwide. The Amens sometimes came as a pause, or a nod, sometimes a smile, a bowed head, or tears. But they came, and they kept on coming. The music had called to Vietnam vets in ways nothing else had.

Something was happening here, Craig and I realized, and while it wasn't always "exactly clear" what it was, what we were witnessing lacked the customary ugliness, pain, and acrimony that characterized too many conversations about Vietnam. The music of the 1960s and early 1970s helped all audience members, veterans primarily, to feel safe and accepted. Everyone listened respectfully. No one pointed fingers. The affirmation of the veterans' experience—whether it was in Vietnam, Thailand, Japan, Germany, Korea, or Kansas—and the respite from judgment meant more than todays' formulaic *thank you for your service* phrase, which doesn't come close to addressing what servicemen and women have endured. The musical affirmations, and Amens, pointed to a way out of America's Vietnam quandary.

Part of the reason for this is because military combat experience is, in some ways, non-verbal, as is music. It calls for a musician-veteran like Country Joe McDonald to describe it.

"Music can help explain some of the military experience like nothing else can, especially for civilians," the former Navy sailor and consummate hippie told us when we interviewed him in his Berkeley home in 2009. "This is something more than entertainment. Music is equated with art and prayer...it's a spiritual experience."

But not everyone gets or understands the connection, added Joe, whose best-known song, "I-Feel-Like-I'm-Fixin'-To-Die-Rag" has been widely misunderstood for more than 50 years.

"The song is irreverent, but not political," Joe explained. "It blames leaders and parents, *not* soldiers. It's not a pacifist song, but a soldier's song...gallows humor...only a soldier could get away with it. A lot of Vietnam vets told me I'd put together what they were thinking but didn't know how to say. The 'Rag' kept them from losing their minds."

Another reason behind music's effectiveness has to do with how the music of the Vietnam era expands our sense of what happened and what it meant beyond the usually simplistic versions of the story that have taken over popular myth and memory (see Counterpoint section for more on Vietnam myths). When veterans share their response to a particular song, they broaden and deepen our sense of what Vietnam meant, and means. The binaries that separated America during the Vietnam era, many of which—right or wrong, hawk or dove, war or peace—continue to divide us today, weren't present in the places we presented. Yes, our audiences had self-selected—they chose to engage with us in churches, bookstores, VA Hospitals, museums and more—thus they do not speak for, nor represent, all veterans or non-veterans. But in all those settings and during all those conversations, the conflict and trauma so identified with Vietnam had left the room.

Was it just the music? Or the music and something more?

Waves of exhilaration, exhaustion, and sorrow came at me as I left the stage at TPT that Veterans Day weekend in 2017. It was then I realized that I needed to write *Who'll Stop the Rain* to share what I had witnessed and to exemplify the power of "call and response" in the Vietnam unburdening for the thousands of men and women who joined us and shared their personal stories. And I wanted America to appreciate how Vietnam veterans, either individually or in groups, were thriving and were promoting therapeutic activities like writing groups, veterans courts, tribal canoe journeys, art, musical composition and more, to help make themselves and their communities complete.

The sections of *Who'll Stop the Rain* reflect the themes that emerged most noticeably in the post-presentation conversations. One overriding refrain is that, for many vets and the society around them, feelings of guilt, shame, misunderstanding, and bitterness keep them stuck, mired in an unchanging past. In order to overcome this paralysis, each individual must be able to express his or her experience as honestly as possible. Only then can we begin to take responsibility for our present and future, both of which we can change. Each section of *Who'll Stop the Rain* emphasizes a particular part of that recovery process and is contextually framed by relevant books, films, music, and solos from veterans and others. Recurring topics include PTSD, survivor guilt, healing, the legacies of the war, lessons learned and unlearned, and public memory. Again, music was both comfort blanket and connective tissue, the non-verbal prompt to the vets' stories and their link to their peers who stayed and didn't serve.

Sonata, "I'll Take You There," emphasizes the myriad *calls and responses* we witnessed. From our first event at Harvard University in October 2015 to the Stax Museum of American Soul Music in Memphis that November to the Rock & Roll Hall of Fame in Cleveland and scores of presentations in 2016 and 2017, this chapter demonstrates how profoundly embedded call and response was in the audience reaction to *We Gotta Get Out of This Place*.

Counterpoint, "Waist Deep in the Big Muddy," examines the way politically motivated myths about the Vietnam war and the veteran experience short-circuit the recovery process for all of us and demonstrates how our presentations could circumvent that gridlock. It highlights stories that reflect the real complexities of vets' political understanding of what they did and what's happened since Vietnam. A consideration of movies and monuments focuses on how America's public memory of Vietnam often contradicts the realities experienced by Vietnam veterans.

Adagio, "Blame It on My Youth," focuses on the debilitating impact of guilt, shame, and bitterness that leaves both veterans and the society around them "waist deep in the big muddy." Survivor guilt often lands vets, and non-vets too, in turbulent waters—and PTSD keeps too many veterans there.

Rondo, "Time to Lay it Down," demonstrates how veterans, either individually or in groups, are promoting therapeutic activities necessary for them and for society. From writing groups and veterans courts to musical composition and more, Vietnam veterans are helping to transform themselves and their communities.

Da Capo, "Who'll Stop the Rain?" features a chorus of voices from veterans and non-veterans who want to stop the deluge of post-Vietnam antipathy. Together these voices intimate new possibilities for understanding the legacy of Vietnam and, ultimately, for bringing the men and women who served their country in that divisive war home for good.

At its heart, *Who'll Stop the Rain* tries to resolve an unsettling question, one that veterans, civilians, and all Americans must answer. Namely this—if we can't stop the rain, if we can't bring about understanding, shape a shared public memory, provide healing, and give succor and redress to our veterans and their Vietnam legacy, then who in the hell can?

Or as Country Joe told me: "The only people who know about war are the people who fight wars. Why aren't people talking to them? If you want to know about killing people...I mean...Jesus Christ. War veterans are all over the fucking place...all you have to do is ask them."

SONATA

"I'll Take You There"

I know a place, y'all (I'll take you there)
Ain't nobody cryin' (I'll take you there)
Ain't nobody worried (I'll take you there)...

—Al Bell, "I'll Take You There",
sung by The Staple Singers (1972)

When you're in the Stax Museum of American Soul Music in Memphis, Tennessee, it's like being in church. Especially if you're lucky enough to be on stage in the famous Studio A, where so many of the classic Stax hits were recorded. Craig and I were there on Veterans Day 2015, right after the release of our book, *We Gotta Get Out of This Place: The Soundtrack of the Vietnam War*. Basking in the glow of Studio A, you feel the presence of Otis Redding, Carla Thomas, Isaac Hayes, and so many other musical giants. You sense the pull that "Dock of the Bay" had for so many homesick, lonesome soldiers stationed in Vietnam. You grasp the fabric of black music in America.

And you can hear the call, as if it were coming from the pulpit, a voice that sings out "I know a place," and you instinctively voice the response "I'll take you there," as if Mavis Staples herself were calling to you. It's a Stax song and a gospel song and a 1969 reggae hit ("The Liquidator"), but most of all, it's a call to close your eyes and listen to the Staples family—Mavis and her sisters Cleotha and Yvonne and their father "Pops." Hearing their voices call, you can't help but respond vocally, emotionally, and spiritually.

I felt it all swirling in Studio A that night as we presented to about 100 Memphis locals, many of them Vietnam veterans, the audience about half white and half black. We'd structured our part of the evening—one of the more than 100 others we'd conduct during our two plus years on the road—upon the African American practice of **call and response**. Our *call* would be an iconic song like "Dock of the Bay" or "Soul Man" and the music-based memory it elicited in a Vietnam veteran, while the audience *response*, be it verbal, musical, or physical—anything that puts the reply across—would usually affirm the veteran's strong attachment to the particular song. Beyond that, we designed the call and response dynamic to move the emphasis from the individual veteran to the broader community, making connections between the historical moment from Vietnam and the veterans' contemporary world.

That night at Stax, we began by playing songs with Tennessee and deep South connections—from the Elvis song "Heartbreak Hotel" and Aretha's "Chain of Fools" to Carl Perkins' "Blue Suede Shoes" and William Bell's "Marching Off to War." Since it's mentioned in the opening paragraph of chapter one of *We Gotta Get Out of This Place*, we threw in "Love Letters in the Sand" by Nashville's own Pat Boone. The veterans' interaction with the music created an intense emotional atmosphere shared by everyone in that sacred place.

"End of the Tour" concert at Twin Cities Public TV studios, November 2017. Photo courtesy Twin Cities Public TV.

The evening inaugurated our pattern: when the members of the audience added their own testimony to the vets' stories and the music, the collective heart commenced its beat. One by one—in voices sometimes quiet, sometimes defiant—the Memphis Vietnam vets responded to Elvis, Aretha, and others, remembered hearing Johnny Cash's "Ring of Fire" on an aircraft carrier in the Gulf of Tonkin or "Hold On I'm Comin'" by Stax artists Sam and Dave being covered by a pretty darn good Korean band at an Enlisted Men's club in the Central Highlands... even Pat Boone, whom I had a slight boy crush on when I saw him in the movie *April Love* in the late 1950s, got some love for his syrupy ballad, echoing the diversity of the Vietnam soundtrack.

We'd issued a call with the music and stories from *We Gotta Get Out of This Place*, and the audience was responding with their own stories, many of them never before voiced. The audience members, which included Cornell McFadden, a long-time Stax session drummer, listened intently and respectfully. We were thrilled, and relieved, realizing in our improvisational approach that maybe we'd hit on a variation on call and response that could serve as a presentational blueprint. For example, if a song like "We Gotta Get Out of This Place" spoke directly and personally to them—a call to the veterans—their response enabled connections to other soldiers and vets, and also to the folks back home. These connections helped them to deal with what was going on in their lives in Vietnam and back home. Maybe what was happening tonight—which would become the crux of *Who'll Stop the Rain*—showed that the book *We Gotta Get Out of This Place* was now the call and the response. Other veterans, family members, and non-vets were willing to share their own strong, personal reactions to the vets in the book, and to those in the room. It wasn't all Nirvana and kumbaya, but there was acceptance, understanding, courtesy, and safety in Studio A that showed us that music helps facilitate a better appreciation for Vietnam and the veteran experience.

Before that insight, though, we noticed that the Memphis vets were talking more to us—treating this session as more of a Q&A—than to each other. As a Vietnam vet, I understood how this stoic distancing worked. None of us wanted to hang ourselves out there publicly, if at all, for fear of another putdown or rejection. But then former Army Spec. 4 Henry Ford, Jr., clutching the hand of his beloved wife Alder, spontaneously burst into song, and you could damn near hear a pin drop.

I stand accused
Of lovin' you too much
And I hope, I hope it's not a crime
'Cause if it is, I'm guilty
Of lovin' you, you, you . . .

Isaac Hayes in front of Stax Studios. Photo courtesy
Stax Museum of American Soul Music.

All of us—authors, audience, and probably the ghost of Isaac Hayes, who'd recorded that song for Stax—were hooked, united in that moment as Henry, now momentarily back in Vietnam almost 50 years earlier, was channeling his loneliness, confusion, and heartache through the song. It wasn't just that Henry communicated how "I Stand Accused" meant Vietnam for him; it was the way he instinctively sang, vocalizing so sweetly and harmoniously as if he were alone, back in Vietnam.

In his rendering of "I Stand Accused," Henry was expressing more than just the unrequited love of a man "chillin' on the witness stand" or for someone else's woman; he was mourning the loss of innocence, the loss of a war, and the accusation and blame often associated with Vietnam veterans, especially black Vietnam veterans like him. "We stand accused," Henry Ford seemed to be saying, found guilty by the rest of America for what went down in Vietnam.

What a sweet, deep voice and rhythmic rendering. Then he stopped. There was some spontaneous applause, but, more importantly, the audience responded with looks of recognition and understanding...of welcoming home.

Henry's song was a dramatic call that elicited potent responses. These, in turn, brought forth new responses as the Studio A conversation went where it needed to go—to honest exchanges, to the differences in the white and black Vietnam soldier experience, to protest, to racism, to compassion. We observed a lively exchange between two veterans, one black, one white, comparing memories on who'd heard the better cover version of Sam and Dave's "Soul Man" at Long Binh Post and assumed, given their laughter and high fives, they knew each other—only to discover they'd just met that night.

Depending on the circumstances in Vietnam—and the year or years when you were there—music could serve to unite or divide. We were told of many occasions where the music black and white soldiers listened to and played was at the center of disagreements and could either bring opposing forces—and musical tastes—together, or send them to their respective corners to come out fighting. Tom Stern, a native of rural Wisconsin who had little contact with blacks before entering the army, remembered one night in Vietnam when a Korean band ended its set "by playing all the Stax tunes."

"This white GI starts using the N word all over the place," Stern recalled. "He's shouting: 'Fucking gooks, all they can play is this fucking nigger music.'"

Needless to say, it didn't end well for Stern and the few white soldiers who were still in the club, and there was a whiff of this disconnect in the air at Stax that night. During his second tour in Vietnam as a brigade commander with the 2nd Infantry Division, Colin Powell came to realize the critical role the jukebox played in race relations.

"The whites wanted rock and country and western," he told Bill Harris in *The Hellfighters of Harlem*, "and the blacks wanted soul, Aretha and Dionne Warwick. The issue got so testy that we summoned the bar owners to see if we could work out a fair formula. They finally agreed that they would feature roughly seven 'white' songs for every three 'black' songs. As a result of this compromise, the whites were unhappy only thirty percent of the time, and the blacks seventy percent."

There's no record of how well, or poorly, Powell's compromise worked, but for Chicano soldiers like Charley Trujillo that wasn't much of a solution. "Where was *our* music?" Charley would remark more than once during our conversations. He pointed out that it wasn't until the arrival of the rock band Santana in the late 1960s that any Latino music got much airplay. Out in the field, troops were united, serving as one. But in the rear, after a few beers or more, well, you needed music to soothe you, speak to you, or transport you to another place. If it didn't, then somebody, someone of a different color, was to blame.

By the time I arrived in Vietnam in late 1970, it seemed like the Army was divided in two, one white Army and one black, a situation exacerbated by the assassination of Dr. Martin Luther King, Jr. in April 1968 and the emergence of the Black Power movement. Black soldiers in Vietnam would take several minutes to DAP with one another—a friendly gesture of greeting, agreement, or solidarity—while others formed groups like the Minority Servicemen's Association, Black Brothers United, the Zulu 1200s, De Mau Mau, and the Black Liberation Front of the Armed Forces. As the renowned journalist Wallace Terry, author of *Bloods*, told *People* magazine in 1987, "In his famous 1963 speech at the Lincoln Memorial, Dr. King said he had a dream that one day the sons of former slaves and sons of slave owners would sit at the same table. That dream came true in only one place, the front lines of Vietnam."

Still, at the end of the day we all were brothers. Our blood was the same color, and we'd all suffered to some degree. We heard that in the music, and we heard it in the voice of Henry Ford, Jr. as he channeled his best Isaac Hayes.

"Witnessing," both as an activity and a process, was constant during our many months of touring and presenting on *We Gotta Get Out of This Place*. From here on, the call and response undercurrents we observed that night in Memphis would reappear, endlessly varied, in museums, hospitals, classrooms, VFW posts, radio and TV studios, community centers, and churches nationwide, as the individual and collective musically merged, separated, merged again.

The Stax Museum experience initiated a pattern that played out from Denver to Durham, from Seattle to St. Paul and everywhere in between, as "question and answer" sessions became "call and response" sessions. Regardless of the size of the audience or the venue, veterans and their fellow audience members spoke up and listened and shared and, in a very real way, found comfort.

Similar moments had occurred during our decade of research and interviews for *We Gotta Get Out of This Place* when Craig and I interviewed an individual veteran and he or she responded movingly and personally to an evocative song. The most powerful of these testimonials became the basis for the more than 30 "solos" we included in *We Gotta Get Out of This Place*, serving as the veterans' unfiltered witness. Often during our presentations we read from one or more of these solos and received intense, emotional responses from the audience. I'll be sprinkling solos throughout *Who'll Stop the Rain*, beginning with one in which Henry Ford expands on the memories released by "I Stand Accused."

SOLO   Henry Ford, Jr.

"I Stand Accused" was always a favorite of mine, although there was a time when I didn't appreciate Isaac Hayes like I should've. Me and some of the guys I grew up with in Memphis used to pretend we were him...we'd imitate something of his and would call it 'Ike's Rap' when we'd talk and sing like he did. Oh my... Later my buddies and I would do that in Vietnam, trading versions of the song as if we had our own special take on what the song meant...

But I was sensing something else that night in Memphis at the Stax Museum when y'all were there...something strong I had to respond to. My wife Alder being by my side, thank God for her and her love which got me through and past Vietnam... and the spirits of Robert Earl Hunt, John Ed Cunningham, Jr., and other young men I grew up with in Memphis whose names are now on the wall of the Vietnam Veterans Memorial in D. C. That pain, and that realization, just tore me up, and well, 'Ike's rap," an Isaac Hays song, seemed the best way at that moment to channel my feelings. It wasn't a black thing or an us versus them thing...But I doubt if many of the white guys I was in Vietnam with would've busted out that Isaac Hayes song to express what they were feeling.

Besides praying, which I did a lot of, music was how I got by in Vietnam. There was just so much good music and it could hook you in the heart and, well, it kept you going...

I got drafted immediately after I dropped out of college during my sophomore year at Memphis State University. I was hoping to be assigned to Fort Gordon in Georgia after my basic training at Fort Campbell, Kentucky. I wanted to be an MP (military police), but I got shipped to Fort Polk, Louisiana with an MOS of 11 Charlie—combat mortar man! By January 1970, I'd just turned 20 years old and I'm in Vietnam.

My first few months in country were fine, but then we—my unit was the 1st of the 22nd Infantry—got sent into Cambodia in May of 1970! That was scary and crazy. Being from Memphis, I was a big Stax fan at that time, and I remember the night before we were supposed to leave Cambodia listening to Eddie Floyd's song "California Girl" over and over. Every time I think about that day I think of that song. That's because the next day I got hit—suffered multiple injuries and was medevacked to a place called Jackson Hole and then to a hospital at Qui Nhon. Spent about a month recovering, but after they patched me up, they sent me back into the jungle as an 11 Bravo, a grunt. Oh, the army tried so hard to kill me...

My unit was called *The Regulars*, and on June 20, we were waging the Battle of the Rock, the largest battle that year for the 1st of the 22nd Infantry. We were in the rugged, triple-canopy mountainous terrain of Binh Dinh Province, north of An Khe. I was 2nd Platoon Bravo Company and was walking directly behind our Kit Carson (Vietnamese) scout as we stumbled upon a reinforced unit of the North Vietnamese Army. I kept asking him if those were RA (Regular Army) soldiers we were seeing in front of us. We couldn't be sure...and then all hell broke loose. Those NVA guys stood their ground. The fighting was fierce and intense. I've never experienced anything like that in my life... Lord, we lived like animals...but I survived.

My wife and I recently watched Steven Spielberg's move *The Post* about newspapers and Watergate and all the rest. I was just so blown away by the lies. I mean, I got the domino theory. I understood it, but the government and the military had given up on Vietnam long before I went over, and hundreds of thousands of other guys too. Why were we there? Why did they lie to us?

All living moments teach us things about ourselves. I learned I was able to endure, what I was capable of, in Vietnam. I didn't think I could do that, but I did, and I learned something about myself...I'm a survivor, but I still gotta keep on going. I gotta sing my song..."

Listening to Henry, you don't come away with an overwhelming sense of bitterness or anger. It feels more like a quiet affirmation of hope, the belief Mavis Staples expressed when she sang "I'll take you there." Whatever it is, it's kept him alive, kept him strong.

Henry's confession tapped into a reservoir of serious and sometimes painful memories—one vet came near tears describing his years of drugs, drinking, and self-accusation. But there were lighter moments, too. A tall, white GI standing in the back of Studio A recalled that while working in one of the large mail receiving stations in Vietnam, he and the other clerks would occasionally "liberate" an expensive stereo or tape deck sent from Japan (the PACEX catalogue was an abundance of mail order riches) to a U.S. soldier in Vietnam. As he explained that night, he and his fellow workers would make sure the deliveries from Japan were insured so that, eventually, a soldier would get his piece of stereo equipment. "It would just be a little delayed is all," he admitted, with only a semi-guilty smile.

Drawing on the experience and insights of the entire community, calls and responses like Henry's aren't simply aesthetic. They form the living, breathing core of African American existence. While the individual does play a crucial role in generating action—his or her carefully crafted call can motivate their peers, even spark demonstrations—the individual does not necessarily maintain control. It requires the members of the congregation, or an audience like ours in Memphis, to recognize their own experiences in the call. Sometimes the responses can reject a call or draw attention to something the preacher or singer has overlooked—the Vietnam veteran's experience for example. The best responses challenge the larger community to take the original call deeper, act on it, make it real.

Thus, the response to a call can affirm, argue, redirect the dialogue, raise a new question. Any response that elicits a response becomes a new call. But, both in its political contexts and in its more strictly musical settings, call and response moves the emphasis from the individual to the community.

Our presentations embodied what Isaac Hayes, Aretha Franklin, Sam Cooke, and a host of other musicians had been doing for years, consciously or unconsciously. For their call to work, they had to receive a response, be it the rallying cry of the community around them, or around some political leader or preacher calling them to action. There were a few rejoinders of "Yes, Lord," and "Tell it!" when Henry Ford, Jr. sang "I Stand Accused" that night. Shades of Reverend King, Mahalia Jackson, and James Brown, a tradition that continues in the classic soul samples of the hip hop music listened to by my son and daughter.

In its purest form, call and response exists in the interaction between people present with one another in the real world. But the underlying dynamic can be recreated in various ways, including recordings in which background singers or choirs stand in for the community. Even in the studio, the best gospel and soul records sound *live* because they capture the irrepressible energy of call and response. The producers and musicians like Sam Cooke and Berry Gordy who turned gospel into Stax soul and Motown number-one hits never forgot the principle. That's why these records were never just commercial products, and why they remain emotional reservoirs for vets.

Craig, who spent 36 years of his academic career in the Department of African American Studies at UW-Madison concentrating on issues of race, remarked that the Memphis exchanges marked "the most honest conversation about race I've ever been a part of." That inspired us to place call and response at the heart of what we would do in our post-presentation conversations for the next two years. Structurally, it followed this pattern:

Hearing the call: It all starts with a call, either from us or from a veteran's song, story, or memory. Hearing that call can require some contextual information—history, biography, etc.—which we were able to supply through the hundreds of Vietnam vets we interviewed for *We Gotta Get Out of This Place*. But truly "hearing the call" demands active listening, audience members fully concentrating on what is being said.

Responding to the call: Responses can agree, or disagree, with any aspect of the "call," saying "yes, but" or connecting the moment to the contemporary world or commenting on links with other written or musical texts, or the audience members' own knowledge. These responses then become new calls from individuals to the other members of the community—in this instance the Stax recording studio in Memphis. While we didn't openly choreograph it, the audience often framed their contribution to the conversation as a response to a previous call.

Exploring the calls and responses: Exploration often occurs in a more structured environment such as a classroom. We spoke with students in classes at Loyola University, Wabash College, the University of Texas at San Marcos, Rhodes College, and others. But exploring the calls also occurred naturally in multiple public settings, because these settings had evolved into safe spaces where we could trust audience members to validate, and respect, what they'd heard. In this way, audience members could respond directly to one another without our interpreting, or parsing, what they'd heard. For the most part, Craig and I tried to shift the focus from the stage to the audience.

One of our favorite touch points for understanding this dynamic comes from the talented African American jazz musician Herbie Hancock. Explaining how the legendary Miles Davis would put together his jazz bands, Hancock noted that "Miles brought interesting people together in a room and let us do our thing. But if we were heading into chaos or a dead-end, he'd play a few notes and swerve us away from the cliff."

Vietnam was a steep enough cliff, and we did our best to keep the conversations from heading into chaos or finger pointing. Frequently, we'd mix in another song to help redirect the energy. Of course, none of this was by the numbers. And since we placed a premium on discovery and surprise, there was a lot of improvisation. But it was what was happening.

Henry Ford, Jr., had shown us that, as did Isaac Hayes, Otis Redding, Aretha Franklin, Wilson Pickett, Carla Thomas, and all the great Memphis and Stax artists. So too did the Staple Singers on "I'll Take You There" with its haunting, gospel-infused refrain. I kept hearing that song in my head, not just because of that catchphrase, but because it was pure, unadulterated call and response. And, like so many great songs steeped in gospel, blues, and country traditions, "I'll Take You There" struck a resonant note with me, harkening back to my own Vietnam and my own response to the call to serve...and now to here, to Memphis and the Stax Studio that felt like the culmination of a long pilgrimage to the rock-and-roll holy land.

While my Memphis epiphany infused everything that came after, it also reinforced patterns that had begun to emerge during our very first presentation in late October at the Mahindra Humanities Center at Harvard University. Our talk was sponsored by Harvard's Committee on Ethnicity, Migration, and Rights. According to Gregory Dunne's *The War that Won't Go Away*, "Of the 1,200 men in the Harvard class of 1970, only 56 served in the military, just two in Vietnam." It sure didn't seem like the proper place to do our first *We Gotta Get Out of This Place* public presentation. But, that's where we were, at 5 p.m. on a late October afternoon in 2015, and the curtain was going up whether I liked it or not.

But like it I did, in part because Harvard had invited University of Massachusetts professor and Vietnam scholar Christian Appy, author of *Working Class War* and *Patriots*, to serve as moderator. The surprisingly large crowd included an abundance of grey-haired Baby Boomers and scores of eager students of all races and genders and outfits. There were a good number of Vietnam veterans in the audience, and they shared their own insights on "Leaving on a Jet Plane" and "What's Going On." One of them offered his own take on James Brown's 1968 tour of Vietnam. And to our surprise, Peter Davis—the director of the 1974 Academy Award-winning documentary film about Vietnam, *Hearts and Minds*—was in the audience. He introduced us to a young Cambodian woman who was making a documentary about her country during, and after, the war in Vietnam.

Was it working? Hell, yes! *The Harvard Crimson* reporter who was there observed that "during the event, the audience, which was dominated by members of the Baby Boomer generation, sang along to hits by artists such as Bruce Springsteen and Aretha Franklin." Plus, our call brought an unexpected response from the diverse audience and made us aware of other calls, like the young Cambodian filmmaker's. While Harvard wasn't quite a Memphis-type call and response, it wasn't just a Q&A session between experts and audience. It was more of a dialogue, a shared, safe conversation. As we'd soon learn, audience responses varied greatly with context, especially the cultural grounding of particular settings. Nevertheless, the evening at Harvard marked the beginning of calls and responses, of veteran testimonials and international connections.

What happened at Memphis and Harvard occurred repeatedly during the next two plus years, in venues large and small, in spaces overwhelming and intimate. From a grass roots arts center in Ventura, California to the King Veterans Home in Waupaca, Wisconsin; from the studios of Twin Cities Public Television in St. Paul to a hallowed chamber in the Library of Congress, there came a chorale of responses to the songs and veterans' stories. For sure the setting and venue mattered—the "First Draft" space in the Changing Hands Bookstore in Phoenix, Arizona, for example, featured a brew pub, hence the audience was, shall we say, a little more steeped in the presentation than the pious parishioners of St. Luke's Lutheran Church in Middleton, Wisconsin. And here's where the extraordinary variety and diversity of the music and stories shined. If we were in the Elliott Bay Book Company in Seattle, for example, we could play songs by Vietnam veterans we'd interviewed from that part of the country and highlight hit records made by artists and groups from that area. Thus, we were able to riff on the classic '60s instrumental "Walk Don't Run" by the Ventures, who hailed from nearby Tacoma, sprinkling anecdotes by vets who'd heard that song played by the many Vietnamese, Korean, or Filipino cover bands in Vietnam, alongside Army medic Allyn Lepeska's recollection of hearing "Angel of the Morning" by Seattle's own Merrilee Rush on the Dawn Buster show on AFVN, the Armed Forces Vietnam Network radio broadcast. Of course, we zeroed in on music by Seattle's greatest talent, Jimi Hendrix, including "Purple Haze," "Machine Gun," and "All Along the Watchtower."

By contrast, the St. Luke's playlist had a more spiritual flavor, highlighted by Bob Dylan's "With God on Our Side" and Sam Cooke's "A Change is Gonna Come." We shared many local vets' music memories from the book, a few of whom were members of Middleton's VFW Post 8216. The quantity, quality, and variety of great music during the Vietnam era allowed us to establish deep connections with local audiences and amplify riveting veteran anecdotes like that of Burke Salsi, a Vietnam vet who was in my graduating class at Thomas Jefferson High School outside Pittsburgh in 1965. Serving in the "brown-water Navy," Salsi recalled "there was no spit and polish in the rivers."

"Basically, the uniform was cut off shorts and boots. No shirt," he continued. "No concern of hygiene and shaving. You could only get a shower once in a while, and a lot of guys had wild crazy beards like Tom Hanks in the movie *Castaway*. The songs I loved in the rivers were on the Beatles' *White Album*. But there were lots of others. That's one thing we had. We had a PsyOps cassette player and learned that the Vietnamese liked the 5th Dimension more than the PsyOps tapes.

"Why does 'While My Guitar Gently Weeps' linger in my mind?" Salsi wondered. "I guess because of snipers and dodging B-40 rounds. And who's gonna be next, and does that have my name on it."

Nowhere was this more apparent than the evening we spent in March 2016 at VFW Post 101 in Craig's hometown of Colorado Springs, Colorado. Craig describes his hometown as "one-third military, one-third evangelical, and one-third hippie." For the evening, we'd put together a Rocky Mountain playlist reflecting that mix, featuring Denver East High School graduate Judy Collins's take on Dylan's "Masters of War," John Denver's version of "Leaving on a Jet Plane," and El Chicano's "Brown-Eyed Girl" in honor of the Chicano bands that had been a central part of the Colorado Springs rock scene. I was more nervous than usual, wanting to hit a home run in front of Craig's family, friends, and neighbors while anxious about the political polarizations in the room. A couple of Craig's old hippie carpenter pals were engaged in a friendly argument over who was farther to the left, and we knew that our Vietnam vet friend Jay Maloney was the most conservative of our attendees. Before we began, Jay introduced us to a local veteran activist who acknowledged that she'd been reluctant to attend because our book had received accolades from *Rolling Stone*, which she considered a source of leftist propaganda. And neither of us knew how to read the cluster of Iraq and Afghanistan vets from nearby Fort Carson, a key base during the Vietnam era and into the 21st century, who were there. Was this the night where the wheels would come off?

The event went well enough, somewhere in the middle of our range, elevated by Jay's tearful reading of his solo, which concludes *We Gotta Get Out of This Place*. I watched his wife Dawn reach over and touch him to give him the strength he needed to finish the story of how the death of his friend, nurse Sharon Lane, one of the small number of women killed in action in Vietnam, had haunted him over the years, and his determination to savor every moment remaining to him and his loved ones.

But the best part of the evening came after we'd finished signing books and adjourned to the basement of VFW 101 along with Jay, a handful of Iraq and Afghan vets, Craig's leftist friends Dan Croseey and Charles Waters, and, crucially, Joe Barrera, a Chicano veteran from south Texas who'd spent his year in Vietnam almost entirely in the field. Taking requests, Craig played songs on his computer and these spurred conversations about loneliness and anger, love and politics. Joe introduced us to Spanish-language songs that tugged at the heartstrings of his fellow Mexican-Americans (not yet "Chicanos" when he went to Vietnam). Jay brought the Top 40 from his youth in Rye, New York, to life. We talked about the Blood, Sweat, and Tears song "And When I Die," the Beach Boys' "Sloop John B," Martha and the Vandellas' "Jimmy Mack" ("When are you coming back?")," and pretty much every song in the Creedence Clearwater catalog covered by Craig's Colorado Springs band back in the 1970s. When politics entered the conversation, as it did when the playlist shifted to Edwin Starr's "War" and Tom Paxton's "Lyndon Johnson Told the Nation," the emphasis stayed with the vets rather than the politicians who'd turned their literal blood, sweat, and tears into ideological hash.

Joe Barrera, who served with Bravo Company, 1st Battalion, 8th Infantry, 4th Infantry Division, in the Central Highlands of South Vietnam, helped guide that evening's unique call and response. Among other things, Joe is the founder and publisher of *The Almagre Review/La Revista Almagre*, a Colorado literary journal that includes writing by veterans. "It's been fifty years since I came home, but how fresh the memories are," he told me, admitting he "felt sad" when his tour of duty was over. "I wanted to stay in Vietnam. I wanted to keep on fighting the war. For me it was not finished."

Is it ever?

SOLO   Joe Barrera

Vietnam veteran Joe Barrera. Photo courtesy Joe Barrera.

We were on the big jet but then they told us to get off. Quickly, we filed out of the plane and sheltered in the revetment next to the runway. The Viet Cong mortars landed some distance away. Our plane was not touched. We ran up the stairs of the Freedom

Bird and took our seats again. The pilots gunned the engines and we were airborne. The men cheered when the wheels left the ground. I sat in my seat silently. My tour of duty was over but I felt a strange emotion: I felt sad—I wanted to stay in Vietnam. I wanted to keep on fighting the war. For me it was not finished. I had come up against the wall, what every combat infantryman faces. I had stood there, pushed against that wall and overcome my fear, I had done my duty. But I had not done enough. I had not gone through the wall. Yes, I had stepped into it but I had not gone far enough into the other side. I had not finished my war. I had not been true to fallen comrades. The other soldiers didn't see it that way. They were just glad to go back to "the world," but I felt differently. "There must be something very wrong with me because I am not happy."

In Japan there was a layover. We went to the PX to buy duty-free cameras, radios, and, of course, liquor. The place was full of Marines on their way to Nam. Their uniforms were brand new, their buzz cuts very tight, their faces so young and innocent. "You'll be sorry," the other guys said to the youngsters.

It's been fifty years but how fresh the memories. We landed at Travis Air Base, late at night, the end of August, 1968. We cleared Customs, dumping the Cambodian Red and other contraband in the amnesty bins. Then they took us to a big warehouse and made us take showers. After that we filed down a row of tables and senior NCOs dressed us in new Class A uniforms. They had to help us put on the Army insignia, lining it up properly. We didn't remember how to do that, but nobody cared. The sergeants offered us the obligatory steak dinner. I was hungry and wanted it. But all the others loudly refused. Then buses pulled up and we were on our way to the Oakland airport. By this time the sun was up. How different "the world" looked.

In those days, you could walk up to any airline counter in any airport and pay cash for a one-way ticket and nobody took you for a terrorist. I paid $80.00 for a ticket to San Antonio. Finally, it started to sink in. I was going home. In the waiting area, people were sitting in what looked like school desks, the fronts fitted with single curved arms. At the ends of the arms were small black-and-white televisions. You could put a quarter in a slot and get fifteen minutes of TV time. Everybody was staring intently at the TVs. I stood behind one man and looked over his shoulder. Just then on the screen I saw a policeman in a white helmet with a raised club chasing a hippie, catching the long-haired young man and beating him mercilessly with the stick. It was a shock. I didn't know what to think. The violence sucked me in. I didn't want to but I was compelled to see it. The riot on TV was the scene outside the Democratic National Convention in Chicago. "My God," I thought, "I've been gone a year and the country is falling to pieces."

Nobody in the airport talked to me. I was a soldier in uniform and I was invisible. I may as well not have existed. People looked right through me. Later on, I realized something. The myth of spit and words in airports was invented by Vietnam veterans to deal with the deep wounds our countrymen gave us. Better to get spit on than to be completely shunned.

The small San Antonio terminal was full of people. I saw a tall soldier in Army green standing in a corner. Around his neck he wore the unmistakable broad blue ribbon of the Medal of Honor. Three or four other soldiers stood around him. The crowd ignored them. I joined the soldiers. The man with the medal told us how he had saved the lives of other men in one of those forgotten Vietnam firefights, so bravely won but so uselessly fought. The profile of the ancient Greek warrior on the medal seemed to approve. The word "Valor" was inscribed above the face of the warrior.

I turned away, looking for home. My fellow citizens ceaselessly rushed past me, past the tall soldier wearing his nation's highest award for honor, for courage and devotion. Nobody stopped, nobody cared.

Calls sometimes evoked responses we couldn't have anticipated. One wintry February 2016 evening we were presenting at Boswell Book Company in Wisconsin's largest city, Milwaukee. Daniel Goldin, our hard-charging, independent bookstore host, had stirred substantial interest among Milwaukee veteran, music, and literary communities, and my old friend and fellow Vietnam vet Bill Christofferson, a major Milwaukee mover and shaker on veteran and political fronts, had roused his sizable local networks. Milwaukee-area print and electronic media had also done several interviews and stories about us and the book, so we beamed as the Boswell folks brought in extra chairs to accommodate an overflow crowd.

I felt confident this would be a special night too, not just because of our Wisconsin roots or because Bill was going to read his entertaining solo about Nancy Sinatra and her number one song from 1966, "These Boots Are Made for Walkin'." What would make tonight even more special was if by chance another Milwaukee Vietnam veteran, Tim Staats, would be here.

Tim had been among the first Vietnam veterans to contact us in early 2005 when the initial word got out that we were working on *We Gotta Get Out of This Place*. When Tim contacted us via letter, he confirmed the significance of "We Gotta Get Out of This Place" for him and his fellow soldiers. He'd been in Vietnam in 1968-69, stationed at Qui Nhon as a helicopter door gunner with the 196th Aviation Company 1st Aviation Brigade. "'We Gotta Get Out of This Place" was *the* Vietnam song," Tim wrote, recalling that every Vietnamese, Filipino, or Korean band that performed at a club on a base anywhere in Vietnam ended their set with that Animals song. Tim added his own special take on the Vietnam vets anthem by telling us "we'd change the lines in the song's refrain from 'work, work work' to 'short short short' as we got closer to the end of our tours!"

That exchange had occurred more than a decade before our presentation at Boswell, and now Tim and his recollection were in our book, on page 11, so I had a good feeling we'd be able to give him a well-deserved shout out and public thanks. We hadn't kept in touch, but there had been enough articles about the book and interviews with us by Wisconsin media, that I figured Tim knew what was happening. After Daniel's introduction, I stepped up to the microphone, thanking the audience for coming out on such a dark and stormy night.

"Is Tim Staats in the audience?" I began. "Tim, if you're here please stand up or wave your arms or do something!" I said to a little nervous laughter from the audience. "No, seriously," I continued, trying to properly set the stage for this special moment, "take a bow."

A hand shot up in the back of the packed room, and I could tell as soon as the man stood up—he was wearing a boonie hat and an old Army field jacket—that he was a Vietnam veteran. *There it is*, I thought.

"Tim, welcome home." I smiled and waved, preparing to tell the audience about his distinction regarding the book when the man who'd just stood up interrupted me.

"Tim's dead," he said with very little emotion. "He died almost two years ago. Pretty sure it was Vietnam related..."

A painful silence descended as all of us, veteran and non-veteran, male and female, young and old, succumbed to one of the more sobering legacies of Vietnam. Bill Christofferson choked up later, as he added a reminiscence to his solo about a fellow Marine he'd served with who was killed in Vietnam. Damn, twice in one night Vietnam had grabbed us by the throat and brought many of us to tears.

The vet in the boonie hat came over to where we were signing books later and just shook his head. I wrote something personal to him and then added *RIP Tim Staats*. He nodded, turned, and walked away. Behind him in line were a middle-school teacher and several of his students, with fresh faces and big smiles.

"I use a lot of music in my classes," the blond-haired teacher smiled, "and I think it's important that my students understand what happened in Vietnam. Listening to the music and the stories is the perfect way into it." He and the students kept smiling, and I wondered if they'd be confronting their own Vietnam some day.

Truth is, there was as much laughter as there were tears during our interviews, presentations, and conversations. Some of that came from what our old friend Joe McDonald talked about in the Introduction—gallows humor. Case in point: Bobby, a happy-go-lucky Vietnam vet I met in Kansas City, joked that "Fire," a 1968 psychedelic hit by a group called The Crazy World of Arthur Brown, was his Vietnam song because he'd walked into a napalm strike and nearly burned to death. "But I'm here ain't I?" he grinned at me at the Harry Truman Presidential Library, proudly showing off the burns on his arms and hands. The folks gathered around us didn't get the joke.

In New Orleans, an Army officer who'd served with PsyOps drew gales of laughter when he confessed that the song which defined his two tours in Vietnam was Phil Ochs's "Draft Dodger Rag." "I knew I had a job to do and I did it well," he said as a broad smile broke out beneath his perfectly groomed hair, "but every single day I ask myself, 'why didn't I have the guts to stay out of that mess?'"

There was Fred, a grunt who joined us in Fort Collins, Colorado, declaring to an audience of 400 that he would never again listen to "Wolverton Mountain" by Claude King, an early 1960s country hit that crossed over to the pop charts. "Not just because it wasn't a very good song," he confessed, "but because I was stationed on a damn mountain, Marble Mountain, in Vietnam in 1971, and I kept thinking of Charlie (Viet Cong) as Clifton Clowers in that damn song because like Clowers, Charlie was 'handy with a gun and knife.' Lord help us!" Fred shook his head and sat down to waves of laughter.

Call. Response. Song. Memory. Sharing. Healing. We heard so much during those many months of presentations and conversations. And we learned a lot. About veteran homelessness, for example. We did a benefit for Housing Initiatives, a terrific, non-profit organization in Madison, Wisconsin that provides a permanent home and supportive services to men and women, many of them veterans and many of them mentally ill. The organization has been especially helpful in combatting veteran homelessness, and we were joined on stage by two people they'd helped, Paul Thormann and his long-time partner Julie Heuer. As a Marine, Paul had served two tours in Vietnam and was awarded the Purple Heart. He'd worked for decades as a furniture mover, but now he was unemployed, homeless, and suffering from Post Traumatic Stress. He and Julie had been living in an old Dodge Aerostar van for four years before it was hit and totaled by another vehicle. Then they lived outside, sometimes staying under a bridge on Madison's south side. But this night their dream had come true. Thanks to Housing Initiatives, Paul and Julie now had an apartment where they'd pay 30 percent of their income for rent, with the rest covered by a federal grant— and they would also receive ongoing case management.

"There were people who helped us along the way," Paul told the audience that night, his voice barely audible. "We knew there had to be some agency out there. You never give up hope."

Craig and I were almost speechless, but, fittingly, several of the songs we played that night were largely unknown pieces by Vietnam vets. We opened with "Shell Shock PTSD" by Blind Albert and closed with "Time to Lay it Down" by Martin and Holiday. In between we played "Veteran's Lament" by Jim Cook and Vietnam veteran Taylor McKinnon about forgotten Vietnam vets like Paul Thormann. Their song includes the line, *he can't get no welfare 'cause homeless vets don't get no mail.*

⊖   ⊖   ⊖

In the spring of 2016 in Seattle, we learned about Native American healing and rituals during a presentation at the University of Washington's Intellectual House. Known officially as wələbʔaltxʷ, this sacred place is a longhouse-style facility constructed of local cedar and serves as a learning and gathering space primarily for American Indian and Alaska Native students, faculty, and staff. Phillip Red Feather, a Vietnam veteran and accomplished poet, writer, and artist, told us afterward that "When you come home from Vietnam, you're really different." He admitted that the only place he felt comfortable was in a canoe or camping out during a Tribal Canoe Journey, a tradition begun by Emmett Oliver of the Quinault Nation in 1989. "I've helped to make more than 6,500 copper rings that are used as part of a Copper Ring Ceremony during the journeys," he explained. "We warriors in Vietnam had a different experience that pushed us into another world, a different realm, and we need to be pushed back in, we need to bring the warrior back to the circle. In our culture, canoe journeys and ring ceremonies are some of the ways to do this."

Audience responses intensified during the handful of presentations that included live bands playing our focal songs. Having the sound front and center, and not our words, audience members were more animated—laughing, shouting, crying, and dancing. The first of these, at the Barrymore Theater in Madison in late September 2016, featured a razor-sharp, soulful local band assembled by Sean Michael Dargan. In addition to Vietnam vets, we were joined by a host of Afghan and Iraq vets who volunteered to read solos from our book. Former Army Staff Sergeant Will Williams spoke eloquently, the audience silent and intent, about Vietnam, fear, death, and redemption. He fired up the crowd—this was Madison after all, the town that famed AFVN disc jockey Adrian Cronauer, so rebelliously portrayed by Robin Williams in the 1987 film *Good Morning Vietnam*, referred to as "the people's republic of Madison." Will didn't just reflect on his own service or his PTSD but urged the crowd to put a stop to "endless wars" and halt the tyranny of U.S. military forces overseas.

At the end of each reading, Sean's brilliant "Back in the World Band" would kick into "For What It's Worth," or "Piece of My Heart," or "What's Going On," and the audience responded immediately by clapping and singing along. Several audience members even got up and danced. It was eerily reminiscent of the Vietnamese bands that covered the songs at the EM clubs I frequented in Vietnam.

Amid the thunderous applause and rousing music, the most heart-rending moment occurred when Tom Deits, author of one of the most moving solos in *We Gotta Get Out of This Place*, paid tribute to his dedicated, driven, guitar-playing sergeant Tom Davies. Davies died in 2008 at the age of 60 due to Agent Orange exposure. Tom Deits told the audience that Davies's widow, Wendy, and their two daughters, were in the audience that night—and that they had brought along the guitar that Davies had played for Tom and the other GIs under his command in Vietnam! An avalanche of wails and moans and cries and applause and tears followed. Then the band played a moving version of "Masters of War," one of Davies's favorites.

Poster for September 2016 live concert at Barrymore Theater in Madison, WI. Photo courtesy Doug Bradley.

We repeated the live band accompaniment—outdoors—at the Perrin Brewery in Grand Rapids, Michigan—partnering with WGVU public broadcasting at Grand Valley State University. Detroit rock and soul master Stewart Francke brought a hard-rocking band that nailed cover versions of "The Letter," "Gimme Shelter," and a Credence Clearwater Revival medley that included "Fortunate Son." In the most powerful moment, Stewart played his Iraq War song, "Summer Soldier (Holler if ya hear me)," strumming his guitar as he sang *England's dreaming across the water/Summer soldiers, lambs to slaughter/Wives and daughters tying yellow ribbons in the sun/Holler, holler, holler if ya hear me...*

The Perrin audience hollered.

And then there was the fantastic concert at the TPT studio in Minnesota (see Overture) which is available online at https://www.mnvietnam.org/concert/

The live events were interspersed with dozens of interviews and call-in shows, television and radio programs, podcasts, online events, and emails that extended the call and response. On Kathleen Dunn's show on Wisconsin Public Radio, we played "Reflections of My Life" by a little-known Scottish band named Marmalade, that elicited a call from a former Vietnam helicopter pilot recalling Marmalade's other hit, "Rainbow," which neither of us remembered. As the caller described the image of the surreal beauty of the sky in Vietnam and the always-present sense of doom, he choked up, unable to continue. If this had happened at one of our presentations, someone in the audience would've put a hand on his shoulder, helped him to finish his testimony. On air, all we could do was thank him for sharing and welcome him home.

What has stayed with me? The specter of guilt and shame, the necessity of recovery and forgiveness, and the depth of misunderstanding about Vietnam and Vietnam veterans. Also, the rehabilitating power of call and response. Henry Ford, Jr. had personified it that November evening at Stax, and his hometown did too. Like other southern cities, Memphis had witnessed its share of tumult and pain, namely the Civil War, Reconstruction, the Memphis Riot of 1868, yellow fever, and the struggle for civil rights. The city's racial tension came to a head in April 1968 when Dr. Martin Luther King, Jr. was assassinated at the Lorraine Motel in Memphis. When citizens rioted in the streets after Dr. King's murder, only one building was left untouched—the home of Stax records located on McLemore Avenue in Soulsville!

As I've said, tensions were off the charts in Vietnam following King's assassination. Because they feared a revolt by black soldiers, the military delayed announcing his death until after they'd contacted the commanders of all units in Vietnam. As a result, many GIs first learned of MLK's death from Hanoi Hannah, the North Vietnamese equivalent of Tokyo Rose.

"The first thing I wanted to do was kill the first honkie I met," David Browne recalled after he heard the news in Vietnam. A member of the 101st Airborne, Browne instead went back to his hooch and put on a tape of Aretha Franklin's *Lady Soul* album. "I listened to it over and over," he said, "and 'bout the fourth time 'Chain of Fools' came round, I thought, 'that's my story,' and from then on it was a different game."

From then on, Browne stopped fighting.

"The death of Martin Luther King created a lot of hostility in Vietnam," added Dave Gallaher, a photo interpreter at Tan Son Nhut Air base in 1968. "Things were always cool until the assassination, when the racial situation got tense and it was hard for people to get along. Even those (blacks and whites) who'd been friends had a hard time associating. There were several times I would be playing with a band, would be the only white guy in the place. Overall, when you were on stage, there was never a problem. But you get off to take a leak, someone would be in there drunk. They'd see your white face and would start trouble."

Ironically, it took a visit to Vietnam by James Brown, the god-father of soul himself, in June of 1968 to maintain racial calm. Brown's inclusion of a white musician in his six-piece band helped, too. "Because of the hostilities that had developed racially, I think James showing up with a white musician just put everyone on a little bit of notice about cooling out," noted Gallaher.

Again, music—in the recordings of Aretha Franklin and the person of James Brown—served as a quieting response to a com-bustible situation. Memphis, too, had responded to its call; Henry Ford, Jr., to his; Al Bell and The Staples Singers to theirs. I'm still waiting on America to "respond" to Vietnam...

In the meantime, I'll always be hearing Henry sing "I Stand Ac-cused," and I'll always be responding to the call *I know a place* by chanting *I'll take you there*. And I'll keep visiting the Monona Ter-race Community and Convention Center in Madison, near the site of Otis Redding's untimely death. His call can still be heard there.

As we were entering the final stages of writing *We Gotta Get Out of This Place* in late 2010, we collaborated with the Wisconsin Veter-ans Museum to put together a two-day conference to coincide with the release of *Next Stop is Vietnam: The War on Record 1961-2008*, a superb 13-CD collection put together by Bear Family Records. The highlights of the conference included a presentation by "Funky Drummer" Clyde Stubblefield, the heart and soul of the James Brown band that toured Vietnam in 1968, and a session featuring Stax artist William Bell and cyber griot Art Flowers, who provided a lively and respectful conversation on the changes in black Mem-phis vets' perspectives from Civil Rights to Black Power.

Among the conference's dozens of songs, Otis Redding's "Dock of the Bay" occupied the spiritual center. Our location, less than a quarter mile from Lake Monona where Otis's plane had gone down on December 10, 1967, added a deep, bittersweet feel to the many vets' stories about sitting on beaches gazing out at the South China Sea with Otis's whistle echoing in their heads and hearts. As his plaque next to Lake Monona says, "King of the Soul Singers."

Earlier, in 2007, Wisconsin Veterans Museum educational director Jeff Kollath—now overseeing the Stax Museum in Memphis—had invited me, Craig, and our friend and music historian Charles Hughes to make a presentation on "Dock of the Bay." When Otis's widow Zelma was sent a recording of the event, she wrote and thanked us, telling us that just before his ill-starred trip to Madison in 1967, Otis had eagerly accepted an invitation to make a tour playing for the troops in Vietnam, the same place the U.S. government called me to as a soldier in 1970.

Otis Redding. Photo courtesy Stax Museum of American Soul Music.

My response to that call, with "Dock of the Bay" ringing in my ears, is to weep, wishing like hell I could have thanked Otis personally for his heart-rending song that saved so many of us Vietnam vets from despair when we were over there...and when we tried to get back home.

COUNTERPOINT

"Waist Deep in the Big Muddy"

But every time I read the papers
That old feeling comes on;
We're waist deep in the Big Muddy
And the big fool says to push on.
—Pete Seeger, "Waist Deep in the Big Muddy"

Rarely did Craig and I encounter any open conflict during our presentations, but the exceptions were memorable. Case in point: early December 2015 at the Rock and Roll Hall of Fame in Cleveland, Ohio. Despite a cold snap that brought frigid winds off Lake Erie and dropped the mercury to single digits—the Rock Hall sits on the waterfront—the room was filled, and our presentation was being streamed worldwide.

We'd prepared a playlist featuring songs by several notable Ohioans—"Houston," by Steubenville's Dean Martin; "Detroit City," by Bobby Bare, who hailed from Ironton; a cover version of the Herman's Hermits' hit "There's a Kind of Hush" by a Franklin, Ohio, garage band named Gary and the Hornets; and, of course "Ohio" by Canadian Neil Young.

As good as the event was, I kept watching the furrowed brow and dismissive body language of a well-kempt gentleman in the front row. He sat there in his London fog raincoat the whole night. This guy was not enjoying himself. Was it our song selections? The vets' commentaries? Or that I'd admitted to serving my time in country as a REMF (Rear Echelon Mother Fucker)? Rifts among some Vietnam vets still lingered, and a lot of it centered on what

Craig and I refer to as the "3 W's" – When you were in Vietnam; Where you were stationed; and What you did, as your military job in Vietnam. And that's without adding service stateside or in Germany or Korea, or on a ship in the U. S. Coast Guard, into the mix of who's a Vietnam veteran....

Take my Vietnam service, for example: I was stationed in Vietnam from November 1970 to November 1971, a relatively quiet period of the war when the troops' mantra was *nobody wants to be the last GI killed in Vietnam*. I worked in a corporate-esque, shine-and-polish public information office at the U.S. Army's headquarters at Long Binh, a safe, rear-echelon location jokingly referred to as "the air-conditioned jungle" because the Army brass for whom I toiled wanted to work in comfortable surroundings. Finally, as an Army journalist I carried a pen and not a rifle, reporting, writing, editing, and publishing Army newspaper and magazine articles intended to boost the morale of the soldiers in the field doing the fighting and dying. Now, contemplate the myriad permutations of the three variables at any particular time: 200 or more different military jobs times 11 or 12 years of jungle guerrilla warfare times an area of 67,000 square miles. The possibilities are inexhaustible...meaning there is no one Vietnam story; rather, there are almost three million of them, one for every service member who was there.

Meanwhile, back to my disgruntled comrade. He remained silent during a lively Q&A call and response session, but he was first in line to purchase a book for us to autograph. He still had that look

as he positioned his copy in front of me.

"Where did you get the picture on the cover?" he asked pointedly. The cover of *We Gotta Get Out of This Place* is an iconic photo from the siege of Khe Sanh in February 1968. It shows a weary Marine waiting for a helicopter ride away from the bloody madness, an M-16 rifle slung over one shoulder and a guitar over the other. My interrogator interrupted me before I could finish my explanation.

"The photo's a fraud," he said angrily. "It's staged."

Momentarily taken aback, I could feel myself getting steamed. Luckily, Craig, typically less likely to show his emotions, intervened.

"Where were you in country?" he asked my nemesis.

"I Corps, 3rd Marine Division, where the shit hit the fan," the guy volunteered. "No Marine wore pants with creases up there."

"You're pissed off about the pants?" I interjected. Craig put his hand over my arm to calm me.

"Worst combat ever." Craig looked the guy in the eye. "Glad you made it home, man." The fellow nodded and tempers cooled.

"I'm dead serious about that picture," the guy repeated. "None of us had pants like that, much less wore them during Tet."

I turned my attention to less belligerent buyers as Craig and the Marine kept on talking. Later, as we hunkered down at a nearby bar to watch the Packers, damn if this same guy didn't walk in and sit down. Now the Vietnam vet in me was getting a little paranoid. Was this dude following us? Who the hell was he, and what did he want?

While I turned my attention to the TV, Craig spotted the fellow, ordered him a beer, and sat down next to him. The two of them were deep in conversation the rest of the evening. Debriefing the next morning, Craig told me how much the Marine vet had on his mind and how angry he still was about Vietnam, how vets were treated when they came home, what most Americans didn't know and didn't care to know about Vietnam.

"The photo just brought out everything he felt was dishonest about the war," Craig explained. "The image doesn't square with his memory of what happened, and it pisses him off."

"So, what in the hell are we supposed to do about that? About him?" I asked.

"Change the conversation, for one," replied Craig. "Help build a fuller, more honest shared story, even if it contradicts some of what we believe to be true. Guys like him need to have their experiences validated, their memories included."

"Did you get his name?"

"Not really, but he's still convinced the cover photo is a fake."

I was particularly bothered by the fake-photo claim because as an Army information specialist in Vietnam, I knew all too well the enormous power of the visual image. My words could get edited or censored, but a photo, well, that was hard to hide. In fact, so much of the fury and folly of Vietnam was reflected in a handful of iconic images—from Malcolm Browne's burning Buddhist monk to Eddie Adams's execution of a Viet Cong soldier to Nick Ut's Napalm girl. Several of the guys in my Information Office at USARV were damn good photographers too, and their images would still hold the eye today. What's changed now is our relationship to the media and whether an image, a story, or a song conforms to our own public memory of the war, or what we want the Vietnam War to represent. If we had never seen those three photos, or others like them, would we still feel the same about Vietnam? Or if we see them now, do we brand them as mere propaganda...or corporate merchandise?

It took me a while, but I was beginning to appreciate why maybe that Marine was so upset about that particular photo—he'd been at Khe Sanh, he'd almost died and some of his buddies were killed, and, damn it, nobody got out of there with creases in their pants. So many of the intense visual images from Vietnam now seemed to be reinforcing what people wanted to believe, or disbelieve, about Vietnam, rather than what really happened.

One of the more rewarding moments of our Cleveland Rock Hall visit occurred on WCPN's *ideastream* radio program. Host Mike McIntire had invited Mary Reynolds Powell to join us as we fielded responses from callers. Mary was an Army nurse in Vietnam, and her memoir, *A World of Hurt: Between Innocence and Arrogance in Vietnam,* is a must read. She shared her memories of Creedence Clearwater Revival and Peter, Paul, and Mary's "Leaving on a Jet Plane," as well as "And When I Die" by Blood, Sweat, and Tears. In stark contrast to the anger we'd encounter later at the Rock Hall, Mary spoke with elegant honesty about the possibility, and difficulty, of recovery. Hers.

U.S. Army nurse Mary Reynolds Powell in Vietnam 1970.
Photo courtesy Mary Reynolds Powell.

"I've always said that nurses are the hub of the wheel," Mary told us. "We took care of the soldiers, we administered to them daily, and we became their confidants and caretakers. By far the toughest part of our job, and one that still haunts me, is that once we got these guys healthy—recovered from wounds or malaria or typhus or some major illness—we sent them back out to the field, to the war. We watched them get better and then they walked out the door and...I can't bear to think about what happened to some of them..."

Mary's fellow Army nurse Sue O'Neill echoed Mary's words, admitting that after a few months in country, she'd stopped learning the names of the soldiers she was treating. "It was just too hard patching them up so they could be torn apart again."

The U.S. got torn apart, too, ruptures we're still trying to mend, or understand. And while many of us have moved on, too many of the veterans we've met have not. But what we found is that if you take the time to listen respectfully to what the veterans of that misunderstood war have to say, you'll frequently find a song at the heart of what they remember. And that same song resonates with their generational peers, those who stayed or served, ones who participated or protested.

The callers we heard from on *ideastream* shared their music-based memories of Jimi Hendrix, the Doors, and the famous AFVN deejay Adrian Cronauer. And they also leveled a good deal of criticism of presidents and politicians and Jane Fonda. As much as the music seemed to connect us, too many of the old Vietnam differences still persisted. I attributed it to the medium—radio—because our *We Gotta Get Out of This Place* experience demonstrated that when people sat together in person and listened to the stories and songs, they found common ground. Was it just the medium? The setting? The music? Or something else?

In *Say Nothing*, Patrick Radden Keefe's brilliant book about the troubles in Northern Ireland, he talks about the "collective denial" of both sides of the conflict not wanting to acknowledge the reality of what really happened. Or as my Vietnam hooch mate and fellow information specialist George Moriarty parsed it, *collective denial* for us Vietnam vets occurs when the public memory of Vietnam doesn't jibe with our personal experience "That's where some of the myths about Vietnam come from," George alleged, "more as a way to cope than anything. You and I believe what we did in Vietnam was solid, honest journalism and that it was the military brass and the devious politicians who messed it up. Maybe, and maybe not. But we accept that rationale in order keep sane."

To quote George, "maybe, or maybe not?" Scholars of memory have demonstrated again and again that the mind creates narratives that take on the power of reality, especially with traumatic events, a theme I'll return to in the section titled *Adagio*. And these narratives can take on mythic stature, either as something to be embraced or debunked. It keeps happening with Vietnam, but, in our *We Gotta Get Out of This Place* presentations, rarely when music was what centered the conversation.

Another way of looking at this is to ask how much the authentic Vietnam veteran experience represents America's public memory of the war. How does that experience square with all the noise surrounding accounts of the spat-upon vet, the Gulf of Tonkin invention, the legacy of McNamara's Project 100,000, "killing anything that moves," fragging, racial antagonism, PTSD, Agent Orange, the Vietnam Veterans Memorial, and more? If you dip your toe into this water, you may just sink like a stone. Get caught in the quagmire. Find yourself with Commander-in-Chief Lyndon Johnson "Waist Deep in the Big Muddy," as the World War II veteran and pacifist Pete Seeger once sang.

Welcome to Vietnam.

Or some not-so-reasonable facsimile thereof, which remains to this day a part of the problem regarding Vietnam and our public take on it. Vietnam veterans know the persistence of this mythical Vietnam—one of the birthplaces of "fake news"—all too well. Edwin Moise's brilliant study *Myths of Tet* provides chapter and verse on how almost everything you're likely to hear about Tet—from the military realities to the media coverage—is disconnected from what actually happened. Nonetheless, veterans sometimes signed up for those narratives and have had to live with them for more than 50 years. That leaves the rest of America wrestling with competing perspectives, biased documentaries, film fictions, and thousands upon thousands upon thousands of books, novels, memoirs, personal narratives, and revisionist histories.

And however obsessive and thorough your quest for truth, somebody else will tell you that you don't know what the hell you're talking about. Maybe that's precisely why we treasure the music of that era. It calls from its own truth, and we respond in ways that are personal, intimate, and genuine.

But even the music gets caught in the Vietnam crossfire, to wit the conflicting responses to Country Joe McDonald's "I Feel Like I'm Fixin' to Die Rag," Neil Young's "Ohio," Merle Haggard's "The Fightin' Side of Me," and Bruce Springsteen's "Born in the USA," songs heard one way by one group of listeners and very differently by others. You could despise Country Joe for callously conjecturing if parents wanted *to be the first ones on your block/to have your boy come home in a box* or laugh your ass off at his gallows humor. You shouted "right on" to "Ohio's" indictment of Richard Nixon or gave Neil Young the finger and told him to go back to Canada. You could dismiss Haggard as a right-wing redneck or hear his empathy for the soldiers facing criticism from all sides. You felt the pain of the disregarded Vietnam veteran in "Born in the USA" or, like President Ronald Reagan, you waved the flag and exhorted U. S. exceptionalism.

These conflicting, opposing interpretations of individual pieces of evidence reflect the opposing premises of absolutist points of view over the Vietnam war, its meaning, and its aftermath. For every Vietnam veteran who stood up during our call-and-response sessions to remind us that more than 90 percent of Vietnam veterans said they are glad they served in the war or that nearly three-quarters of Vietnam vets claimed they'd serve again, another veteran would stand and dispute those findings, offering counter-stats that showed quite the opposite—higher numbers of Vietnam vets in prison; higher suicide rates among vets; higher unemployment rates among veterans, and so on. Not to mention the frequent insights about Vietnam offered by draft resisters and anti-war protesters. Five decades on, and America continues to construct a public memory of Vietnam that often contradicts some of the realities as excavated by historians and experienced by Vietnam veterans. The necessity of an accurate, comprehensive public memory of Vietnam emerges from the narrative of Vietnam veteran Susan O'Neill, a nurse in operating rooms and surgical and Evac hospitals in Vietnam from May 1969 until June 1970.

SOLO Sue O'Neill

Vietnam veteran Sue O'Neill. Photo courtesy Sue O'Neill.

We Vietnam vets haven't missed or misunderstood much about the war, although, of course, we interpret our own experiences in as many different ways as we have different veterans. The rest of society, non-Vietnam vets, however, do seem to have some misconceptions. One is about the nature of our service. There's information out there, based on various figures, that contends the majority of Vietnam military were volunteers. What that fails to take into account was the tendency of guys to "volunteer" for Vietnam because with the draft hanging over their heads, they enlisted, hoping to find themselves in a better job than one that would put them in the line of fire. That sure strikes me as more of an imposed "career choice" when you're thrown into the military involuntarily, without signing up. Also, some of those who served signed up for distinctly non-war reasons. A good friend of mine left school to become a Marine because his home life was in chaos, he wanted to pass his GED and get his high school diploma, and generally add the structure to his life that his mess of a family couldn't provide. He was trying to find himself, at age seventeen. He died in Vietnam.

Another thing that I think is misunderstood—and this leans on that first point I just mentioned—is that the ratio of non-combat troops to combat troops in Vietnam was quite large. I've heard figures like five- or six-to-one, and I wouldn't be at all surprised if it was even more.

This is something Ken Burns and Lynn Novick missed in their documentary *The Vietnam War*. There was way too much emphasis on combat and killing. I know that's what war is about. I saw enough of what war does putting broken bodies back together, but what was missing (in the series) was the role of the REMF (rear echelon soldier) in Vietnam, given that it was so disproportionately large. I mean, it takes an enormous number of support staff to stage a war. Hospitals like the one where I worked, need to be staffed, supply depots must be manned, and the paperwork part of a war requires many, many people. Trucks don't drive themselves; food on basecamps doesn't magically fall from trees. Logistics don't just happen. There are engineers, clerks, the troops who build Quonset huts [lightweight, pre-fab structures used by the military] and lay cement walkways. People who fly helicopter cranes; people who fly Chinooks and airplanes to bring in materials, troops, and vehicles.

Of course, everybody has a preference of their own choosing, a penchant for looking for their own job in the presentation, so even though Burns and Novick did a decent job, given the many, many facets of the time and the war itself, I also thought they did very little to show the medical support elements, all the folks who were fighting a different war in the rear...yeah, too much emphasis on combat.

They also missed the chance to show what really happened to women from the other side, North Vietnamese fighting women, who, more often than not, were left unmarried and childless because they sacrificed their younger, "marriageable" lives to the cause, or because they feared the effect of exposure to malaria and our good old Agent Orange on their lives and those of potential children. They were left, for the most part, without financial support—their country did not give them a pension or benefits, so they were left to do whatever they could to make money or had to rely on the goodwill of those who held them in esteem for their work. Instead, the documentary concentrated on a couple who met and married doing the work, which was, from what I read, a novelty...

When I left Vietnam, I was *so* bitter about our invasion, about how I'd actually witnessed the destruction of their economy— the herding of farmers and villagers into the desperate-looking, hurricane-fence-topped-with-barbed-wire enclosed camps of shacks and dirt I passed in a jeep going from Phu Bai to Huế, the people at the sides of the roadways selling black market GI stuff; the bar girls and massage parlors that catered to GIs—and how horribly disrespectful we were to their culture...how we flat-out didn't understand the country and its customs, history and people. I remember I thought, the *one* good thing we Americans just might have pulled from our experience in Vietnam was that we would never do something so ill-advised, unfounded, and outright stupid again as to invade a country that we didn't understand (or maybe even *like*) for some obscure political reason, spilling our and their blood recklessly, wasting lives and money and tearing both countries apart.

And then we invaded Afghanistan and Iraq.

As Sue O'Neill reminds us, our public memory of the past constructs our responses in the present to determine our future.

In their article of January 2017 titled "Public Memory," professors Matthew Houdek and Kendall R. Phillips observed that "the term *public memory* refers to the circulation of recollections among members of a given community." They go on to explain that such recollections are "far from being perfect records of the past; rather, they entail what we remember, the ways we frame it, and what aspects we forget." The 18-hour PBS series *The Vietnam War* by Ken Burns and Lynn Novick made it clear just how powerful and influential a role film plays in public memory, arguably second only to music in its reach. The young students who take our UW-Madison course on the Music of the Vietnam War are more schooled in *Platoon, Good Morning Vietnam,* and *Apocalypse Now* than in the Gulf of Tonkin, the Tet Offensive, or My Lai. And at just about every book presentation, Craig and I were asked to name our favorite Vietnam film.

The military provided us with music (see Meredith Lair's *Armed With Abundance*) and showered the rear with movies. There was a real theater at MACV (Military Assistance Command, Vietnam) headquarters in Saigon, and numerous movie venues on Long Binh post, where I spent my 365 days in country. In most cases, those venues were nothing more than a large, blank, white wall and a projector, but the equipment worked, and the movies evoked their intended effects of distraction, nostalgia, and interruption. My best friend and fellow information specialist George Moriarty often joined me on lazy, tropical evenings, to stare at celluloid and try to forget we were in Vietnam.

SOLO   George Moriarty

The Army did its best to provide us soldiers in the rear with distractions other than dope and beer. There was always a nightly volleyball game, weather permitting, and there often was a Filipino band with a female singer, wearing a suitably short skirt, murdering Tina Turner's "Proud Mary" at the non-commissioned officers clubs...But the movies Uncle Sam provided for our enjoyment were also well attended, and a cause for celebration.

My favorite memory of movie night was the long-awaited arrival of *King Kong.* I cannot really remember how the movies were transferred from company to company, but we knew it was a coming attraction. The day Kong arrived we set up our beach chairs early so that we would have front row seats. No doubt, by the time the film began, there was a buzz (beer and dope) in the audience.

If you remember the film, you have to admit that the men leading the expedition to Skull Island left much to be desired. Fay Wray, on the other hand, as Ann Darrow, the damsel in distress, was quite high on the desire scale to a bunch of female-starved soldiers. During the film we cheered on the natives at some points, but not when they sacrificed a young maiden to Kong. As far as Kong was concerned, he was the hero of the film, and we cheered lustily as he fought off dinosaur after dinosaur to protect the beautiful Ann.

Things did not end well for Kong on the island. We find him in chains in New York and a spectacle on display by Mr. Carl Denham. Kong, having other ideas about his future, not only manages to escape, but also retrieves Ann. Cut to the Empire State Building scene and the Vietnam soldiers assembled are cheering on Kong and booing the fighter pilots who have been called in to restore order. Kong succumbs. Dumb Mr. Denham manages the final word in the film, "It was beauty killed the beast." We went and had another beer!

P.S. Fifteen years or so after my King Kong experience in Vietnam, I was attending a summer stock theater in Tamworth, N.H. called "The Barnstormers." They were having a fundraiser and were selling a chair autographed by the one and only Fay Wray. She had once appeared there in a play. I was dying to buy the chair, but my wife was not in the market. I guess you had to be there.

Harkening back to the 3Ws I mentioned earlier, movie nights in Vietnam for REMFs like George and me in 1970–71 were more than just an escape—they were a way to either protest, albeit timidly, the bullshit of the Army—as we did the night we had a shouting match with the Lifers during John Wayne's *Ballad of the Green Berets*—or construct an alternative reality to what we were experiencing. King Kong did that for us one hot, silent night in Vietnam. Little did we and our fellow REMFs know, but Hollywood filmmakers would eventually construct their own alternate Vietnam reality, one that in most cases didn't reflect or include our experiences. More than 40 years ago, I obsessed over what filmmakers would present about Vietnam. Even if I didn't know a damn thing then about public memory, I had a strong sense that movies would define the Vietnam war and Vietnam veterans for decades to come. So, if the war in Vietnam was the call to America and Hollywood in the 1960s and early 1970s, what was Hollywood's response?

Nearly universal silence.

Except for arguably one of the worst films of all time, John Wayne's western cowboy approach in *The Green Berets* (1968), the film industry steered clear of Vietnam. Well, almost. While Hollywood could not, and would not, address the unpleasantness and ambivalence of Vietnam, the industry did find a convenient scapegoat for what was wrong about Vietnam and ailing America—the Vietnam veteran.

Presented as either victim or vanquisher, or both, Vietnam vet characters like Billy Jack (*Born Losers*, 1967), John Rambo (*First Blood*, 1982), and Travis Bickle (*Taxi Driver*, 1976) portrayed the Vietnam veteran as loner, loser, and killer. Even if you're the good guy in these films, with titles like *Angels from Hell*, *The Angry Breed*, and *Satan's Sadists*, you take no prisoners. And you leave behind a swath of death and destruction that would make General William Tecumseh Sherman proud.

There were some feeble attempts to make a different statement, but they were few and scattered. Well into the 1970s, Vietnam was radioactive, and Hollywood shunned it. Even high-caliber filmmakers like Samuel Fuller and Stanley Kramer had Vietnam-related film projects rejected. Movies about the Vietnam war started to appear in the late '70s. In 1978 alone, *The Boys in Company C, Go Tell the Spartans, Coming Home,* and *The Deer Hunter* all debuted, to be followed by *Apocalypse Now* in 1979. The race was on, and Stanley Kubrick, Oliver Stone, Brian DePalma, Martin Ritt, and other prominent directors were waiting in the wings with their own Vietnam projects.

I decided I needed to see these films for myself, accompanied by a few of my fellow Vietnam veterans, whom I'd interview afterward about their responses; I'd even convinced the local newspaper to publish these veteran-based reviews of Vietnam films. My rationale was that rather than just take as gospel what some Hollywood director was telling you about Vietnam, you should compare it to the real experiences of actual Vietnam veterans to see if the film was in any way accurate.

None of the vets with whom I watched those films found any of them to be credible. *The Boys in Company C,* for example, which advertised itself with the slogan "To keep their sanity in an insane war, they had to be crazy," elicited howls of derisions from my fellow vets, one of whom, former Marine Charlie Piper, stated emphatically that the "cliché-ridden film in no way resembled our training, actions, or experiences in Vietnam."

The most notable exception was *Go Tell the Spartans,* which made a serious effort to look at the American combat experience in the early phase of America's war in Vietnam. Set in the early 1960s, prior to the Gulf of Tonkin Resolution, the film focused on the role of U.S. advisors working with the South Vietnamese Army. And it had a big-name star in Burt Lancaster. But those of us who spent 365 days or more in Vietnam after the Gulf of Tonkin couldn't relate to a group of assorted lifers who wanted to be there and wanted to stop Communism at any cost. U.S. Army veteran Chuck Goranson, who served in Vietnam in 1966–67, did have something good to say about the film's close. "At least the firefight at the end had the feel of real combat," he deadpanned. "Nothing like the main battle in *The*

Green Berets, which looked like a John-Wayne-against-the-Indians shootout."

Not that it mattered anyway, because like *The Boys in Company C*, *Go Tell the Spartans* didn't attract a large audience. Both films quickly passed from view...but then along came Michael Cimino's *The Deer Hunter*. Hailed as "the great American film of 1978," and "one of the boldest and most brilliant American films in recent years," *The Deer Hunter* won five Academy awards and almost single-handedly changed the calculus on films about Vietnam being a financially viable subject for filmmakers. Still, none of the films I watched with my fellow veterans elicited the kind of disapproval and outright anger as *The Deer Hunter*.

"This fucking movie is about as accurate in its depiction of the Vietnam War as *West Side Story* was in its portrayal of Spanish Harlem," former soldier Chuck Goranson remarked bitterly.

"From looking at the movie, you'd think a lot of the guys who served in Vietnam were in their mid-20s or early 30s," added Charlie Piper. "That's way off base. Most of the guys I served with were in their late teens or early 20s—high school grads and dropouts—those were the ones who fought the damn war and they were the ones who got killed."

It wasn't just that *The Deer Hunter* distorted history, we concluded. What really got us riled was the film's central metaphor, the recurring game of Russian roulette. "Hell, you'd think it was the Vietnam national sport," scoffed Wayne Horner, an Army veteran with three Purple Hearts who was wounded in Vietnam. "I never saw or heard of anyone playing Russian roulette in Vietnam before or since. It's a damn lie."

Equally hollow for us vets was the film's closing sequence where everyone sings "God Bless America."

"Both God and America died in Vietnam," Charlie muttered as we left.

The passage of time confirmed my fears about our public memory of Vietnam being too heavily influenced by *The Deer Hunter*,

Apocalypse Now, Good Morning Vietnam, and *Full Metal Jacket.* They are the Vietnam touchstones for too many Americans. There's now a *Battlefield: Bad Company 2: Vietnam* videogame—and an *Apocalypse Now* videogame was released in late 2018.

By the time the POWs had returned home and Nixon had been impeached, Francis Ford Coppola of *Godfather* fame and his planned BIG Vietnam film *Apocalypse Now* began to dominate the celluloid landscape. We Vietnam vets knew it was coming, and given the rash of ugly, brutal biker-vet films, we were fearful that *Apocalypse Now* would be another dagger in the heart, again portraying Vietnam vets as disturbed zombies, violent killers, or latent maniacs.

In 1976, as president of Vets House in Madison, I and several other Vietnam veteran organizations wrote an open letter to Coppola asking him to present a fair and sympathetic portrayal of Vietnam soldiers. Curiously, the response we received was not from Francis Ford himself but from Charles Champlin, the film critic of the Los Angeles Times, who cautioned us to not "prejudge Francis" but to wait and see the finished product. "Having seen the completed script," added Champlain, "I'd say overall that Mr. Coppola has not cast the Vietnam veteran in a negative light."

Still, many of us were anxious for Hollywood to "set the record straight," to have our fellow countrymen get beyond the "living room war," as Michael Arlen described the TV-version of Vietnam, to see it on the big screen in all its nuance and complexity. Maybe some astute director would even make a Vietnam-version of *Best Years of Our Lives* (1946), the amazingly popular and positive film portrayal of World War veterans? But then again, this was our war, the one we lost, not the one our fathers had won...

In October 1979, nearly a dozen of us went to see *Apocalypse Now* when it opened, this time accompanied by a reporter with Wisconsin Public Radio. Unlike previous films, *Apocalypse Now* felt more like the real Vietnam to the combat vets. "I was just about on the floor when that first sapper attack came," said Wayne Horner. "That was too damn real to be funny."

"It's obvious that Coppola had solid technical assistance for the helicopter scenes," observed Chuck Goranson, "but it's equally obvious that he didn't know anything about the USO, night maneuvers, or explosives."

The verdict on *Apocalypse Now* was, and remains, mixed. "There's nothing accurate about *Apocalypse Now*," added Charlie Piper. "No issues are expressed, no historical overview of the Indochina conflict. Nothing. Vietnam was evil all right, but the evil was in Washington, not Vietnam."

Why was I subjecting myself and others to this? Whether I liked it or not, these films were having an impact. Oscars were awarded, artistic accolades came like monsoons. *Platoon*, in 1986, was the crest of the wave, and all the great directors of that era—Kubrick, Scorsese, Coppola, and more—made their Vietnam film. In the process, they helped construct a flawed public memory.

My obsession with film and verisimilitude came to a head in March 1980, when I performed my own version of the disgruntled vet who objected to the cover picture of *We Gotta Get Out of This Place*. Francis Ford Coppola arrived in Madison to direct a live half-hour television show for his friend, California Governor Jerry Brown, then a presidential candidate. We tried to get Coppola to add Vets House to his itinerary, but he passed. So, I followed him around town, showing up at every venue, asking pointed questions about inaccuracies in *Apocalypse Now*. By the third or fourth time I ambushed him publicly, the audience was as unhappy with me as Coppola was. Looking back, I may have been working thorough some of my own PTSD, my anger at the time being projected onto films and filmmakers. Much like the disgruntled Marine who didn't trust our cover photo, I just couldn't believe the American public was falling for this celluloid fiction. And goddamn Francis Ford Coppola and his people wouldn't even engage with us in a letter or a face-to-face meeting.

"Were any Vietnam vets involved in the creation or production of the film?" I hollered from the rear of a packed classroom at West High School.

"Plenty," Coppola smiled.

"Didn't they tell you the USO scene with the Playboy bunnies was bogus? That the massacre on the sampan reeked of My Lai? That the Montagnards were our friends? That nobody likes the smell of napalm in the morning?" I was pretty fired up.

"Listen," Coppola interrupted me sternly. "I had a laundry list of over 200 things I wanted to show about the Vietnam experience. I couldn't get all of them in there and I had to compress a lot of the others. So, sue me."

Laughter and applause from the audience.

I got a similar response to my questions in Russ Merritt's film class. By then Coppola was on to me and lectured more than responded: "We made the film the way Americans made war in Vietnam," he pronounced. "There were too many of us, too much money and equipment, and little by little we went insane." Huge groan from me. "We took this very seriously," he went on. "We commissioned pollsters to discern the public's tolerance level on the Vietnam experience. You know what they told us? Most people wanted to forget about the war, they wanted to be entertained and not lectured to, and they wanted to see lots of action."

More applause from the audience.

"My film is an anti-lie, not an anti-war film," he wrapped up, "it's honest, pro-human, and therefore very pro-American. It can enable us to put the Vietnam war behind us."

INTERMISSION

What does reside, and resonate, are the soundtracks to so many of these Vietnam films. Even as we shook our heads over the cinematic distortions, my fellow veterans and I could at least tap our toes to their soundtracks, with Motown and Creedence, and swivel our heads at the Doors and Jefferson Airplane. Here are some of the more notable soundtracks from among the many celluloid treatments of the Vietnam war:

Born on the Fourth of July—includes "Soldier Boy"; "My Girl"; "The Times They Are a Changin'"; "San Francisco"; "Born on the Bayou"

Casualties of War—includes "Hello I Love You"; "Time Has Come Today"; "Magic Carpet Ride"; "Hold On, I'm Comin'"

Coming Home—includes "Time Has Come Today"; "Hey Jude"; "For What It's Worth"; "Just Like a Woman"; "White Rabbit"; "My Girl"

Dead Presidents—includes "Say It Loud (I'm Black and I'm Proud)"; "Love Train"; "Keep on Pushin'"; "What's Happenin' Brother"

Full Metal Jacket—includes "Hello Vietnam"; "Wooly Bully"; "I Like It Like That"; "These Boots are Made for Walkin'"

Good Morning Vietnam—includes "Nowhere to Run"; "I Get Around"; "Ballad of a Thin Man"; "I Got You"; "In the Midnight Hour"; "Puff, the Magic Dragon"

Hamburger Hill—includes "Sittin' on The Dock of the Bay"; "Ruby, Don't Take Your Love To Town"; "Fixin' to Die Rag"; "We Gotta Get Out of This Place"

Heaven and Earth—includes "Can't Take My Eyes Off Of You"; "Mellow Yellow"; "Sugar Sugar"; "Cry Like a Baby"; traditional Vietnamese music

Music Within—includes "Papa's Got a Brand New Bag"; "Sunshine Superman"; "Midnight Rambler"; "Somebody to Love"; "We Gotta Get Out of This Place"

Platoon—includes "Tracks of My Tears"; "Okie from Muskogee"; "White Rabbit"; "Sittin' on the Dock of the Bay"

Who'll Stop the Rain—includes "Proud Mary"; "Gimme Some Lovin'"; "The Golden Rocket"; "Hey Tonight"; "Who'll Stop the Rain"

Because Hollywood did a better job with music than with many other Vietnam issues, public memory includes both a critical deejay, Adrian Cronauer, and an essential band, Creedence Clearwater Revival. Robin Williams immortalized Cronauer, the celebrated AFVN disc jockey, in his tour-de-force performance in the 1987 movie *Good Morning Vietnam*.

Good Morning Vietnam credits Cronauer with adding Top 40 hits and comedy to AFVN, all the while battling military censorship, fighting with the higher ups, and educating Vietnamese. Hollywood, of course, altered the Vietnam truth to suit its own entertainment ends. Yes, an Air Force broadcaster named Adrian Cronauer in Vietnam in 1965–66 hosted a popular AFVN radio show from 6 a.m. to 9 a.m. every morning and taught English to Vietnamese during his off-duty time. But that's where the parallels end. In fact, the real-life Cronauer played within the bounds of the approved Armed Forces Radio format. Cronauer, who described himself as a "lifelong, card-carrying Republican," (in contrast to all the "card-carrying liberals" in Hollywood) worked for the U. S. Department of Defense and was active in both the Dole/Kemp (1996) and Bush/Cheney (2000/2004) presidential campaigns. "Once people get to know me, they realize very quickly that I'm not Robin Williams," he told Jim Barthold in a March 2005 interview. "Anybody who has been in the military will tell you that if I did half the things in that movie, I'd still be in Leavenworth right now," Cronauer observed. "A lot of Hollywood imagination went into the movie."

Robin Williams was quite aware of the real Adrian Cronauer. "He's a very straight guy," he told *Rolling Stone* magazine in a February 1988 interview. "He looks like Judge Bork. In real life, he never did anything outrageous...He didn't want to buck the system, because you can get court-martialed for that shit. So, yes, we took some dramatic license. But he did play rock & roll, he did do characters to introduce standard army announcements, and 'Goooooood morning, Vietnam' really was his signature line. He says he learned whenever soldiers in the field heard his sign-on line, they'd shout back at their radios, 'Gehhhhhhht fucked, Cronauer!'" Undeniably, too much of the film is pure Hollywood and manic Robin Williams, not true Vietnam war nor Adrian Cronauer. But the film did put a reasonably representative cross section of music at the center of the Vietnam War. Maybe the only thing missing from *Good Morning Vietnam* is a song by Creedence.

In an interview for Craig Werner's book *Up Around the Bend: An Oral History of Creedence Clearwater Revival,* John Fogerty claims he wrote "Fortunate Son" in about 20 minutes. But, according to a February 2018 article by Zach Schonfeld in *Pitchfork,* the music Fogerty and CCR produced "has soundtracked the Vietnam War in public memory for what feels like an eternity." CCR saw the war through their own circumstances and experiences, believing that the war in Vietnam was being fought by too many like themselves. So, for CCR it was personal—Fogerty did a brief stint in the Reserves, and the band's drummer, Doug Clifford, served in the Coast Guard Reserve between 1966 and 1968. So, when President Nixon's daughter Julie married Dwight Eisenhower's grandson, David, in 1969, Fogerty lost it.

"You'd hear about the son of this senator or that congressman who was given a deferment from the military," he wrote in his 2015 memoir *Fortunate Son: My Life, My Music.* "They weren't being touched by what their parents were doing."

Full of righteous indignation, Fogerty penned "Fortunate Son." Among other themes, the song highlighted the class disparity of the war. "Fortunate Son" is "really not an anti-war song," CCR drummer Doug Clifford told Schonfeld, "It's about class. Who did the dirty work?"

Perhaps more than any of their other songs, CCR's "Fortunate Son" aligned them with their peers, and, in a way, with films. As soon as Hollywood focused on Vietnam, one or more CCR songs roared on the soundtrack. *Forrest Gump?* CCR is there. *Born on the Fourth of July? Air America? Tropic of Thunder?* The 1998 cult hit *The Big Lebowski?* More Creedence. Even Spielberg's 2017 film *The Post* includes a Vietnam scene counterpointed by CCR's "Green River."

So how did America's best swamp rock band become the de facto soundtrack to the Vietnam War? According to Schonfeld and others, it started with *Who'll Stop the Rain,* a 1978 drama about a jaded journalist (Michael Moriarty) and a Vietnam vet (Nick Nolte) trying to smuggle heroin from Vietnam to the U.S. The film's soundtrack features three Credence numbers: "Proud Mary," "Hey Tonight," and, of course, "Who'll Stop the Rain." A decade later, writes Schonfeld, "the CCR trend started to really catch on: *1969*, a meditation on the war's impact on a small town released in 1988, used 'Green River.'"

For a change Hollywood had it right. In conversation after conversation during our ten years of research and interviews for *We Gotta Get Out of This Place*, vets talked about Creedence. Peter Bukowski, who served with the Army's American Division near Chu Lai from December 1968 to December 1969, summed up the music of the war by saying, "Two words: Creedence Clearwater. They were the one thing everybody agreed on. It wasn't any one song, there was just something about their sound and the way they brought what you were feeling into the music and the words."

Doug Clifford underscored the depth of the connection Creedence felt with the soldiers on active duty and the veterans returning home. "We were very much aware and we supported the guys and we knew what it was like to be in the military and be forced to do what you didn't want to do," he told Craig in *Up Around the Bend*. "We didn't look at them like some of our peers and call them pigs and baby killers. The poor bastards were guys our age who were going over there and getting their asses shot off. Our heart was with them. It wasn't them, it was the administrations. Kennedy basically got us in there, but it escalated under Johnson and Nixon. They were lying to the American people."

Fogerty, who'd grown up in a downwardly mobile lower middle-class family in El Cerrito, California, emphasized the importance of his service in an Army Reserve unit to the songs he wrote and sang: "The military experience was key in my motivation. I was writing songs, I was doing it with no instruments, no connection, I was not even in the outside world, but somehow this was better.

Something had happened to me, and I resolved at that point to not be mediocre, to write real songs."

Several of CCR's biggest hits were inspired by their awareness of Vietnam. Even "Proud Mary," CCR's ode to the countercultural vision of a hassle-free life on a half-mythic river, has a Vietnam connection, according to Fogerty: "In the middle of July 1968, this envelope containing this little thing that's like a diploma had been sitting on the stairs of my apartment building for a couple of days," he revealed. "It said, 'Official Business,' or something. Well, I didn't bother to look close at it. Finally, one day I was coming into my apartment, and I look on the stairs, and, 'Hey, that's got my name on it!' Well, son of a bitch, I opened it up, and I'm discharged from the Army. Holy Hallelujah! I actually went out on the little apartment building lawn and did a couple of cartwheels. At that one moment, it was like, 'Wow, all the troubles of the world have been lifted off my shoulders.' If it didn't happen within five minutes, certainly within a week and a half I had written, 'Proud Mary.' That's where 'left a good job in the city' comes from."

Perhaps most importantly, the band's political position—antiwar and pro-veteran—appealed to Vietnam soldiers and veterans. "Military guys loved us," noted Clifford. "A lot of them said, 'Hey, you got us through Vietnam.' My answer to that was, 'No, you got yourself through. We might have helped you a little bit. But we were behind you a hundred percent and we still are today.' People don't realize unless they've been in the military what it's really like."

"These guys put their lives on the line," CCR bassist Stu Cook added. "We got tons of fan mail from Vietnam. Guys would send us stuff...We felt like we were doing something, helping there even though we weren't there. I really identify with the vets even though it wasn't something I experienced."

In his memoir, Fogerty describes being thanked in the 1990s by a Vietnam veteran who told him that his squad routinely played Creedence to prepare for combat: "Every night, just before we'd go out into the jungle, we would turn on all the lights in our encampment, put on 'Bad Moon Rising,' and blast it as loud as we could."

In his *Pitchfork* article, Zach Schonfeld points out that something else about CCR's music made them appealing to Hollywood music supervisors—legally, their music was readily obtainable because Fogerty had signed away distribution and publishing rights to Fantasy Records, a decision he regrets to this day. And, culturally, the band's roots-rock hooks functioned as a nostalgic shorthand, immediately situating a scene in the late '60s or early '70s. Although "Run Through the Jungle" is frequently misinterpreted as being about Vietnam—Fogerty says he wrote it about gun violence in the U. S.—most CCR songs contain no direct reference to the war. They do, however, strongly evoke a period when the war dominated American life.

The sentimental 1994 drama *Forrest Gump* sealed CCR's status as the distinctive Vietnam sound. The film's soundtrack reads like a who's who of rock and roll stardom—Elvis, Dylan, Aretha, the Four Tops and Supremes, Simon and Garfunkel, the Byrds, Jefferson Airplane, and more. But it is the arrival of Forrest Gump in Vietnam via helicopter to the sounds of "Fortunate Son" that "acts as trigger to the memory of the song's codified message," observed writer Hilary Lapedis. I watched the film when it came out in 1994 with my then 14-year-old daughter Summer, and during that helicopter scene, she squeezed my hand as hard as she's ever squeezed it, proof that the combination of Vietnam visuals and a CCR Vietnam-related song had made a lasting impact.

There's another story about media, Vietnam, and public memory that doesn't center on Hollywood; it's about public radio and TV.

"Really, a 'brief' summary of our Vietnam work?" questioned Mik Derks, a producer with Wisconsin Public Television (WPT) in Madison, Wisconsin. He and his WPT colleagues were responsible for *Wisconsin Vietnam War Stories,* an award-winning series broadcast statewide in 2010. "How could I ever be brief about my years spent interviewing 300 Vietnam Veterans, laughing and crying with them?" Mik continued. "About wrangling those interviews, each deserving a show of its own, into three hours that used the experiences of soldiers, sailors, Marines, and Air Force to tell the larger story of the Vietnam war? About those years crossing the state to convince and listen to veterans about a long overdue welcome home that should instead be a party, and those three amazing days of hugs and tears at LZ Lambeau in May 2010? About watching WPT photographer Jim Gill capture the soul of the veterans in his portrait project? About marveling at how a documentary project took over an entire station? About the years since then working with PBS affiliates in other states to do what we did in Wisconsin?"

Mik wasn't being facetious about all that went into *Wisconsin Vietnam War Stories* and LZ Lambeau (The letters refer to "landing zone" in Vietnam parlance.). With both achievements, WPT set the standard for how public media contribute to our Vietnam public memory. Extensive veteran outreach, hundreds of interviews, school curricula, education days, the three-hour documentary, two books, community engagement, and three days of robust and well-attended welcome home activity at LZ Lambeau. Drawing on the Wisconsin experience, numerous public media nationwide sought out Vietnam veterans in their communities and encouraged them to open up about their experience for radio, TV, and web programs. LZ Lambeau inspired public media and veteran organizations in Texas, Michigan, California, Oklahoma, New York, Ohio, Louisiana, Utah, and Maryland. It was cathartic, healing, therapeutic.

Mik interviewed me for *Wisconsin Vietnam War Stories,* and though a non-veteran, he was naturally adept in his questioning. He helped us interviewees to get at the heart of what Vietnam was, and is. *Wisconsin Vietnam War Stories* received broadcast Emmys both statewide and nationally; it inspired other public media— Penn State (WPSU) and Minnesota (TPT) and Grand Rapids (WGVU) and Kansas City (KCPT)—to engage and encourage their own veterans to talk about Vietnam. It wasn't Ken Burns and Lynn Novick, not Oliver Stone and Francis Ford Coppola. It wasn't glamorous or hyper Hollywood. It was pure and true. Real.

It was us telling our stories.

How we got to tell those stories affected *what* we could tell. Public radio and television were working in a different genre from the Hollywood film, with its director's vision and its production necessities and its eye to profit.

SOLO Mik Derks

Mik Derks. Photo courtesy Wisconsin Public Television.

If you're like me, you don't appreciate people telling you how to do your job. But if you're someone who's planning to combine archival footage of the Vietnam War with the stories of the veterans who fought it, and you haven't had many opportunities to talk to veterans about their experiences, it might be helpful to know what I've learned in the course of interviewing hundreds of veterans from World War II, Korea, and Vietnam.

First off, be prepared when you first approach Vietnam veterans about sharing their stories—they will most likely tell you they don't want to talk about it. They will insist that they have put the war behind them and want to keep it there. That's not true, of course. They think about the war every day, still trying to figure it out. But the memories are indeed painful, of friends lost, of lives changed, of endless fear and tension, the guilt of surviving, the reception received when they came home, accusations that they lost their war, anger over the way the war was fought and things they were asked to do. And for many, previous attempts to tell their story have gone badly—war is not something you want to share with your wife or children, and reporters seem more interested in hearing something sensational than listening. That is why so many veterans have found it easier to pretend they never served. And that is why people are often shocked to find out after many years that their neighbors, friends, and workmates are Vietnam veterans.

The public image of the typical Vietnam veteran as the troubled homeless guy who wears tattered fatigues is false. There are, unfortunately, some of those, but there are far more school principals and mailmen, CEOs and social workers, storekeepers and factory workers, doctors and ministers, and anyone else you see when you look around.

It's also extremely important to keep in mind the wide variance of Vietnam experiences. Veterans have said that Vietnam was not a ten-year war, but ten one-year wars, because each year was so different. Similarly, the type of war waged on the border with North Vietnam was totally different from that in the Central Highlands, which was in turn totally different from the guerilla war in the Delta. Add to that the difference of experience in the Army, Marines, Air Force, Navy and Coast Guard...

Your first contact with the veteran is critical. At any mention of television or interview or telling their story, they will envision the worst. You have to let them know up front that you understand what they have been through, both in Vietnam and on their return home. They may be quick to anger, so remember that the anger is not directed at you, but at the unfairness of their experience. Tell them about your project and what you hope to accomplish, such as clearing up some of the confusion people have about Vietnam veterans. Tell them that you believe the best way to do that is to let veterans tell their own story rather than having it interpreted by a producer or reporter. Then, get their information. They don't like to talk about their bad experiences, but they will happily share with you the dates of their service, their unit, where they were in Vietnam, and their job in the military. Providing this information may very well start them talking about their experiences, and if they sound comfortable, you can ask them if they would be willing to share their story with you in an interview. But if you sense that there is still hesitation on their part, don't force the issue, because once they say no it's hard to change their mind.

There is a sad phenomenon that appears to be connected more with Vietnam than any other war—people who never served pretending that they did, and people who served stateside or in rear echelon positions claiming combat experience and even medals for valor. This is treacherous ground for anyone trying to interview veterans because you don't want to include stories in your program that can later be proved bogus, and neither do you want to give real veterans the impression that you don't trust what they are saying. I had the luxury of having Butch, a videographer who is a Vietnam veteran, to help me watch for things like a story that's just too good to be true, full of heroic actions and fuzzy on specific details. These stories tend to focus only on the storyteller, whereas veterans who were in the thick of it speak mostly of the people they were with, and especially the people they lost...Still, it's not an easy call, because these memories are forty years old, and things like names and dates and the order of events can get a little confused.

One of the difficulties veterans have when it comes to telling their stories is that it takes time. It takes time for them to let the memories flow, and it takes time to tell a story of such complexity and emotion, and it takes time to come back out of the telling. Television production, on the other hand, is more of a "get in, get the story, and get out" process. In this case, I think we have an obligation to change that process because we can actually cause damage by asking the veteran to delve into those memories and then abruptly pulling away because we have to move on to another interview. For this reason, we chose to do our interviews as oral histories, allowing time for vets to tell their two-hour story, even though we would only be using a few minutes in the program. The added benefit of this approach was the creation of an extensive archive that will benefit historians and families for generations.

Whenever we scheduled an interview, we made sure to explain clearly what would happen. Most people hear the word "interview" and think of what they've seen on television, with a reporter asking the questions and the interviewee on the spot to come up with cogent answers. That's a lot of pressure. I always tell veterans that it will be more of a conversation than an interview, with just the two of us talking about their experience. I tell them I will ask questions, but only to clarify my understanding of their story. We will start at the beginning of their service and talk until there's nothing more to say, with them having full control over what they choose to talk about...I never went into an interview with a list of questions (though I had them in my head), because I've found that if you ask a formal question you get a formal answer, and what I was looking for was the flow of memory—the story...I also found that silence can be productive. Many of the veterans we interviewed, perhaps the majority of them, had never before talked so much about Vietnam. They were processing memories that they had not allowed to surface for decades, so they did not come out in an organized narrative, but jumped around from incident to incident, place to place, person to person, as triggered by something else that had been said. Silence provided the room for more memories to surface, and they always did.

I told the veterans repeatedly that they were in full control of what we talked about in the interview, that I would never try to lead them into memories that made them uncomfortable. And whenever I asked a question that might have that result, I reminded them that I wasn't trying to push them into anything and just to say no if they didn't want to go there. But even without my actively looking for it, the raw stories came pouring out as if they could no longer be contained—as if they were just waiting for someone to listen, without judgment, without horror, without fear. Of course, tears and sobs and valiant struggles to stay in control would accompany the stories. How could they not? But we learned not to be embarrassed by these shows of emotion, and because we weren't, the veterans weren't embarrassed either. They would let it out, then regain their composure and continue.

What WPT did with its Vietnam veteran initiatives still resonates here in Wisconsin. Craig and I sensed it when we made presentations about our book in communities across the state. The distance, the apprehension, the tension, the blame, the bullshit that usually surround Vietnam and veterans were greatly reduced, replaced by a continuous openness we could build on. That's one of the many upsides of WPT's broadcasting, streaming, and distributing *Wisconsin Vietnam War Stories* so that it reached hundreds of thousands of viewers. Our dear departed friend, and founding member of our Deadly Writers Patrol, Howard Sherpe, put it best in a letter he wrote to WPT after the first statewide broadcast of *Wisconsin Vietnam War Stories*. Howard was a medic in Vietnam in 1966–67, where he saw more than his fair share of pain, suffering, and death. Like me, Howard was interviewed by Mik for *Wisconsin Vietnam War Stories*.

LETTER   Howard Sherpe

U.S. Army medic Howard Sherpe in Vietnam 1966. Photo courtesy Howard Sherpe.

I've been meaning to write to you and let you know how much I appreciate what you have done for all Vietnam vets. As you know, I was very reluctant to be a part of the interviewing process and tell my story. You remained true to your word that if I didn't like how the interviewing process went, I could tell you I didn't want any of it used. I'm so thankful you didn't give up on me and made me realize how important it is to tell our individual stories.

I'm honored to be included in the documentary. You have put together a very powerful, honest, gut-wrenching portrayal of the Vietnam veteran and let us tell it in our own words. I thank you. As one friend said, "I had no idea that the war affected people to such a deep degree, even after all these years." She saw how deeply it affected so many and how hard it was to talk about it without the emotions coming to the surface. It's also good for all of us Vietnam vets to see that emotion too and know we aren't the only ones who were so deeply affected. My friend, author Ben Logan, said it best when I asked him about his World War II experiences. He told me, "You never come completely home from the war, you come part way home." Thank you again for all you've done...for us Vietnam vets.

Mik Derks and WPT had responded to veterans' call for recognition with their own call for interviews; Howard Sherpe, I, and so many other vets responded. When other public radio and television stations became interested, the statewide call-and-response took on a more national scope without losing its local focus.

What truly set apart WPT and its partners most clearly from commercial media and film was LZ Lambeau. The project partners, seeking an opportunity to thank Vietnam and Vietnam-era veterans for their service and sacrifice, collaborated with the Oneida Tribe, the greater Green Bay community, and the Green Bay Packers to create LZ Lambeau. On the weekend of May 21–23, 2010, an estimated 70,000 people—Vietnam veterans, their families, friends and neighbors—traveled to Green Bay for three days of tributes, memorials, reunions, camaraderie, and brotherhood.

An "Honor Ride" opened the event. Exactly 1,244 motorcyclists rode from La Crosse to Green Bay in honor of the number of Wisconsin service members killed, or still missing, in Vietnam. As the ride made its way across Wisconsin, communities came out in force to greet, applaud, and salute the motorcycles. In the tiny town of Freedom, Wisconsin, the local school students waved flags and the fire department mounted a huge American flag above the street. WPT videographer and Vietnam veteran Butch Soetenga was part of the entourage, joined by four of his five sons. "To experience that ride with four of my sons was one of the most memorable and emotional moments in my life," he recalled. "To hear my sons tell me that it was an honor for them to ride beside me was music to my ears and brought tears to my eyes. To roll through the town of Freedom with those boys at my side and surrounded by all of my Vietnam brothers was a moment too awesome for words. To receive a welcome home like that was overwhelming."

LZ Lambeau featured museum and photography exhibits, a music stage, Vietnam-era vehicles and aircraft, The Moving Wall™, community events, school outreach, an ecumenical service, and a Tribute Ceremony inside historic Lambeau Field. Craig and I gave one of our best presentations to a packed house in the Paul Hornung Room of the Legends Club. Later that Saturday, more than 27,000 people from 30 states attended a special welcome-home ceremony inside Lambeau Field for a "thank you" to Wisconsin's Vietnam Veterans. Of course, the gala event featured music—our friend Kimo Williams was there doing his best Jimi Hendrix simulation with Gary Sinise's Lt. Dan Band, and Ben E. King gave a mighty rendition of "Stand by Me." There was poetry from Anishinaabe vet Jim Northrup, who spoke movingly about the thousands of vets who had died following their service, felled by Agent Orange, desperation, and suicides. The 1,244 empty chairs standing silent on the expansive playing field served as a painful reminder of those Wisconsin service members killed or missing in Vietnam. Live broadcasts on Wisconsin Public Television and Radio shared the event with all Wisconsin citizens, including thousands of veterans who could not attend.

Kimo Williams performing with the Lt. Dan Band at LZ Lambeau,
May 2010. Photo courtesy Wisconsin Public Television.

But for me the crowning achievement of LZ Lambeau was the "Big Map," a 105 by 140 foot vinyl map of Southeast Asia that filled one of the Lambeau Field parking lots. The brainchild of Jeff Kollath, who at the time was director of programming at the Wisconsin Veterans Museum, the Big Map became the spiritual center of LZ Lambeau. Hundreds of Vietnam vets returned again and again to retrace their tours of duty and connect with fellow veterans. Guys who'd tried for 40 years to put Vietnam behind them proudly wrote their names on the map, wrote memorials to those they had lost, and for the first time shared their stories with their families. One wry vet scrawled his name across neighboring Cambodia and said "I wasn't here, 1969." The map is now a treasured artifact of the LZ Lambeau permanent collection of the Wisconsin Veterans Museum.

Vietnam vet looking at LZ Lambeau's "Big Map" May 2010.
Photo courtesy Wisconsin Public Television.

LZ Lambeau was conceived of and executed as a participatory project, structured with opportunities for non-vets to acknowledge service and for vets to express their experiences in public spaces. The music and the Big Map gave vets ways to say, "I heard this; I felt that; I was *here*." LZ Lambeau was what historian John Gillis calls a "commemorative event," one that impacts our public memory such as a celebration, parade, or vigil. "Commemorative activity is by definition social and political," Gillis writes, "for it involves the coordination of individual and group memories, whose results may appear consensual when they are in fact the product of processes of intense contest, struggle, and, in some instances, annihilation" Mik Derks, WPT, and their many partners were using a form of ritual and celebration to give life to a *public* memory based on the *private* memories of Vietnam veterans. Whereas our public interpretations of Vietnam would often lead to diverse, conflicting claims about the war, other activities at LZ Lambeau like the Big Map, the Honor Ride, and *Wisconsin Vietnam War Stories* had validated the experiences of Wisconsin Vietnam veterans. As a result, scores of community events engaged residents across Wisconsin in conversation about the Vietnam War and its legacy. After decades of keeping their stories inside, veterans had shared their experiences with their communities and built a public memory that was more authentic and personal. WPT had responded to the call of Vietnam veterans who, to quote from the lyrics of a powerful 1968 song by the Dells, had been asking for years, "Does Anybody Know I'm Here?"

Thanks to public media, there were similar affirmations in other states. Some station activities—LZ events in Texas and Maryland—predated the PBS 2017 Burns-Novick The Vietnam War series, while others—led by KCPT in Kansas City, KCTS-TV in Seattle—were linked to it. Still others—our TPT friends in Minnesota whom you've read about in the Overture and Penn State's WPSU—launched ongoing efforts.

Led by senior producer Frank Christopher and Jerry Zolten, a Penn State professor, radio producer, and folk singer, WPSU decided to create a complementary cross-platform media project about Vietnam and reached out to me, since I was a native Pennsylvanian, for input. The WPSU project became *The Vietnam War: Telling the Pennsylvania Story*, a major, cross-platform effort that encompassed TV, radio, Web, and community engagement. Among the highlights, broadcast throughout Pennsylvania, were a one-hour TV documentary, *A Time to Heal*, and a two-hour radio program, *Time to Lay it Down*.

Meanwhile, Patty Lindley, digital director with KTCS 9 in Seattle, asked me to help put together a highly interactive timeline of the Vietnam War featuring the music in *We Gotta Get Out of This Place*. The timeline contained a "greatest hits by the years" assessment of the music from 1964–73 and was featured in the Vietnam Veterans Memorial Fund's newsletter.

"Finding a timeline that connects to history, music, events within the United States, and Vietnam is an epic challenge," observed newsletter editor Callie Wright. "KCTS 9, out of Seattle, has done just that. This timeline helps remind us that while 1964 may have produced the enchanting "I Want to Hold Your Hand" by The Beatles, it was also the year that three young men were murdered while working to register black voters in Mississippi and on the other side of the world four Americans and two Vietnamese soldiers were killed at an airbase attack on Bien Hoa. Check out *On The Record* at http://origin.kcts9.org/vietnam-war-timeline/

With *Minnesota Remembers Vietnam*, Katie Carpenter, Randal Dietrich, and their colleagues at TPT launched events, programs, testimonials, broadcasts, outreach, and the Veterans Day Concert mentioned in the Introduction. In all, TPT raised more than $2 million, produced 17 original documentaries with six Minnesota PBS stations; garnered five Emmy nominations, and reached well over 20,000 people at its numerous public events. The outpouring of support and enthusiasm was astonishing. Richard Timmerman, a Vietnam veteran who was in the audience for the *We Gotta Get Out of This Place* concert, said it best: "This event had a life-changing effect on me and my spouse. Let me explain. It became evident to me during the readings and discussions, as well as the musical numbers, that *my* Vietnam can now be viewed in a healthier manner as 'historic' rather than primarily political. My spouse, who is five years my junior and who was not as personally involved in Vietnam...has told me how much better she now feels regarding an understanding of who I am and how I have become that person. We talked for more than an hour that evening with a [new] depth."

Jim Pagliarini, president and CEO of Twin Cities Public Television, reflected on TPT's Vietnam initiative.

SOLO   Jim Pagliarini

"End of the Tour" concert at Twin Cities Public TV studios, November 2017. Photo courtesy Twin Cities Public TV.

Our year-long, statewide initiative called Minnesota Remembers Vietnam, was conceived well over two years ago when we learned that filmmakers Ken Burns and Lynn Novick were going to present to America their comprehensive and definitive work on Vietnam. We took pause at Twin Cities PBS and asked, "What could we do to bring this story home? What might we do to honor and give voice to the men and women in Minnesota whose lives were touched by this confusing, divisive, and tumultuous period in American history? And what might we do to create understanding and healing?"

We set our sights very high, and over the past year we have undertaken what has been the largest and one of the most important projects in the station's sixty-year history. We produced four incredibly powerful documentaries that will live for generations. We also produced a remarkable Veteran's Day concert based on *Rolling Stone*'s #1 Music Book for 2015, *We Gotta Get Out of This Place*, which used the music of the era to stimulate and tell stories of the Vietnam experience. Music, storytelling and imagery came together to create an unforgettable community experience at two concerts held at Twin Cities PBS-TPT Veterans Day weekend of 2017.

An all-star band performed iconic music from Jimi Hendrix, Buffalo Springfield, Aretha Franklin, Bob Dylan, Janis Joplin, Creedence Clearwater Revival, and many more. These musical performances were punctuated with readings by Minnesota veterans and activists, selected from *We Gotta Get Out of This Place*.

The audience danced—I know I did—sang along, and even shed a few tears as music joined the past to the present in a moving musical experience.

A Vietnam veteran attendee said, "This was the welcome home celebration I never had." Another commented, "Music doesn't just make you remember. It makes you feel."

With our colleagues across Minnesota, we explored the war from all sides, giving it a 360-degree view. We traveled the state to collect stories and artifacts from veterans, family members, activists, protestors. We gathered stories at class reunions, veteran reunions, community centers, museums, VA hospitals, and libraries. We worked with students and educators and made our Vietnam work a centerpiece for this year's Minnesota History Day. To date, we have collected over a thousand stories from people in Minnesota, and we're still counting. Some found their home in documentaries that I mentioned, but all of them found a home in what has been the centerpiece of this endeavor, the Minnesota Vietnam Digital Story Wall that you can explore at MNVietnam.org. There, you'll find a remarkable collection of videos, written work, art, and audio, each telling a personal and moving story about the Vietnam War era.

And as part of the culmination of the project, we brought to Minnesota *The Wall That Heals,* a replica of the Vietnam Memorial, and we brought that to our state's capital and have held numerous events to honor the men and women who served. Over 15,000 people visited over several days, and it was a moving and memorable experience to watch the community of people who have come together to remember and to honor....

It has been a deeply moving experience for all of us at Twin Cities PBS, and we feel much richer for having been a part of this...I can tell you very sincerely in my four decades of working with PBS, I've never been involved in a project that was so universally embraced.

The unifying message that I heard time and time again from those who supported the war, those who demonstrated against it, and those who only learned about it through the history books, now was the time to seize the moment to honor the men and women who served their country during this tumultuous and confusing time, men and women who were shunned and endured hardships upon returning home, and who, until very recently, did not feel welcome to tell their stories, to share both the joyful memories of friendships and camaraderie and the haunting, painful memories of battle.

Twin Cities PBS is honored to have played a small role in helping us all remember, honor, and understand.

Obviously, far fewer Americans have seen *Wisconsin Vietnam War Stories* or been a part of *Minnesota Remembers* or listened to "Time to Lay It Down" than saw *Apocalypse Now* or *Platoon.* But the public media programs for Vietnam veterans had, and have, restorative power. When will public media give the same level of and programming to the veterans of America's more recent wars?

Our debates over public memory and Vietnam are more than differences of opinion about the historical record. Rather, they center on fundamental questions about the structure and legitimacy of our social and political institutions, questions that public media, and we the people, grapple with. In *Remaking America: Public Memory, Commemoration, and Patriotism in the Twentieth Century*, historian John Bodnar notes that the real focus of a public memory dispute "is not the past, however, but serious matters in the present such as the nature of power and the question of loyalty to both official and vernacular [informal] cultures."

Vietnam vets could explain to you just why this is so, which underscores the importance and necessity of their voice, and their take, on Vietnam and public memory. John Fogerty and CCR could too, as "Fortunate Son" perfectly illustrates:

Some folks are born made to wave the flag
Ooh, they're red, white and blue
And when the band plays "Hail to the chief"
Ooh, they point the cannon at you, Lord
It ain't me, it ain't me, I ain't no senator's son, son
It ain't me, it ain't me, I ain't no fortunate one, no

In their respective books *Forever Vietnam* and *The Vietnam War in American Memory*, authors David Kieran and Patrick Hagopian have examined public memory as it relates to the war in Vietnam. In his introduction Kieran calls attention to the use and misuse of Vietnam War history: "This book argues that the evolving and contested memory of the American War in Vietnam has shaped Americans' commemoration of other events in ways that inform the understanding of themselves, their nation, and the global interests of the United States...to delineate more fully the contours of many Americans' enduring embrace of militarism, often uncritical acquiescence to the use of military force abroad, and continued failure to acknowledge the crises that those interventions prompted in the lives of veterans, their families, and the civilians who experience them."

An important contribution to the emerging field of Memory Studies, *Forever Vietnam* demonstrates how the legacy of the Vietnam War has shaped American conceptions of historical events such as the Alamo; World War II and the overdue acknowledgment of post-traumatic syndrome (PTSD); the infamous Andersonville prison camp of the Civil War; the "Black Hawk Down" incident in Somalia; Flight 93 of 9/11; and the War on Terror. In each of these examples, Kieran shows that the experience of the Vietnam War provided an interpretive construct, and he concludes by arguing that the war in Iraq has become the "new Vietnam," a lesson of the past that will be invoked whenever the U.S. faces new challenges abroad or engages in a period of national soul-searching.

Forever Vietnam is a provocative evaluation of public memory, but I was having a hard time seeing my Vietnam reflected in the Alamo and Andersonville and Somalia, no matter how entrenched those examples are in our public memory. On the other hand, Hagopian's *The Vietnam War in American Memory: Veterans, Memorials, and the Politics of Healing* brought my own memory of Vietnam front and center. Reading it, I kept seeing the names listed in order of death on the Vietnam Veterans Memorial, including that of one my fellow information specialists. I kept revisiting the music-based memories of the hundreds of Vietnam veterans we'd interviewed for our book...and I kept hearing those young Marines at Khe Sanh playing guitars and singing "Where Have All the Flowers Gone?" as they endured a daily barrage of artillery from the North Vietnamese Army—sometimes as many as 1,200 rounds a day—during the 77-day siege of Khe Sanh during the Tet Offensive in early 1968.

Crucially, Hagopian scrutinizes the central role assigned to Vietnam veterans in the evolution of our public memory of the war. He shows us how the public perception of Vietnam veterans evolved from alienated malcontent to traumatized victim to noble warrior. And he delineates how efforts to commemorate the war have increasingly downplayed the political divisions it generated in favor of a more unifying emphasis on honoring veterans and promoting national healing.

U.S. Army soldiers strumming guitars at Khe Sanh, Vietnam, 1968. Public domain.

Perhaps it's fitting that Hagopian centers his argument around the most revered, and controversial, direct outcome of the war, the Vietnam Veterans Memorial ("The Wall") in Washington, D.C. He follows its development painstakingly from idea to plan to design, then to the heavily politicized public dispute, through execution and more disagreement, to the hallowed place it now holds in public memory.

"I think it is actually a miracle that the piece ever got built," recalled designer Maya Lin in a November 2002 essay for *The New York Review of Books*.

Still, Hagopian encourages us—all of us, including Maya Lin—to move on: "Memorials are not simply the products of their designers' imaginations and their planners' motives. Once a memorial is constructed it ceases to be the 'property' of those who created it. As visitors enrich the site with their own thoughts and feelings, a memorial becomes a *public* possession [emphasis mine]. A clear example of the way the memorial experience differs from its original conception involves the segmentation of the granite wall."

Hagopian notes that Maya Lin had imagined that the public's relationship to the memorial would be essentially passive and contemplative because the war was still so raw for many Americans: "I made a conscious decision not to do any specific research on the Vietnam War and the political turmoil surrounding it," Lin wrote. "I felt that the politics had eclipsed the veterans, their service, and their lives. I wanted to create a memorial that everyone would be able to respond to, regardless of whether one thought our country should or should not have participated in the war...(thus) the two walls were positioned so that one pointed to the Lincoln Memorial and the other pointed to the Washington Monument. By linking these two strong symbols for the country, I wanted to create a unity between the nation's past and present."

The Vietnam Memorial, Washington, D.C. Public domain.

Maya Lin and her detractors, as well as Vietnam veterans and the American public, got much more than they bargained for. When the first panels went up, the public didn't just respond dynamically to the memorial, they approached the stone and touched the name of a deceased soldier as if they could be in actual contact with the real person.

"It was like the wall was alive," said one visitor, quoted by Ha-gopian. Another, a young Boston father, was overheard telling his rambunctious son, "Hush, Timmy—this is like a church."

Maya Lin understood the power that a name, and the memories associated with it, could have. "What then would bring back the memory of a person?" she posed in her article. "A specific object or image would be limiting. A realistic sculpture would be only one interpretation of that time. I wanted something that all people could relate to on a personal level...The use of names was a way to bring back everything someone could remember about a person. The strength in a name is something that has always made me wonder at the 'abstraction' of the design; the ability of a name to bring back every single memory you have of that person is far more realistic and specific and much more comprehensive than a still photograph, which captures a specific moment in time or a single event or a generalized image that may or may not be moving for all who have connections to that time."

The first time I approached the wall, on a damp, cloudy May morning in 1984, I could still see my own reflection, my connection, to the wall...and with the names. And then I did what most visitors to The Wall do—I searched for a very special someone. I found his name on Panel W5 Line 104, "Stephen H. Warner."

Guys like Steve Warner weren't supposed to get killed in Vietnam. Steve was a Phi Beta Kappa National Honor Society graduate of Gettysburg College; he'd been drafted in June 1969 after his first year of law school at Yale and had a first-year law student's keen sense of actions that were lawful and unlawful. Steve and I were meant to spend our 365 days in the rear, working in a bright, shiny, almost corporate public information office in the U.S. Army's headquarters at Long Binh, a former rubber plantation 15 miles from Saigon. And while we didn't necessarily write the truth about what was going on, or going wrong, in Vietnam, we could at least stay out of harm's way: there was no requirement that we accompany troops into combat.

But Steve did. Like a lot of us who were drafted into the Army and sent to Vietnam during the later stages of the war (1970s), Steve was not an admirer of U.S. policy in Vietnam. But, unlike most of the rest of us REMFs, Steve put his principles where his mouth was and took every occasion to go out into the countryside and see exactly what was going on. He made a point of interviewing, photographing, and connecting with the grunts in the field who were doing the fighting and dying.

U.S. Army combat correspondent Steve Warner, Vietnam, 1971. Photo courtesy Gettysburg College library.

What Steve discovered increased his consternation about the war. I remember his being especially angry when he was told to "paint out beads" at the bottom of one of his field photographs. During this time (1970–71), many soldiers were wearing a plethora of physical adornments, including "Love Beads," a direct violation of military dress regulations. Steve stood his ground with the military censors, absolutely refusing to remove the beads from his shots.

While the rest of us Army "journalists" cursed the military under our breath, Steve raised the volume. By the time we shared an office, he'd dedicated himself to being the Vietnam War's version of Ernie Pyle, the great WWII war correspondent. "What sold me on Ernie Pyle, " he wrote to his parents, "was a book by him...it said, 'He hates war but loves the men who have to fight them.' That about sums me up too!"

Stephen Warner was killed in an ambush near the Laotian border on February 14, 1971. He didn't have to be there. But for me, Panel W5 Line 104 says it all because it is, like so many other Vietnam war deaths, a terrible waste. The online Vietnam Wall provides additional, albeit sobering, details:

STEPHEN HENRY WARNER
SP4 - E4 - Army - Selective Service
5th Infantry Division Mechanized

His tour began on Mar 21, 1970
Casualty was on Feb 14, 1971
In QUANG TRI, SOUTH VIETNAM
Hostile, died of wounds, GROUND CASUALTY
OTHER EXPLOSIVE DEVICE
Body was recovered

Visitors to the Memorial have testified about seeing their reflection in the black gabbro wall. Among them is the heralded poet, Yusef Komunyakaa, a Vietnam veteran who wrote an amazing collection of poems, *Dien Cai Dau*. In "Facing It," he writes:

My black face fades,
hiding inside the black granite.
I said I wouldn't,
dammit: No tears.
I'm stone. I'm flesh.
My clouded reflection eyes me

like a bird of prey, the profile of night
slanted against morning. I turn
this way—the stone lets me go.
I turn that way—I'm inside
the Vietnam Veterans Memorial
again, depending on the light
to make a difference.

One popular painting, *Reflections*, by Lee Teter, shows a middle-aged man, head bent in grief, as he reaches out to place his hand on the wall. The man has set his briefcase, suit jacket draped over it, on the ground. From the "other side," where one would expect to see his reflection, the image is a younger man, helmeted and in military fatigues, flanked by four other troops. Palm against reflected palm, the visitor is touching his younger self, flanked by his buddies. Or perhaps he is encountering five comrades lost in the war? As Hagopian observes, "The scene suggests that time and space collapse at the encounter across the wall, as if the scroll of time were punctured and two points separated by years pinned together."

Hagopian closes *The Vietnam War in American Memory* by quoting from President Ronald Reagan's "Farewell Address to the Nation" on January 11, 1989. Reagan, whose administration redefined the war in Vietnam as a "noble cause," told his fellow Americans that "If we forget what we did, we won't know who we are. I'm warning of an eradication of the American memory that could result, ultimately, in an erosion of the American spirit." And then Hagopian shows us the stakes: "It is not only, as Jonathan Schell once said, Americans' souls that are at stake, but the moral order of the world. Americans' decisions about how to remember the Vietnam War will help determine whether we live in a world where justice is possible or a world where the powerful forgive themselves anything, and then, without shame, move on. America remains a city upon a hill: the world is still watching."

⊖ ⊖ ⊖

One of the goals of academic historians is to share our past with future generations, but as I thought more about the hundreds of music-based memories and war experiences that veterans had shared, I knew I hadn't found them in even the best political-military histories (those by Stanley Karnow, Marilyn Young, and John Prados). Henry Ford, Jr. wouldn't be singing "I Stand Accused," Mary Reynolds Powell wouldn't be waxing poetic on "And When I Die." *We Gotta Get Out of This Place* had added an important layer of personal, informal reminiscence to public memory. All we needed to do was get the word out to more and more of our fellow citizens.

But we still live in the world of *Forever Vietnam*, with strong, conflicting claims about the past that still cause controversies like John Kerry and the Swift Boat vets, or Bob Kerrey's being branded a war criminal for leading a deadly attack on Vietnamese civilians. As Kieran noted, these and other conflicts over public memory disagreements are not only about the historical record but also about social and political institutions, about the very nature of power.

This point was driven home by CBS News correspondent and Vietnam veteran David Martin, who was among the many presenters at a superb symposium put on by the University of Nebraska-Omaha, "The Vietnam War: Lessons and Legacies," on October 27 and 28, 2016. We gave two well-received presentations there, and it's where I first met Chuck and Tom Hagel, two exceptional public servants and Vietnam veterans, who've written the Prelude to this book.

"The Vietnam War began with the false belief that North Vietnamese torpedo boats attacked American destroyers in the Gulf of Tonkin," Martin explained during one of the panel discussions. "The war in Iraq began with the false belief that Saddam Hussein was hiding weapons of mass destruction. I blame the press for that as much as I do the government. We too willingly reported every little scooplet we could get from the government about the latest evidence that Saddam really did have weapons of mass destruction, and we did not as an institution, the press, question it strongly enough, and if a few of the more powerful news organizations had raised any doubts about the intelligence, we might not have ended up in Iraq."

"Obviously, this is lesson we did not learn from Vietnam," Martin concluded, showing us the power of false public memory to determine events in the present. Later during that same panel, decorated Vietnam veteran and former U. S. Secretary of Defense Chuck Hagel, shared some similar sentiments about public memory: "In 1981, I became the Deputy Administrator for the Veterans Administration under President Ronald Reagan," Hagel recalled. "I had a problem with the then-current VA administrator [Robert Nimmo], who went on ABC's 'Good Morning America' and stated publicly that Vietnam veterans were cry-babies, that Agent Orange didn't produce anything more than a bad complexion, that PTSD was a bunch of hocus pocus and so on. That was the formal position of the Reagan administration. They were changing the conversation about Vietnam, and Congress didn't want to touch it. Everybody wanted to walk away from it because the Reagan administration essentially wanted to dismantle any more conversation or programs about any funds being expended for epidemiological surveys and studies to see if there were any consequences for our veterans exposed to Agent Orange...I actually resigned that VA job a year later."

Always the optimist, former Secretary Hagel believes the U.S. has an uncanny ability to adapt and adjust, to get the story right, ultimately. "We have an amazing society and culture and system that allows us to self-correct," he told the audience at the UNO Symposium. "We have twenty-seven Amendments to the United States Constitution, because we didn't get it all right the first time, and we're still working on a lot of things. We fought a Civil War, but since then we've done pretty well with our differences. I mean we have our episodes, but we have this process of self-correction, and if we're wise enough and learn enough—about what the Constitution guarantees as a nation of laws—and we respect each other and listen to each other, we can bring this around and come back.

"After fifty years, roughly, we do learn things and we are influenced by what we learn and what we see," Hagel concluded. "Like in any war, the legacies of Vietnam have quite unattractive dimensions...how did we get there and why did we go? But the legacy of questioning the policies of our government itself has affected and shaped our country...the Vietnam War may have been the first time that an entire society began to question the legitimacy of its government and the truthfulness of the government and the policies of that government. And I think that's as good a legacy as we have— the questioning of government and its policies—and I see that as a healthy thing."

We don't necessarily have to agree with Chuck Hagel, or David Martin. But we need to listen to them and include their sentiments and perspectives in our Vietnam public memory. If these two Vietnam veterans can critique our government and its policies, and even criticize themselves in the process, then we need to pay attention, and perhaps consider adopting a "both-and" dialectic rather than our default "either-or" for Vietnam.

I recalled reading a letter from a Vietnam vet in Cody, Wyoming who claimed that when he returned from Vietnam the VFW in Grand Island, Nebraska "treated me like garbage and made it known that they didn't want any 'baby killers or any commando types' in their precious organization...they didn't want anything to do with 'Nam vets back then." A salvo of letters came to the VFW's defense, expressing sentiments like these: "I am a Vietnam vet who was the subject of ridicule by anti-war protesters but never a fellow vet. When I returned home to South Dakota, I was welcomed by members of the VFW in grand fashion. I have passed through the doors of many a VFW. Every VFW post I have been in I found very cordial people."

Were they both right? Both wrong? Does that matter? They felt strongly about their experiences as Vietnam veterans and maybe, just maybe, that's good enough?

Or not? As Exhibit A, let's examine the concept of the spat-upon veteran. When Craig and I made a music and memory presentation at LZ Lambeau, I made the mistake of telling a fellow Vietnam veteran that he was wrong about being spat on.

"Jerry Lembcke, a Vietnam vet we know," I told the vet, "wrote a book called *The Spitting Image* where he details that there's no contemporary documentation of spitting and presents evidence that the myth was promulgated in order to demonize protestors." Next thing I knew, I was surrounded by a group of Vietnam vets, all of whom told me that "I didn't know shit" and that they all were spat upon by anti-war protesters. It was as if they'd all been programmed—every story was the same. Fresh out of Vietnam, off the plane at Fort Lewis, Washington or Travis Air Force base near San Francisco, Vietnam vets were greeted by anti-war protesters who called them pigs and baby killers and spat on them.

I shut my mouth. But when I got back to Madison, I reread the notes from Craig's conversation with Jerry Lembcke. And I started to dig a little deeper myself since that "spitting image" was by far the most powerful Vietnam War "meme"—a term used by Diane Mazur, a specialist in civil-military relations and advisor to the National Institute of Military Justice, to refer to "a cultural unit of information passed from one person to another, like a biological gene because it can be deployed instantly to silence difficult but necessary conversations about the military."

In many ways, this spat-upon not-spat-upon conundrum was the crux of the Vietnam public memory gridlock and is still the focus of our current military-civilian divide. Whether it ever happened—and it certainly didn't happen anywhere near as frequently as myth claims—the image of the spat-on Vietnam veteran is ingrained in public memory. During a presentation in Monroe, Wisconsin, a Vietnam veteran told me that an anti-war protester had urinated on him when he returned from Vietnam. Had the veterans' mistreatment come to this? And who benefits from keeping that ugly public memory alive?

Lembcke suggests one answer. In *The Spitting Image: Myth, Memory and the Legacy of Vietnam*, he documents the efforts of the Nixon Administration to drive a wedge between military servicemen and the antiwar movement by portraying democratic dissent as a betrayal of the troops, effectively redirecting blame for failure in Vietnam onto protesters. Combined with society's exaggeration of drug abuse among veterans to the point of broadly vilifying us as mentally unfit, emotionally volatile losers and victims, the collective memory about Vietnam had been refocused onto the veteran and away from the war. In her recollection, Army nurse Sue O'Neill lamented America's invasion of Afghanistan and Iraq as results of not having constructed accurate public memory of Vietnam; Lembcke's research confirms the continuing oppression of false public memory.

But the written record, like the spoken record, is contested ground. Bob Greene's 1989 *Homecoming: When the Soldiers Returned from Vietnam* included hundreds of letters from Vietnam veterans who responded affirmatively to Greene's call about whether they'd been spat on when they returned home. In his 2009 book *War Stories*, however, historian and Vietnam veteran Gary Kulik devoted a whole chapter to Greene's book of letters, Lembcke's research, and other data; he concluded that Greene had "arrogantly dismissed the surprising number of veterans who 'refuse to believe' the spitting stories...Greene was not just credulous, but negligently irresponsible," Kulik wrote. He concluded that the spitting stories were formulaic and unbelievable, and that they were propagated to serve the political goals of those vilifying the antiwar movement: "The image of 'hippie' men and women hawking up gobs of phlegm to hurl at the ribbons of veterans, as a pervasive and commonplace act, is surely false."

Historian Christian Appy, the author of three books about the American War in Vietnam, offers a balanced assessment of the evidence. Appy observed that Lembcke "is quite persuasive" in arguing that "there was no hostility or tension at all between veterans and protesters" to the point that Lembcke characterizes their relationship as "empathetic and mutually supporting." But he faults Lembcke for insisting on "a strict either/or argument: Veterans and peaceniks were either enemies or comrades...Antiwar activists could not have been spitting on veterans while at the same time befriending them in off-base coffeehouses..."

Appy goes on to share his own perspective, based on his extensive interviews with Vietnam veterans since the early 1980s: "My own view is that the spitting stories are largely mythic but that the myth itself reflects the deep anger and animosity that many veterans harbored toward the antiwar movement. Their anger often reflected a sense of class injustice that gave their more privileged peers greater freedom to avoid the war..."

I can confirm from my own work with Vietnam veterans from 1974 to 1977 at Vets House that much of this antipathy seemed class oriented. Vets House was a grass roots, community-based service center for Vietnam era veterans that we veterans established in Madison, home of the University of Wisconsin and a hotbed of anti-war protest. A large number of the vets we helped were the sons of fathers who worked in blue collar jobs at factories such as Oscar Meyer and Madison Kipp. As Appy and others remind us, some 80 percent of the 2.5 million enlisted men who served in Vietnam—out of the 27 million men who reached draft age during the war—came from working-class and impoverished backgrounds. They didn't have a lot in common with the college students protesting the war from the safety of places like UW-Madison.

I'll never convince those guys at LZ Lambeau or the Vietnam veteran in Monroe who said they were spat on, or worse. Fact is, they and their Vietnam service were disrespected, and the less privileged they are and the more they believed in the war, or lost a buddy, or did something horrible and unforgivable, the more they feel disrespect, as if a gob of phlegm had been hurled in their face. As my co-author Craig Werner observes, "The myth took root because vets felt like they were being spat on, by both the protestors and many older vets who looked on them as dirty hippies who'd 'lost the war.'"

Our good friend, Vietnam vet and poet extraordinaire, Bill Ehrhart has written what he calls "A True Spat-Upon Soldier Story."

SOLO Bill Ehrhart

Vietnam veteran poet Bill Ehrhart. Photo courtesy Bill Ehrhart.

One of the most widely promulgated and enduring myths of the American War in Vietnam is the belief—indeed the conviction among countless Americans young and old—that soldiers returning from Vietnam were accosted by antiwar demonstrators, spit on, called baby killers, verbally and even physically assaulted and abused.

That does not accord with my own experiences. I returned to the U.S. from Asia twice, in full military uniform, March 1968 and June 1969, both times passing through San Francisco airport—the heart of hippiedom—on my way home to Philadelphia. No one ever accosted me.

In May 1970, after the killings at Kent State, I joined the anti-war movement, but I did not spit on myself or call myself "baby killer." Moreover, I never saw anyone else around me abusing soldiers or veterans. I, however, do have a true "spat-upon veteran story." It goes like this:

The day after I came home from Vietnam in early March 1968, I took the money I'd saved in those thirteen months and went to West German Motors in Fort Washington, Pennsylvania, and bought a brand-new Volkswagen Beetle. Red with black interior.

Only I didn't buy it. I had to give the money to my father, and he bought it because I was not legally old enough to buy a car. The owner's card remained in my father's name for the next year and a half until I turned twenty-one, which was the age of majority then in Pennsylvania.

The day after that, I went to McKeever Insurance, in my home town of Perkasie, to get insurance for my car. But Mrs. McKeever told me I couldn't get a policy in my name. I would have to be carried on my parents' policy as a dependent child.

Understand what I'm saying here: I had just spent thirteen months fighting in Vietnam. I was a combat-wounded Marine Corps sergeant, but the state of Pennsylvania recognized me only as a child dependent on my parents.

Indeed, I could not even legally buy a beer in my own hometown.

And when I began college in the fall of 1969, unlike the World War II and Korean War veterans who received full college tuition plus monthly living expenses in recognition of their service, I got $135 a month for every month I spent in the Marines, which was hardly enough to buy my books and cover the cost of my dorm room; it didn't begin to cover my tuition.

You want to talk about abuse and disrespect? I was indeed abused and disrespected when I came home from the Vietnam

War, but it wasn't the antiwar people who were abusing and disrespecting me.

And in perpetuating the myth that I was abused by the very antiwar movement I joined, rather than by the government that sent me to Vietnam in the first place, my fellow citizens are distorting history, placing blame where it does not belong, and allowing the real abusers to avoid responsibility for the terrible damage they caused."

Back and forth. Forth and back. Who's right? Who's wrong? The music of the era can help ground us, get us out of the quagmire, by moving us away from these polarizations. Music truth is complex, an implicit recognition that no one voice can tell the whole story, that our public memory is inescapably plural. If we can value that Country Joe McDonald is a veteran and that gallows humor is part of the soldier experience; if we can grasp how Johnny Cash, after his tour of Vietnam, could describe himself as "a dove with claws"; if we can understand why Freda Payne would want to record "Bring the Boys Home" in 1971; and if we can appreciate why, until his death, Merle Haggard was conflicted about his song "Okie from Muskogee," then maybe there's room in our public memory for dichotomy and diversity?

And for call and response, because during our Q&A call and response sessions after presentations on *We Gotta Get Out of This Place*, audiences didn't do the usual griping or head shaking; instead, they listened, intently and respectfully, to what all sides had to say. Maybe that's why just about every conversation eventually moved somewhere to the middle, and, in the end, toward some type of communal healing, with every person who stood up and shared—veteran and non-veteran—feeling as if they had been heard.

Having engaged in innumerable conversations about Vietnam for more than 50 years, I'm here to tell you that this is *not* what usually happens. It was more than extraordinary; it was redemptive. Music gets credit for this positive development, and for creating a more accepting, and authentic, environment. But the participants themselves, albeit self-selected, deserve credit too—credit for their patience, tolerance, and courteous listening. Those sessions have important meanings for our processes of forming public memory.

In order to be accurate, our public memory has to be fundamentally different from the endless, recycled assertions of polarized interpretations of Vietnam, the U.S., Vietnam veterans, and non-veteran Americans. These interpretations seek to define in unchangeable terms what our collective and individual histories mean. While they're argued with emotional intensity, they totalize; they move from the individual to the abstract and general.

Our experiences interviewing veterans for *We Gotta Get Out of This Place*, and during the call-and-response sessions after our presentations on the book, suggest an approach that can preserve both the universal and the individual. Music's call invites a multiplicity of response: *Where were you when you first heard this song? What did you feel? Who was with you? How do you feel when you hear it now?*

Likewise, LZ Lambeau and other public media events issue calls that evoke multiple responses. They are events, not interpretation. Unlike the assumptions of a politician, sociologist, or historian (whether veteran or not), these communal activities are participatory, they create a shared experience of the event itself, and they both call forth and witness recollections. Gathering these testimonies into permanent homes in the public spaces of the internet, museums, libraries, and other historical repositories ensures that we will preserve those individual experiences. They will remain part of the historical record. And maybe they'll influence public memory.

For millions of Americans, Vietnam and the mid-20th century are ancient history. But Craig and I realized that the music and nonjudgmental sharing helped audiences to reflect on thorny issues of their responsibilities and duties as citizens; the meaning of patriotism, loyalty, and morality; and the authority of government. The Vietnam War, as Chuck Hagel and others have observed, severely tested our democracy. But that war also speaks to the depth and resilience of the foundational aspects of American life—an important lesson at the present moment.

The strains of CCR and Pete Seeger, the soundtracks of innumerable Vietnam movies, and the testimony of Vietnam veterans like Sue O'Neill and Bill Ehrhart echo in my ear. It's their voices, their stories, and their songs that should populate our public memory. And maybe if we listen hard enough, we can hear them when we touch a name on the Vietnam Veterans Memorial.

"People cannot resolve that war, nor can they separate the issues, the politics, from it," Maya Lin wrote. "As for me, the first time I visited the memorial after it was completed, I found myself searching out the name of a friend's father and touching it. It was strange to realize that I was another visitor...and I was reacting to it as I had designed it."

ADAGIO

"Blame It On My Youth"

If I cried a little bit,
When I first learned the truth
Don't blame it on my heart
Blame it on my youth

—Edward Heyman "Blame It on My Youth"

Given that my World War II veteran dad, Jack Bradley, fancied himself a Big Band crooner—he even sang in USO Clubs with Army bands during the war—I was surprised that I didn't immediately recognize Heyman's 1930s standard. But I heard it, meaning that I absorbed its meaning and power and passion, in the Oakland, California home of Alfredo Véa, Jr., a defense lawyer specializing in capital crimes. One of the most interesting and articulate Vietnam vets I've ever met, he's also the author of four novels, one of them— *Gods Go Begging*—centrally concerned with the Vietnam war. In late fall of 2009, Craig and I were completing interviews with several California veterans for *We Gotta Get Out of This Place*, and Alfredo, whom Craig already knew, was the last stop on our west coast tour. Véa's world consists of soldierly Mexicans and Yaqui Indians, of war and violence, and vulnerable youth. Any conversation with him brings into relief the complexities and contradictions of war and killing, injustice, guilt and healing, usually in the context of music. Véa simply loves music. Repurposing the expertise he'd honed in the Army, he built his own stereo system because he didn't like the sound of store-bought equipment. Now, Véa uses music to create, motivate, and inspire.

For him, music is not just good for the soul, it catalyzes his creativity: "If I'm writing something serious, I'll put on Thelonious Monk or Miles Davis's *Kind of Blue*," he explained. "If I'm editing, I like piano trios...When I'm writing dialog, I might put on Merle Haggard. There's something about his voice that really gets me jazzed up. I listen to him over and over, and suddenly it's three hours later."

All of this was a part of Véa's own therapy, I surmised. He was working through what he saw and did in Vietnam, for sure, but also what he saw on the streets of a dysfunctional America and in the eyes of the death penalty offenders he represents. More than most Vietnam vets we interviewed, he has a clear sense of how war and violence intoxicate young men, teenagers like he was in Vietnam, when he thought he could handle anything and everything the world threw at him.

"As seventeen-year-old boys, we danced with the apocalypse, and it cooked our hearts," he told us, his curly hair and rounded face sparkling in the candlelight. "War begins...when we are boys longing for the initiation rite of the warrior and everything it promises: sexual prowess and sexual license...but war is the opposite of sexual prowess. Things haven't changed a whole lot," Alfredo continued. "Watch any commercial during a football game. Men are still the cars they drive, the size of the engine, the pulling power. They're still at it, selling prowess and sexual license. They'll never stop."

Véa's Vietnam story is as compelling as the rest of his life story, and his captivating novel *Gods Go Begging* is unique, one of the best explorations of the war, and of America. "I didn't want to write another anecdotal book of Vietnam war stories," he said. "I wanted to get into why kids start at infancy getting ready for war. It's personal prowess. It is the cult of celebrity that is insidious...John Wayne was in every boy's head. War was really emotional castration.

"I was seventeen when I was in the field in Vietnam," he continued. "I had no sleep, it was dawn. The place was filling with

North Vietnamese Army regulars. What we were about to do, we didn't want to do, and neither did they. I like to say that war is desire stripped of humanity." He paused and shook his head. "I'm still trying to define war. It's what every vet does."

Many veterans have this "figuring out" of experience as a lifetime project. America called us baby boomers to service in Vietnam; we responded by serving in all of that war's challenging roles, and, now, how do we explain all that happened over there? Who will listen? And why won't those damned unpleasant memories of war just go away?

Writing can be one way out. Or in. Music too. Or, in Véa's case, pursuing justice while writing and listening. Late that evening, we were listening to *A Love Supreme*, the John Coltrane jazz masterpiece that figures prominently in *Gods Go Begging*. Coltrane's composition seemed to fit our mission of listening intently to what veterans had to say about the music that helped them to survive Vietnam. "Psalm," the last of the four parts of *A Love Supreme*, sounded like Coltrane's homage to the sermons of African American preachers, a response to the call from the pulpit, his way of saying *amen*.

"I made it home safe," Alfredo grudgingly admitted, then added, "in body." *Where was the rest of him?* I wondered that night in his living room. Still in Vietnam? At the jail or the courthouse? Wandering the Arizona desert where he'd grown up? Coursing within the jazz aficionado, the writer, the lawyer, there's still a lot of that fierce 17-year-old man in him, a lot of Vietnam in him.

"War begins long before battle…and lasts long after the last bullet is fired," he said.

"Into old age and death, we go carrying a secret knowledge that no one wants to know about."

Another carrier of that secret knowledge, Karl Marlantes, voices these ideas, especially about the youthful penchant for violence. A First Lieutenant in Vietnam in 1969–70 with Company C, 1st Battalion, 4th Marines, 3rd Marine Division, he was awarded the Navy Cross, Bronze Star, two Navy Commendation Medals for valor, and two Purple Hearts. A graduate of Yale University and a Rhodes Scholar at Oxford University, Marlantes is the award-winning author of *Matterhorn: A Novel of the Vietnam War* (2010) and *What it is Like to Go to War* (2011).

"War is the result of the failure of diplomacy, and kids become our best weapons," he informed Craig and me in the fall of 2011 when he came to Madison to talk to our students at the UW. "I'm no pacifist—there are times when war is necessary. But you'd better be damn sure."

In the PBS documentary *The Vietnam War*, Marlantes expands on the notion of young men as "our best weapons." "People talk a lot about how the military turns kids into killing machines," he told filmmakers Burns and Novick. "But I'll always argue that it's just finishing school...We are a very aggressive species. It is in us."

Alfredo Véa, Jr. and Karl Marlantes are survivors. But that doesn't mean they're home free, or even completely home yet. Too many Vietnam veterans must constantly struggle. "Growing up with a PTSD father was hard on my kids," Marlantes honestly admitted. "They learned to not wake up their dad by touching him, that I didn't like fireworks...I'm sure they were baffled by my behavior, which probably seemed inconsistent to them...if they dropped something behind me, the PTSD startle reaction would take over and my body would sense danger and prepare to fight...It wasn't rational, but it was very real."

PTSD is the war's legacy; survivor guilt, almost universal among vets, often accompanies it. While clinical explorations and analyses for survivor guilt abound, I've found the explanation offered by my friend and fellow Vietnam veteran Steve Piotrowski to be the most instructive.

SOLO   Steve Piotrowski

Vietnam veteran Steve Piotrowski. Photo courtesy Jim Gill.

I grew up in a small town in rural Wisconsin. Three days after high school graduation in 1969, I joined the United States Army. I volunteered for Airborne training and found that jumping from perfectly good airplanes was as big of a thrill as I expected...I arrived in Vietnam in February of 1969 and was assigned to Charlie Company, 3rd Battalion, 503rd Infantry Brigade, 173rd Airborne Infantry Brigade. I served a year in the field with the "Herd," primarily as a Radio Operator. I came back home unwounded physically, but deeply changed.

Because the Vietnam War was so divisive, the term Vietnam Era Vet came into use. It was initially used to separate those who served honorably and had a cleaner conscience from the so-called Vietnam "baby killers." Later, while working at organizing vets, Vietnam vets in particular, I would encounter these so-called "Vietnam era" vets who told me they didn't deserve to be called Vietnam veterans because they didn't serve "in-country" or some variation of that. "You never heard anyone talk about a WW II era vet, did you?" I'd ask them. There was honor for all who served in the great cause that was WW II. But it was hard to convince so many of these guys who felt guilty for not going to Vietnam.

The simple truth is that once you enter the military, your assignments were no longer in your hands. If the military wanted to send you to Antarctica or to the Equator, your personal preferences had no influence on the outcome. So, when someone argues that since they didn't serve in combat, their service is lessened in some way, I tell them not to feel guilty, because we all feel guilty about not doing enough.

Here's how I break it down:

• The guy who served stateside feels guilty because he didn't go to the war zone;
• The guy who was stationed in the war zone but spent his time in the rear feels guilty because he didn't serve in the front lines;
• The guy who served in the front lines but didn't get wounded feels guilty because he didn't sacrifice his blood;
• The guy who got wounded feels guilty if he didn't lose a limb, since he spent hospital time with many who did;
• The guy who lost a limb feels guilty because his buddy died;
• In the end, the only person who doesn't feel guilty is the one who died.

We the survivors are the only ones who can tell the story. The dead cannot talk. We must talk so others can understand the terrible cost of war. In the end, we all feel guilty, all of us, because someone else gave more.

Craig and I heard this sentiment time and again. Bruce Meredith, for example, didn't consider himself a "real" veteran for years "because I wasn't involved in actual combat." But he was in Vietnam, and that experience shaped his path. That later journey included the Deadly Writers Patrol (DWP) writers' group which I've been a part of for years.

"After my retirement, I had the good fortune to join DWP, a writing group comprised primarily of Vietnam veterans based in Madison," Meredith said. "They helped me to understand that the Vietnam War also affected those who weren't involved in actual combat, and that these veterans, people like me, also had stories they needed to tell."

What eventually became DWP began at the Madison Vet Center where the counselors incorporated writing in their therapy group sessions with vets in the 1990s. I sat in on a few of those sessions myself since I knew the counselors and figured I could serve as a positive role model. Little did I know that the sessions were helping me and my own post-Vietnam issues and would eventually lead to the publication of *DEROS Vietnam: Dispatches from the Air-Conditioned Jungle* in 2012.

During that early phase at the Vet Center, a graduate student from the University of Chicago proposed doing a research study about writing and therapy. The study didn't last long, but the writing group continued to meet on a weekly basis, initiating a magazine also called *The Deadly Writers Patrol* in 2006. At the beginning, the magazine was primarily an outlet for writing by local Vietnam vets like me and Bruce, but it now publishes work by vets of Korea, Vietnam, Iraq, and Afghanistan from all over the United States. On several occasions, it has included prose and poems by the children of Vietnamese soldiers.

While writing served as a path to healing for Bruce and other DWP members, the road home for Linda McClenahan, was full of detours. The first occurred when she decided to enter the Army instead of the convent: "I didn't want the government or the protesters telling me what was going on in Vietnam," Linda explained during one of several visits to Madison to talk with our students, "so I decided to go see for myself and serve my country first."

Vietnam veteran Linda McClenahan ("Sister Sarge"). Photo courtesy Jim Gill.

Linda served for three years as a communications specialist, followed by six years in the U.S. Army Reserves. In 1969–70, she worked with the Army's First Signal Brigade at Long Binh, Vietnam. Our tours nearly overlapped. But like Bruce Meredith and others, she denied, or downplayed, her Vietnam veteran status for years—"Others gave more," she insists. But her losses were profound.

"I lost God over there," Linda confessed. "It was rough. And after I got back, I didn't cry...I didn't have any emotions except anger. I was either numb or pissed off, you know, for years and years and years. I was suffering from PTSD—Post Traumatic *Spiritual* Disorder." Eventually Linda found her way back to her true calling, her vocation, and came to realize that her status as a Vietnam veteran qualified her as a veteran caregiver, enabling her to provide better support for younger veterans, especially women, and their families. Linda is now known as "Sister Sarge" within her order of Dominican nuns in Racine, Wisconsin. Working as a psychotherapist at the order's sponsored HOPES Center outreach and at Psychological & Counseling Services, Sister Sarge connects her clients with other veterans, helps them deal with trauma, and wades through governmental red tape. Along the way, she's become outspoken about who she is and what veterans need: "Vietnam veterans need to lose some of the shame that society imposed upon them and move forward," she emphasized. "So many vets were led to believe they should be embarrassed or should hide the fact they served in Vietnam. That has to stop."

With her example, her master's degree in counseling, and her religious standing, Sister Sarge is doing her part. She's been there, that place where a lot of veterans are. "I think it's important for everybody to tell their story," she added. "The only thing we can truly give each other is our stories. We need to share those."

Amen to that, Sister.

We heard in the Counterpoint section from Vietnam veterans Susan O'Neill and Mary Reynolds Powell, who still harbor the "guilt" of mending broken bodies only to send them back into war. Montana native Rick Smith, who served with me in the "air-conditioned jungle" at USARV headquarters in Long Binh in 1971, wrote a powerful solo for *We Gotta Get Out of This Place*. When I was in Phoenix for a presentation at Changing Hands Bookstore in March of 2016, I asked Rick, who lives nearby, to join me and read his piece. He's also an accomplished guitar player, so we counterpointed my veteran stories with Rick's acoustic versions of "The Ballad of the Green Berets" and "These Boots Are Made for Walkin'." Then Rick delivered his solo, in which he describes listening to a Korean girl band cover the Animals' "We Gotta Get Out of This Place" as he watched "three soldiers so emotionally engaged in the lyrics that they were destroying the small card table at which they'd been sitting...[raising] folding chairs above their heads, they slammed the table again and again at a strategically selected percussion moment." Unsure how to respond, Rick watched as an MP (military policeman) refused to arrest the three soldiers because "they've just come in from the bush."

"The bush," Rick notes, "was a part of the war I didn't know. Serving in Long Binh in a support role, I never had to experience the real Vietnam War...these were guys living daily in harm's way. But tonight they were safe. Tonight they could party. Tonight they could drink too much beer. Tonight they could break some chairs. When the music stopped, so did they. I watched as they laughed their way out the door.

"And even though it's forty years later," Rick concluded, "whenever I hear that old Animals song, I still flash back to that night in Vietnam...and I wonder if those three brave souls ever got out of that place."

That warm March night in Phoenix, when Rick got to those last few lines, he broke down, weeping. I went over, put my arm around him, and patted his back, telling him everything was all right. He never finished his reading.

"I'd never read that piece aloud," Rick explained to me later, still emotionally spent. "The sense of loss, the waste of war...it all hit me at that moment. But so too did the guilt. I'd survived, but I'm not sure if those three guys smashing that table had. Or, even if they did, if they'd ever be the same after Vietnam."

Music has been therapeutic for Rick Smith, even though a lot of the songs he writes and plays aren't Vietnam centric. But being able to lose himself in the strumming and humming and singing has helped keep him together. For several other Vietnam vets, a few whom you'll hear from in the next section, crafting their own music has been essential to their survival. Either way, writing—be it a story, memoir, or song—has aided many vets' recovery and restoration.

Dan Naylor, of Waupaca, Wisconsin, an MP in the U.S. Army from 1971 to 1973, subscribes to the Sister Sarge service ethic, and he too knows the sting of survivor guilt. Dan earned two degrees, including a master's degree in Public Administration, and worked for more than 40 years in behavioral health services across Wisconsin, including stints as Director of a Vietnam Veterans service center, an adult correctional halfway house, and a three-county alcohol and other drug abuse prevention and treatment agency.

"Thanks to my religious upbringing by two incredible parents and role models, I never thought twice about serving others—that is just what you do," Naylor affirmed, "and for the last forty-seven years that is what I have done and will continue to do until my dying breath."

I first met Dan in the summer of 1974 when he and fellow veteran Steve Barnes were opening Vets House in Madison. They and a handful of other vets understood that Vietnam veterans were hurting and that the traditional veteran organizations—from the VA and the VFW to the state employment service and the American Legion—weren't providing the help and support the returning vets needed. Working out of two dilapidated houses on Park Street in Madison, a group of us built a highly successful organization which helped hundreds of local veterans get jobs, receive a variety of counseling, return to school, find apprenticeships, earn their VA benefits, or stay out of prison or jail. Vets House was one of the veteran-to-veteran peer organizations that served as a model for the national Vet Center Program established by Congress in 1979 to provide a broad range of counseling, outreach, and referral services to eligible veterans to help them make a satisfying post-war readjustment to civilian life.

In 2006 Dan and I reconnected when he was running for the 40th State Assembly seat in the Wisconsin Legislature. Campaigning as a Democrat, Dan lost the election by less than 1,000 votes in a district that had been staunchly Republican for more than 60 years. What motivated him to run was "being the father of two children who [had] enlisted in the Army and served in combat in Iraq. I wanted to be a voice for veterans and active duty soldiers and their families," he told me. He said he first got energized by pushing the Waupaca town board to adopt a bring-the-troops-home referendum. He also became active in Vets for Kerry during the 2004 presidential campaign and helped draft a resolution at the Wisconsin Democratic Party Convention that called for a timetable to withdraw American troops from Iraq.

"I wanted to return civility to government," Dan said. "I wanted to help veterans and give voice to the voiceless." He not only found his own voice in the process but became an inspiration for his three children, who credit him with "their devotion to helping right the wrongs of the world."

Being connected to those who serve, particularly when you know the personal costs of service, exacted its toll: "It was hard being the father of two children, Joe and Laura, who enlisted in the Army and served in combat in Iraq and a third child Andy, who entered the Peace Corps and served in South Africa," Dan recalled. "Today, my son Joe works at a VA hospital, my daughter Laura is an assistant middle school principal, and my son Andy is a police officer—all serving others." Dan is justly proud of his family's service.

The Naylor family (left to right), Joe, Andy, Laura, Mary, and Dan. Photo courtesy Judith Adrian.

The whole family—Dan and his wife Mary, along with Joe, Laura, and Andy—met with a class I was co-teaching at Edgewood College in the spring of 2016. I asked Dan to share his own music-based memory and to talk about how and why his ethos of service and helping others had been transmitted to his children.

I didn't expect what happened next. Using the old Brook Benton ballad "Rainy Night in Georgia" as his connective tissue, Dan talked about December 1971 and the decisions he and his fellow MPs in training faced at Fort Gordon, Georgia, the week before Christmas.

"It was the sixth week of Advanced Training as an MP," Dan told us, "and at the Friday formation the Company Commander tells us the good news—no one is going to Vietnam. And to top it off, we all got a week off for Christmas break. I spent that week sharing the good news with family and friends," he continued. "At the end of the seventh week, Friday formation, the Company commander says plans have changed. Bad news—we were all going to Vietnam in two weeks. That night in total disbelief and shock, I drove to my best friend's off-base housing to process all this, listening to the radio in the rain, and on comes the song 'A Rainy Night in Georgia' by Brook Benton. I could hear the yearning soul ballad: *But it's a rainy night in Georgia, baby, it's a rainy night in Georgia/I feel it's rainin' all over the world...it's rainin' all over the world.*

The song kept playing in my head," Dan continued. "I spent the weekend with my two best friends from training trying to decide what to do—Canada? AWOL? Vietnam? We finally decided to 'do our duty' and support each other and come home together. During the last week, we all had the opportunity to sign up for more training," Dan concluded. "I was one of thirteen in the entire company to get assigned to additional MP training—everyone else went to Vietnam. Why me?"

Dan stopped. I was still playing the song "A Rainy Night in Georgia," and you could tell he was back there, at Fort Gordon, hearing that song, trying to figure out what to do next, only to be spared from Vietnam while his best, closest friends weren't. He didn't just cry, his whole body was overcome with emotion, 47 years of accumulated survivor guilt. I hugged him as Mary held his hand. She and their children were in tears. So was the entire class.

"I was back at Fort Gordon and two emotions immediately set in," Dan recalled later. "The first emotion was relief...and the other emotion I was unable to characterize, but it was an unbearable pain in my heart that I later identified as survivor guilt."

⊖　⊖　⊖

The term we have for this now is PTSD, Post Traumatic Stress Disorder, which wasn't named or recognized for years. Many of the vets quoted here—Alfredo Véa, Linda McClenahan, Karl Marlantes, Steve Piotrowski, and more—have experienced some variation of PTSD. Hell, now nearly 50 years after Vietnam, I'm convinced I had a mild case of PTSD when I came home in late 1971, exacerbated by my own heavy survivor guilt and a contentious country. Although terms like "soldier's heart," "shell shock" and "battle fatigue" have been applied to soldiers and veterans for centuries, it wasn't until 1980—1980!—years after many Vietnam veterans had endured its scourge—that the American Psychiatric Association added PTSD to the third edition of the *Diagnostic and Statistical Manual of Mental Disorders (DSM-III)*. What took so long? How did we not know what our brothers and sisters were dealing with?

Due in large part to the resentment, antagonism, and cacophony surrounding the Vietnam War, many soldiers and vets were left to their own devices. Or to the instincts and insights of Army psychologists like Floyd "Shad" Meshad and Bob Fraser. In the thick of it in Vietnam in the late 1960s, they personally and professionally responded to the calls of pain they were hearing from countless Vietnam soldiers by helping them "get out of that place."

Not only did Shad and Bob keep hundreds upon hundreds of men alive in Vietnam, they helped the Veterans Administration (VA) and communities across the country to address, understand, and treat PTSD in our veterans. Shad and his California colleagues encouraged the VA to establish community-based, peer-counseling Vet Centers across America. Like Alfredo Véa, Sister Sarge, and Dan Naylor, they've spent their whole lives helping others, especially Vietnam veterans.

I knew Bob before I knew Shad. He and I worked together building Vets House, very much like the work Shad was doing in California. After his stint in the Army, Bob pursued master's degrees in rehabilitation counseling from the University of Southern California and public administration at Seattle University. He was studying for his Ph.D. in rehabilitation psychology at the University of Wisconsin–Madison when we met, and he was instrumental in establishing our vocational rehabilitation program at Vets House. He even convinced a number of crusty old UW professors to volunteer at Vets House to see first-hand what Vietnam veterans were experiencing.

Vietnam veteran Dr. Robert Fraser.
Photo courtesy Robert Fraser.

Since he left Madison, Bob has been on the faculty of the University of Washington's Department of Rehabilitation Medicine, jointly with the Departments of Neurological Surgery and Neurology, and a consultant to the Social Security Administration. He is an active counseling and rehabilitation psychologist, a certified rehabilitation counselor, and a certified life care planner who directs Neurological Vocational Services within Rehabilitation Medicine. Within neurological rehabilitation, Bob has specialized in epilepsy, brain injury, and multiple sclerosis vocational rehabilitation, all the while authoring, or co-authoring, more than 120 publications and four texts. He is now, as he's always been, energetic, committed, witty, upbeat, and very patient-focused.

Bob connected me with Shad, who as a U.S. Army Medical Service Officer in Vietnam in 1970, pioneered treatment techniques for what would later become known as PTSD. After Vietnam, Shad became a tireless advocate and counselor to our nation's veterans, establishing the National Veterans Foundation (NVF), a non-profit that has helped more than 350,000 veterans and their families with crisis and information services. He also co-authored legislation for, and helped found, the VA's Vet Center Program, which continues to this day to be one of the most effective service models the VA operates. A licensed Clinical Social Worker, Shad is one of our fore-most experts on Combat Stress, Trauma Therapy, and the readjust-ment issues confronting returning soldiers and their families.

So, Vietnam is never far away for these two steadfast public servants. In fact, when you listen to them talk about what they confronted overseas, time evaporates and you return there with them in the heat, the insanity, and the stress. You hear the call of the distressed troops and the pain Shad and Bob and their Army colleagues were trying to respond to. They can tell us the whole history of, finally, getting vets treated for PTSD because they were there shaping that history. They did a lot because they cared a lot, then and now.

Vietnam veteran Floyd "Shad" Meshad.
Photo courtesy Shad Meshad.

DUET   Floyd "Shad" Meshad and Bob Fraser

Shad: I received a fellowship to Florida State in 1966, and I chose social work, because I was interested in working with prisoners and the school recommended that track. The social work degree allowed me to transfer out of my commission as an Infantry Second Lieutenant in '66 to the Medical Service Corps as a professional officer. I was assigned to Vietnam be-cause in 1970 I switched duties with another psychologist who did not want to go. I didn't have to go, but military service was a tradition in my family. My father, grandfather, and uncle had all served, going back to World War II. I also wanted to see the Vietnam experience for myself. I didn't want to miss the biggest event of my generation.

Bob: I was drafted out of graduate school at the University of Southern California where I was studying rehabilitation counseling and psychology. Before I left Fort Ord in Monterey, I applied for a specialty as a psychiatric social work specialist. I even wrote a letter to a colonel who was in charge of psychiatry for Vietnam and he responded with a handwritten letter, describing how much the Army needed me and exactly what to do when I landed in Saigon.

Shad: Was I prepared for my job? Absolutely *not* for doing mental health work in Vietnam as a social work Psychology Officer. I had no idea what it was going to be like. There was no way to prepare.

Bob: I thought that I'd been "around the horn" a bit by having grown up in New York City and worked as a case worker for the city's welfare department. And in grad school, I'd been an employment specialist at a rehabilitation hospital. Still, there was no way that I was prepared for my Vietnam assignment. Even though some people in my assigned specialty had had some training in the States, none of us had ever seen anything like the difficulties presented by our troops coming to the mental health center. At the DMZ, I was flipped a psychiatric medication guide and became the main prescriber out of a little shack for two weeks! My job was generally to screen the troops who came into our mental health unit and provide a provisional diagnosis. I'd spend my evenings studying the diagnostic manual and the psychiatrist would provide feedback on a daily basis. We worked six days a week, and the flow of troops to our unit never slowed. There was no dearth of alcohol available on our base, and I essentially drank myself to sleep many nights.

Shad: There were two psych teams in Vietnam when I landed there in January 1970. Not sure they could be called well-oiled since there were only about fifteen mental health workers to support more than five hundred thousand troops. It was really a lot of Band-Aid therapy...These psych teams evolved out of the war in Korea when the military realized that there was such a thing as combat stress and all the other names we used for what we know now as PTSD. They evolved further as the Vietnam war started, and the Army decided for the first time that it needed to have mental-health teams in a war zone. The only problem was the teams were very few and far between. And they didn't have much power with the leadership in Vietnam, even though we did our very best.

Bob: There was one psychiatric team that covered the southern half of South Vietnam and we covered the north up to the DMZ. Morale was at an extremely low point, so when Captain Shad appeared at our door it really was a ray of sunshine. And then the Army, after a medical administrative review, moved a whole team up from Nha Trang—four psychiatrists, two social workers (Captain Shad being one of them), a psychologist, and five to six specialists like myself. There was some jockeying of medications, some limited drug and adjustment counseling...but we never truly understood PTSD.

U.S. Army "psychologists" (left to right) Captain Shad Meshad, Specialist Pete Wilson, and Specialist Bob Fraser, 95th Evac Hospital, Da Nang, Vietnam, 1970. Photo courtesy Shad Meshad.

Shad: The most common psychological problem was "I need to get out of this place." Quite a few soldiers, in 1970, had problems with any kind of authority or leadership. We had significant racial problems, drug problems, officer problems, all going on by that time of the war. After North Vietnam's Tet Offensive of early 1968, troop morale had sunk to an all-time low, so we were dealing with major morale issues. Not a whole lot of psychosis. And a lot of violence.

Bob: With morale at an all-time low, we dealt mostly with anxiety, depression, mixed-mood disorders, and increasing drug problems. The classic "adjustment disorder" involved a 19-year-old male, often based in some difficult, horrible environment, who'd just received a "Dear John" breakup letter from his girl back home. Plus, our troops in the field often were chased by locals who'd sell them French-manufactured speed and other drugs on which they got hooked. In some cases, individual soldiers would move from using marijuana or speed to doing heroin. The heroin problem existed basically in the open right there at our own Evac hospital. And administration just didn't see it...or didn't want to.

Shad: Our level of treatment was, well, you can't just send these soldiers home regardless of whether or not they were a threat to themselves or others. It was a long, difficult process. As a mental health officer, a U.S. Army Captain, I was able to flag soldiers as "unfit" or "unsuitable" depending on their individual case and how bad it was and recommend them for either an other-than-honorable or general discharge. That was the quickest way. The other way was to try to keep them in our MASH hospital for as long as possible. But if they had to return to their unit, we would write a strong note of caution to their CO, which did not have a lot of power, or influence.

Bob: I would explain to a number of soldiers that if they accumulated numerous Article 15s for things like being late for formations or other acts of disobedience, etc., that they could work their way to a general discharge, which was honorable, for unsuitability or unfitness. I thought those lesser incremental steps were a lot better than other, more flagrant destructive behavior. I'd caution the GIs, however, that I did not know how getting the general discharge might affect their life back in the States. We received very little feedback as to whatever happened to these guys after they became veterans.

Shad: Almost ninety-five percent of the troops there in 1970 were either draftees or reluctant enlistees who knew they were going to be drafted. They were not prepared at all psychologically for jungle warfare, even by 1970. There was just really very little training. A minority of the fighting force—special forces, Rangers, and other combat specialties—were trained pretty well for jungle fighting. But, psychologically speaking, I don't think anybody in Vietnam was trained or had any psychological training in what they would face in Vietnam.

Bob: Training for the troops was cursory and in no way prepared you for the Vietnam environment—the heat, the type of fighting, the drugs readily available, the intra-unit conflicts, etc. Also at the time, the Army had dropped the required intellectual level for Army service. These were troops with limited intelligence, some with IQs as low as the high 60s, who totally disassembled within the hostile environment and brutal combat. They'd often endanger their fellow troops with poor reaction to combat and the lack of the requisite quick and accurate decision-making. We'd try to get them out of country whenever possible.

Shad: When the troops got home in the late 1960s, early '70s, there was a lot of chaos, a lot of protests in the country, so the returning soldiers really didn't know where they fit. The soldiers were confused about the war they'd just fought. We'd lost the war, but we never lost a battle. It was all pretty confusing.

In a study by the Vet Center program, about sixty percent of the Vietnam veterans got by and sort of moved on, depending on their economic status, their racial status, whether they were from a strong family, and the amount of combat they had.

Those vets who saw less combat and had more security were better able to get by and move on. Not that there weren't scars.

But it's that forty percent who really struggled, who came back with readjustment issues. There wasn't any real help when they came back, so that made it even more difficult—no Vet Centers, no counseling centers. They did not have a place to go. It wasn't until later in the '70s that programs like the Vet Center were available. Many of those forty percent never really recovered because they were never treated, and many today still have never been treated for their PTSD.

Bob: When we started Vets House in Madison, we initially rented a couple of houses where several of the guys lived and began offering free mental health treatment two nights a week. The numbers that showed up were totally overwhelming. Our first grant was awarded by Paul Soglin, mayor of Madison, for job placement services. Mayor Soglin, who'd been jailed as an anti-war activist, visited Vets House. He definitely saw the need. Later, the VA from Milwaukee awarded us a mental health contract and certification. We then expanded to vocational rehabilitation evaluation and veteran prison outreach.

Shad: There was very insignificant psychological treatment for Vietnam vets when they came home. Absolutely nothing unless a vet could get to a private psychiatrist, but even then, they didn't really understand trauma at the time. The problem wasn't even listed as delayed stress or trauma. It took all of the 1970s to get a definition for that. So, there was very little treatment. If the veteran was lucky, he got some level of treatment, but there wasn't really any quality treatment during that period.

Bob: There were a few VA programs that were better than others and some non-profits, like Vets House. If you lived in a rural area, however, access to treatment was generally unavailable. Another big issue was that many Vietnam veterans would not even consider going to a VA facility—they did not want any more bureaucracy and lime green-painted walls! Since their own military experience had created their problems, they wanted no further contact with any aspect of the service or bureaucracy. My college roommate received the Silver Star in Vietnam for bravery and being wounded as a combat medic. He ate himself up for years because in Vietnam he had to move from soldier to soldier under fire, and he believed that he had missed certain wounds. It took decades for me to convince him to go to the VA. They also screened him for PTSD and he received a one-hundred percent service-connected disability. He is one example among many and his PTSD is survivor's guilt—a tough variant.

Shad: If it wasn't for the Vietnam War, we probably wouldn't even have the term PTSD. What we learned about post-war psychological treatment after Vietnam was that we had none. By 1977, the VA Secretary brought in folks like me to address changes that were needed. One thing was to place counseling centers in the community, where veterans could go, and not have to go to a VA hospital. The Vet Centers, which I co-authored and helped implement in 1979, really were the beginning of the change within the VA to address PTSD. It gave vets a place to go and openly talk about what they'd been through. The VA had to change. It still to this day needs to change. The Vet Centers were the beginning of a very important part of the change.

Bob: Veterans often look at a big VA medical complex and simply won't go near it. Accessible, community-based veteran resources and mental health programs are absolutely the way to go, and the Veterans Administration now understands the need for this option. Having veterans on the staff also alleviates the credibility concern, but this type of staffing may be harder to find.

Shad: Even today, I'd say the treatment is not extremely strong. There's a lot of weakness in treatment around the country. New types of treatment for PTSD—from Eye Movement Desensitization and Reprocessing (EMDR) to Thought Field

Therapy, from Neuro-Linguistic Programming (NLP) to Trauma Incident Reduction—are more effective than just talk therapy or other types of listening and talk therapy. But there's a long way to go still, even today.

Bob: There's more of an emphasis on trauma expertise and certification in treatment. EMDR, trauma incident reduction, exposure therapies...that's all good news. The weaknesses in treatment today, however, still relate to engaging the veteran and to the accessibility of treatment. The Veterans Administration needs to invest more in marketing their mental health services and increasing accessibility. After initial assessment, telehealth and telemental health services may often be an ideal modality. They can be convenient and remove the travel time demands for some individuals and can truly reinforce engagement.

Shad: We're still in the learning process, but the narrative today, and even at the start of the Iraq and Afghanistan Wars, is that the military have set up mental-health teams. They've also tried to market the fact that the leadership of your unit will not stigmatize you for going in and talking about psychological problems due to your in-war experiences, while you're in war, not just after war. But that stigma is still there for real specialized soldiers like Rangers and Special Forces and SEAL Teams. They're not really likely to go get pre-war or post-war psychological care. But there is more care now, with a lot better focus on the need for PTSD pre-war and post-war care preparations, and classes on it. We've learned so much from the Vietnam experience. The Vet Centers are around. PTSD has been around now thirty-eight years as a diagnosis, and it's accepted pretty much worldwide.

Bob: We did learn a lot from the Vietnam war and our ongoing conflict experiences. Soldiers today have more of a pre-deployment preparation program not only for themselves—which had long been overlooked—but also for their spouse and family. One can never be fully prepared for a combat experience, but this is definitely helpful. I remember that the extent of my mental set preparation for Vietnam was by our captain as we graduated from infantry training. His statement was "Look to your left and look to your right, among the three of you, one will be wounded and another possibly killed!" A crash course in resilience perhaps? Coming home, I landed at Fort Lewis late on a Saturday night and woke up the next day, saluted, and they gave me my savings check and cash for a cab. Today there are more transition services and classes to include career and school preparation. I believe that Shad's right about a six-month deprogramming and psychological consult for combatants serving a tour or multiple tours. Transition intervention and routine psychological screening should be standard requirements.

Guys like Shad and Bob would scoff at being called heroes. They were simply doing their job to the best of their abilities. They were also applying call and response in a unique way, not only hearing, and responding to the call of soldiers and vets with PTSD, but also calling on the military establishment to work through their disagreements and misunderstandings to synthesize perspectives that could, and did, save lives.

Even the Donut Dollies—their official Red Cross designation was "Supplemental Recreation Activities Overseas, or SARO—those smiling, upbeat, girl-next-door personnel who worked tirelessly to lift our spirts and hearts—felt the impact of PTSD. Bobbie Lischak Trotter sent us an email in May 2018 when she had finished reading our book and shared her story. A resident of Norristown, Pennsylvania who teaches English and history for Mount Saint Joseph Academy in Flourtown, Bobbie had had a first career as a master sergeant in the Air National Guard.

SOLO Bobbie Trotter

Red Cross Donut Dollie Bobbie Trotter, Vietnam, 1970. Photo courtesy Bobbie Trotter.

I do not believe in accidents; my metaphysics proclaims a reason for all things, even the terrible things that give us wisdom gained from the awful grace of God. It was important for me to find and read this book. *We Gotta Get Out of This Place* is, for me, one of the most honest, complete, inclusive, and compassionate expressions of what my experience was as a Donut Dollie in Vietnam...I cried through many of the solos, especially Jay Maloney's. It invoked memories that forced me to take long walks away from my family before I felt like returning home. There were moments while reading when I realized I wasn't breathing.

My journey began fifty years ago this month, and like for everybody else who was there, it never ends. It took ten years for PTSD to catch up with me, but as the fates would have it, Lynda VanDervanter recruited me to share my poetry for her book, *Visions of War: Dreams of Peace*, and to campaign for the Vietnam Women's Memorial. At that moment, because of my husband's job transfer, I was forced to end my therapy with Doc Robinson, a crusty old World War II vet whom I cherish to this day. I was afraid I'd fall apart if I had to leave him. He told me,

"Use your pain, make it work for you. If you share it to help others, it will heal yourself. Don't be afraid. Face it, and don't let it own you." He was right...yet, there are moments...there always will be.

There were moments of great joy, too, that I experienced in the reading, like meeting old friends. Bill Ehrhart lived in my community. I read almost all of his books. He came to read his poetry to my students when I was teaching at Northampton Community College. We met up again years later when I moved to the Philadelphia area and joined Veterans for Peace, Chapter 31. I screamed with delight when I read Eileen O'Neill's comments. We share the same birthday and were inseparable buddies in the seven months we spent in Da Nang. We still send each other birthday cards and Christmas catch-up notes.

All the references to CCR warm my heart. My son's band almost always plays a CCR song or two for me because they know how much that music means to me. Oh lord, I remember the off-duty hours spent taping music. When I retired after almost thirty years with the Air Guard, my son played the Hendrix version of the national anthem for me and my guests. And then there was the humiliating flashback moment when I was doing photo coverage of our war games for the 111th Fighter Wing at Willow Grove. I was armed with two cameras and a large sign on my chest which read "NON-PLAYER." I was on the flight line where they had set up bunkers. Smoke bombs went off everywhere, there were explosions and lots of shouting. Next thing I knew I was in a bunker when one of the guys said, 'Sarge, what does your sign say?'

Oh yes (big sigh). There's more. The Donut Dollies still seem to be conduits for communication and healing. I was recently approached by another author writing about the DJs who worked for AFVN and wanted to include any Dollies who participated in their broadcasts. This, I did, when I was assigned to Da Nang, so I wrote him. His twenty questions exhausted me and brought back many memories, both good and bad...

Coming home was hard. Unlike the men, we women could hide if we chose to, but most of us did not. We wanted people to know, but mostly no one wanted to listen. I lost all my old friends, struggled with my family and sought company with military people. I was fortunate in that I soon began dating a Vietnam vet. We were very supportive of each other. I later joined the Air National Guard and was welcomed by a lot of Vietnam vets, whom I will admit were surprised by a woman who chose to go to Vietnam...And there's more...

You can find that "more" in the powerful poetry Bobbie has written since Vietnam. "Just Driving Along" is but one example:

The pain runs deeper than death—
to the soul—
thus nullifying any option of escape.
So one must live with it,
try to control it,
master it,
reconfigure it,
transfer it,
anything!
to live with it.
On a particularly beautiful, late, summer afternoon
she rides down a country road.
She tunes the radio to the arts and theater segment
of National Public Radio-
thrilled to hear a discussion of Macbeth,
a play she knows by heart,
until she hears the actor recite,
"Out, out, brief candle . . . "

Instantly ripped
from herself,
she sees another woman standing outside a dingy field hospital
holding a half smoked cigarette in her hand,
watching a distant flair go out,
its tiny parachute slowly descending into darkness.
She hears a woman's voice
weeping in unison with the actor's words,
"...a tale told by an idiot...full of sound and fury, signifying nothing"
Then,
the pain comes, fresh as ever,
and the emptiness.
She pulls to the side of the road,
stops,
hangs her head over the steering wheel,
and sobs for twenty minutes.
Feeling exhausted and weak, she prays
for the strength to go home
and prepare a meal for her family.
It is twenty-five years
after it happened.

None of this is meant to imply that everyone who served in Vietnam is sick or screwed up, has had PTSD, or suffers with survival guilt. Many do not. But it does suggest that regardless of station or rank or gender or race or location or occupation, PTSD and survivor guilt can descend upon you and shake you to your core. Not everyone accepts PTSD as a near-universal veteran condition, however. Author and filmmaker Sebastian Junger has a different take. He was an embedded journalist in Afghanistan, the source material for his compelling book *War* (2010) and his two outstanding documentaries, *Restrepo* (2010) and *Kornegal* (2014). I connected with him indirectly in 2012 when he and Karl Marlantes were trying to get Congress to approve a Presidential Commission on Healing the Wounds of War.

Regrettably, the Junger-Marlantes initiative never received Congressional approval. Since then, Junger, who retired from war reporting, has been vocal about what America is doing right, and wrong, by its veterans. He believes strongly that the over-diagnosis of PTSD does more to disable, than enable, our newest veterans.

"As far as I'm concerned, PTSD is a disorder," he told the interviewers from the *Task & Purpose* website in 2016. "It's treatable and it's usually temporary. Long-term, chronic PTSD afflicts a very small fraction of people who've been traumatized. The problem is that on the one hand the VA says, 'We can treat your problem. Give it some time, and we will help you.' On the other hand, the government—the same government—is giving them lifelong PTSD disability. There's a therapeutic contradiction just in the messages that the government is giving to the soldiers. If you lose your leg, that's a lifelong issue. It's not going away. PTSD is *not* a lifelong problem. When you compensate the soldier for life, you're basically telling the soldier, 'Look, you're ruined for life, might as well accept it.' So, I think one of the problems is that the government itself is incentivizing a view of veterans as psychologically incapacitated. There's a financial incentive for it. There's a social incentive in the sense that if you have PTSD you served your country bravely in combat."

Junger goes on to point out that while only ten percent of the U.S. military experiences combat, nearly 50 percent of the military has applied for PTSD disability. "I think an awful lot of those people are honestly describing something that is actually a transition disorder," he told *Task & Purpose*. "It isn't PTSD, but the only vocabulary we have right now is PTSD, so they call it PTSD...And a lot of these people are honest people, and I think they're probably quite insecure about the fact that they know they were never traumatized, and, yeah, PTSD is the only category that they have available to describe what they're truly feeling."

Junger is particularly incensed by what he sees as the perfunc-tory and often exaggerated valorization of today's soldiers: "There's such reflexive veneration of veterans that no one dares to say any-thing other than the most sanitized, approving sentences about the whole issue. It's political suicide to say anything but catechisms about how valorous they all are. Listen, I spent a lot of time out there with those guys and I'm enormously admiring of those young men. But right now they need to be transitioned back into normal life. And if they're overly valorized, we're basically saying, 'You're not a normal person.' There comes a point where we're actually harming them by over-valorizing them."

You can add the military-civilian divide, embedded journalists, over-diagnosing PTSD and "thank you for your service" to the grow-ing list of Vietnam legacies. They and others were born from Viet-nam, and, like the all-volunteer army and counterinsurgency war-fare, are now not just part of our Vietnam public memory but are part of who we are as a nation and how we go about the business of safeguarding our interests worldwide. All I know for sure is that my generation of veterans dedicated themselves to ensuring that no other generation of veterans would be abandoned by their country.

While Craig and I aren't psychologists, we could sense survi-vor-guilt dynamics during our presentations and conversations, sometimes even from those audience members who were not in Vietnam, or maybe had vigorously protested the war. These men realized that if they didn't go to Vietnam, somebody else went in their place. Survivor guilt. The women echoed the sentiments of Vietnam nurses like Sue O'Neil and Mary Reynolds Powell—our men needed helping, needed saving, and we didn't save them.

Do we blame these problems on our young and reckless selves? On our leaders? On the veterans? Or maybe for once we won't point any more fingers, won't assign any blame. Maybe we pause, exhale, and respond collectively to the hurt that is in the call of Vietnam experience, not just from the soldier or the veteran or the enemy combatant or the revisionist historian or the next great novelist but from the gold-star parent, the anti-war activist, the warrior, and the pacifist. All of us lost something in Vietnam, and it's time we come together, join hands, and move forward. Maybe we could try to emulate what Vietnam veterans like Moses Mora have done to renew themselves, their brothers and sisters, and their entire community.

SOLO   Moses Mora

Vietnam veteran Moses Mora. Photo courtesy Moses Mora.

Despite its location, in the 1950s and '60s, Ventura, California, nestled between Los Angeles and Santa Barbara, was a small, sleepy beach town sometimes referred to as "Bakersfield by the Sea." As the moniker implies, not much happened here. The social upheavals of the 1960s, like the civil rights movement, the women's and anti-war movements, barely registered in Ventura, at least for me and my circle of friends.

I was born in 1949. The 1950s were my formative years, and the 1960s were my teenage years. That means, culturally, I was experiencing live the dance craze era, early soul, surf music, the British Invasion, and the American musical response as it was happening. Trends came and went, but by the time I graduated from high school, in the Summer of Love, 1967, "my soul had been psychedelicized," as the Chambers Brothers cleverly sang. That summer I had seen live The Jimi Hendrix Experience, Frank Zappa & The Mothers of Invention, Country Joe & The Fish, etc. Woefully, by December of 1967, the military had gotten their clutches on me. I was drafted into the Army and sent to Fort Ord, California, eventually bound for Vietnam.

Well, we all know what happened there. Some of my friends might say that I was damaged before I went into the military, but I was damaged goods for sure when I came back. Like many other Vietnam veterans, it would be forty years or more before the VA would enter into our lives...until then we were left to our best, or worst, devices.

To digress a bit, I want to say that I was always a poor student in school. Growing up, I was not interested in, nor did I read, my school books. I read vinyl record labels and album liner notes. That's where my real knowledge came from. The records taught me what 33&1/3, 45, or 78 rpms meant—revolutions per minute. I learned about BMI and ASCAP, the music publishing companies. The records always listed who wrote the songs, sometimes who arranged them, and always the time length of a song, and the performer(s). The record labels' names themselves were often not in my usual vocabulary, like Scepter, Tamla, Atco, Vocalion, Rampart, Argo, Vee-Jay, or Elektra, to name but a few. Sometimes even their address was listed.

My true teachers were those who wrote the album liner notes—Ralph Gleason, John Hammond, Sr., Alan Lomax, Nat Hentoff, Leonard Feather, Orrin Keepnews, Robert Shelton, Ahmet Ertegun, etc. When I was thirteen, I was in a record store reading the extensive liner notes of Bob Dylan's first album, written by Stacey Williams. The liner notes name-checked Bukka White, Sonny Terry, Dave Van Ronk, Ramblin' Jack Elliot, Jelly Roll Morton, Mance Lipscolm, Big Joe Williams, Jesse Fuller, and many others. I didn't buy the Bob Dylan album that day, but soon I was listening to "San Francisco Bay Blues" by Jesse Fuller, and Ramblin' Jack Elliot's entire output was in my budding record collection.

I didn't go to college. I went to record stores. Flipping through albums in record shops was very therapeutic for an angst-filled kid bound for Vietnam in those wonder days and years of the 1960s. By the time I was discharged from the military in December 1969, the era of record albums with liner notes was waning, a lost art.

I survived the Vietnam war. I did what I was told to do, I followed orders, and I came out with an Honorable Discharge. I did not do so well with the war after the war. In 1986, a powerful film that gave a ground-level view of the Vietnam war was released. Promotional info on the movie *Platoon* suggested that Vietnam vets should not see this movie alone because of the emotional impact it might have. After viewing the film, I noticed guys my age were gathering in small groups and talking, I'm sure they were Vietnam vets, but I didn't join them. Instead, I went to the music store next door and started flipping through albums—that early self-medicating act addressed my OCD tendency, and its calming power settled me by bringing brief relief from the anxiety I was experiencing...

After my military service, I didn't go to college, I went to jail—Jail, not Yale; State Pen, not Penn State. I experienced several years in and out of jails. It was known as doing life on the installment plan. In Soledad prison, they had their own radio station. The inmates had earphones that they could plug into a wall jack and listen. At the time the only opening was in the country music slot, midnight until six in the morning. Even though I considered myself a soul man, I took the job and started calling myself Mad Mountain Mike, and I learned a lot about country music. I'd introduce Donna Fargo records as by "Donna Far Gone" and Tammy Wynette became "Tell Me Why Not." I still love the music of Ernest Tubbs. The rule was that after 3 a.m., any kind of music could be played, so drawing from the vast selection, I played a mix of blues, jazz, rock, soul, Latin, and classical music. One morning I played the entire album of Bob Marley & The Wailers *Live*. The last song that I played on air, on the day I was released, was "Ventura Highway," by the group America. I signed off saying, "I'll be going down Ventura Highway."

Fortunately, almost immediately after being released, I met the Lakota medicine man Archie Fire Lame Deer, who was living nearby. He took me under his wing, and I started participating in Native American spiritual ceremonies. Foremost amongst them was the sweat lodge purification ceremony. For the troubled person, veteran or not, the ceremony is a godsend. It keeps me in balance, upright, and centered. The ceremonies are not only for the troubled soul; they are also a wonderful place to give thanks for the many blessings that come our way. Sometimes we have ceremonies just for veterans, men and women. There is a variation of the sweat lodge ceremony called the wash-away ceremony. It's an old traditional ceremony for warriors upon their return from battle. It's for anyone who feels responsible for taking a life, or lives. A person completely covers their body with charcoal and then enters the sweat lodge, where prayers, songs, heat, and steam wash away any negative or remorseful feelings regarding the actions of battle.

Inside the sweat lodges, chants and songs are used to help us focus and endure. The songs tell us to walk in beauty, to honor ourselves and each other, and to see everything in nature as a relation. The ceremonies and songs help us to be better people, mindful of all, the generations, the sacred water, the giver of life.

Music taught me that it was always there from childhood lullabies to soothe us to gospel songs of inspiration, drumbeats, and heartbeats, rhythms to make us dance, move, be happy, chants in a sweat lodge, melodies that bring beauty and heavenly harmonies, lyrics to inform. A music store can be a college if we let it and, yes, even flipping through record albums has a cadence to it.

Music and ritual have brought Moses home. And Moses is bringing other vets home. One of our most powerful events took place at the Bell Arts Center in Ventura, California, where Moses brought together a circle of two dozen Chicano vets on a warm April night in 2016. Tapping into his time in the half Anglo/half Chicano garage rock scene in Colorado Springs, Craig had put together a playlist that built up to Al Reyes's Chicano twist in "Vietnam Veterano." With Moses guiding the conversation, every single veteran in the room, including a Mexican vet who was obviously uncomfortable speaking in English, shared stories of their service. A towering vet nicknamed Oso ("Bear" in Spanish) had sat quietly through most of the evening, and it wasn't clear whether he had problems with having a gringo leading the conversation. But at the end of the event, he stepped forward and wrapped Craig in a giant hug. Oso was the artist designing the tee shirt for an upcoming ceremony dedicated to bringing his *hermanos* another step or two on the path home. Moses made it clear that embracing the Native part of the Mexican-American heritage had played a key role in finding a way beyond the self-medication and spiritual paralysis that he and so many others experienced. Gazing reverently at the large ceremonial drum in his living room—his wife is Native American and, as for so many vets, an irreplaceable part of his life—Moses mused that "the ceremonies give us something we hadn't had in our lives. They let us know it's possible to live sane and clean."

And they can do it for the rest of us, too. If there's anything I observed and felt and believed while we were touring, it's that it is never too late to bring all of us home, veterans and non-veterans alike. That's what Sebastian Junger and Karl Marlantes were trying to do with their proposed Presidential Commission on Healing the Wounds of War.

"War takes a toll," they wrote in their memo to Congress in 2012. "It involves staggering amounts of loss and—equally important—of killing. No nation does this easily or without a deep spiritual and emotional cost. Many initiatives exist for our veterans and are providing some help for the men and women who fought. But we must go beyond policy initiatives. In pre-industrial society, leaders were intimately involved in war itself—often sword in hand—and religious or spiritual leaders were fully engaged in the aftermath. Rituals and ceremonies decommissioned the fighters and made the entire community conscious of the soldiers' role in this sacrifice. More importantly, the entire community also experienced the sacrifice. This commission would enable soldiers returned from war to share their experience and unburden their souls."

Unburdening their souls sounds like what a preacher would call from the pulpit, hoping to get a witness to testify, someone to shout, "Amen."

And just what *is* America's response?

BRIDGE: Hugo, Vietnam, and Next Stop

Vietnam teacher Hugo Keesing, Phan Rang, Vietnam, 1970.
Photo courtesy Hugo Keesing.

One of the main things we learned during our more than a decade of research and interviews for *We Gotta Get Out of This Place* was the pivotal role music played in the "laying it down" process for so many Vietnam veterans. Not just the music they listened to, but also the music they created for themselves and their fellow vets. Mere words cannot do justice to the raw, therapeutic power of the many vet-composed pieces we listened to and which comprise the last two of the 13 CDs in the *Next Stop is Vietnam: The War on Record 1961-2008* compilation. Regrettably, most Americans wouldn't know these vets or their music because it, and its creators, remain secluded, private, unshared.

Popular artists—musicians like Bruce Springsteen, Curtis Mayfield, Charlie Daniels, Billy Joel, Marvin Gaye, Merle Haggard, John Prine, Bill Withers, CCR, and others—used music as a way to grasp, illuminate, or to support or condemn the war, but, and this is a critically important point, in almost every case their popular music supported Vietnam veterans. From Springsteen's "Born in the USA" and "Brothers Under the Bridge" to CCR's "Fortunate Son" and Marvin Gaye's "What's Going On," listeners were made aware of the travail and challenges confronting Vietnam soldiers and veterans. Again, even though millions of Americans heard these songs, in many cases they didn't really get what the music was telling them.

"Time to Lay It Down" is a good case in point. According to Hugo Keesing, principal archivist for the *Next Stop is Vietnam* collection, it was "an obvious choice to end the collection."

"Olin Murrell's lyrics say it all," he told us, "but the interpretation by Martin and Holiday, two Vietnam veteran musicians, is extraordinary. Perfect way to close the anthology."

Craig and I have collaborated, and co-presented, with Hugo over the years—we're fortunate enough to have an essay included in the 304-page book that accompanies the 13-CDs in the Bear Family box set—and every time we came away impressed with his encyclopedic knowledge of war music, World Wars I and II, Korea, as well as Vietnam.

Hugo even went to Vietnam—in 1970 as a volunteer! Fresh out of graduate school, he took a job with the University of Maryland's overseas continuing education program. "I was looking for a job that would permit me to teach and travel, but accepting a contract to teach in Asia required that I spend at least one term in Vietnam," he explained. "While I wasn't wild about the idea, I said, 'Fine, I'll do it.' So, I flew to Saigon."

Coming to a war zone straight from an American campus, Hugo stood out, or at least his long hair and muttonchops' sideburns did. "I had long hair and purposely did not get a military-style haircut before I went to Vietnam," Hugo recalled. "I vividly remember the first night, coming out of the officers' mess after my first meal, and being confronted by a gentleman who smelled of alcohol. He was a pilot, I guessed, and he took exception to the way I looked. He said, 'What the hell do you think you're doing here?' I said politely I was just having dinner, and his next question was 'What's that shit on your face?' I said, 'That's hair.' I probably wasn't taking him seriously enough, and it didn't take very long for a circle of people to form around us.

"But what could have turned into an unfortunate situation," he continued, "was broken up when the base commander and wing commander came breaking through this circle of men who were surrounding me and said, 'What's going on here?' I said, 'Nothing as far as I'm concerned,' and quickly left."

The next day Hugo was called in front of his superiors, who strongly suggested he see a barber. "Word got around [about the haircut]," he said, "and at my class the next day the first thing I heard was, 'Don't do it, don't cut your hair!' Most of my students were enlisted men, and I was picking up very quickly on a different attitude if I compared the enlisted—who included a large number of draftees—to the officers."

Hugo kept his hair, but he stayed away from the officers' club. And over the ensuing months, he observed first-hand the importance of music to everyone who was in Vietnam, officers and draftees alike. Guys like me who were there in 1970 and 1971 brought our own records and cassettes, tuned in to broadcasts over AFVN, and listened to cover bands from the Philippines and Korea. Music was everywhere and it was our salve. Hugo observed this first hand. He knew what we GIs were struggling with, what we were listening to, and, in some cases, why. That makes his selection of "Time to Lay It Down" as the final song on such an impressive collection all the wiser.

RONDO
Time to Lay It Down

I've been carrying this hate for eighteen years
And it's time to lay it down.
—Olin Murrell, "Time to Lay It Down",
sung by Michael Martin and Tim Holiday

This powerful song is the last of 332 tracks on the monumental
13-CD collection *Next Stop is Vietnam: The War on Record 1961-2008*
released by Bear Family Records in 2010. Olin Murrell's haunting
lyrics—and the uncompromisingly authentic interpretation by Michael Martin and Tim "Doc" Holiday, two Vietnam veterans—con-
vey the urgency and necessity confronting the song's Vietnam veteran narrator who stands before "The Wall." He realizes that if he is
going to maintain his sanity, move on with his life, and get beyond
Vietnam, he has to shed the weight of guilt and shame he's been
carrying around since he came home from the war. Indeed, he has
to "lay it down."

So must we all.

A number of the Vietnam veterans Craig and I encountered
over the years have been able to "lay it down," and, in doing so,
have found their own peace. For many, it's not a quiet, isolated
peace, but rather one that ripples across the communities around
them through vehicles such as veterans courts, art, music, ritual,
poetry, writers groups, and memorials. Although many of these en-
counters centered on eliciting a music-based memory for *We Gotta
Get Out of This Place*, we were struck by how many of these men and
women were not only rebuilding themselves, but were also helping

support the current generation of younger veterans all the while enriching our wider world. Giving witness to their voices and following their examples could help America to broaden its Vietnam public memory, and in the process, become more supportive and understanding of its veterans.

None of this is easy. Just ask a Vietnam veteran. The weight some have been carrying for 50 years or more manifests itself in challenges that range from jobs and benefits to Agent Orange poisoning and PTSD, from homelessness to homecomings, and lots in between. Each unique burden requires a different response. Music often counterpoints these efforts, but, unlike *We Gotta Get Out of This Place*, is not at the center of the activity. Still, as with the music that comforted them, the compassion, understanding, listening and attentiveness that accompanied these various activities made all the difference.

My fellow veterans and I knew this when we launched Vets House in Madison. In 1974, very few of the traditional veterans organizations and resources were providing the support many Vietnam vets needed: jobs, counseling, housing, help staying out of jail, and more. Those of us who were better off—Steve Barnes, Dan Naylor, Bob Fraser, Steve Schoch, Bob Cook, and other vet volunteers—realized that if we could help these beleaguered vets, we'd also be helping ourselves, and maybe helping our city, Madison, and our state, Wisconsin, to be more compassionate toward its newest generation of veterans. Shad Meshad and his colleagues were doing similar work in California.

This was before the days of anyone using music to help vets to center and cope, so I don't recall an abundance of music filling the halls of Vets House, just a lot of intense conversation and typewriter clatter. Still, co-founder Steve Barnes, who was with the Army in Germany, told me that he would often listen to music by himself in his office there, recalling that when he left the States "it was the Beach Boys and stretch levis and penny loafers," but when he returned "it was Led Zeppelin and drugs—clothes, art, music... everything had changed and it took a long time to catch up."

Every now and then one of the vets we were helping at Vets House would invite us to hear a band they were playing with at some local venue. I'd often go and watch the vet musician, for some reason he was frequently the bass player, as his band covered all the great Vietnam tunes—CCR, Motown, Stax, James Brown, and more—and wait for the smile or the uplift. It usually came, and I wondered why I wasn't able to do that during our counseling sessions. I later discovered that in California Shad was engaging musicians—Bruce Springsteen and the Doobie Brothers among them—to help with his Vet Center fundraising efforts and to use their music as a way to connect with veterans and help express the Vietnam vets' experience.

Nevertheless, the vet-to-vet approach worked for most of the men and women who walked through our Vets House doors. But what about the rest? Helping them to "lay it down" would require similar commitments but different approaches—to housing, to therapy, to criminal justice, to healing. And, in most cases, Vietnam vets would take the lead, determined to establish organizations so that the next generation of veterans would not have to carry the same heavy burden by themselves.

Getting a job is hard enough, but it's that much harder if you're homeless and wondering *where* you can lay it down. Regrettably, it's nearly impossible to get a credible count of homeless veterans. Historically, veterans are a disproportionate share of the homeless population, and Vietnam veterans in particular are over-represented. Under the direction of the U.S. Department of Housing and Urban Development (HUD), a semi-annual *Point in Time* census is conducted to seek out and identify the homeless. HUD's 2017 survey placed the number of homeless veterans in the U.S. at about 40,000, of which 15,000 were living on the streets.

The numbers, federal officials say, are down 56% since their 2010 count, when the Veterans Administration and the Obama administration established a goal of ending veteran homelessness by 2015. It was an ambitious objective that focused more attention and resources on homeless veterans, but, without adequate funding and the appropriate mental health resources, it fell far short. Regardless, don't ever believe the numbers and the surveys. There are a helluva lot more Vietnam veterans adrift on the streets of America, as veteran Bill Christofferson discovered in Milwaukee.

I've known Bill for more than forty years, but it wasn't until Craig and I began our interviews for *We Gotta Get Out of This Place* that I realized Bill was a fellow 'Nam vet. His "solo" about Nancy Sinatra and "These Boots Are Made for Walkin'" is one of the best we collected. He's also one of the most politically savvy persons I've ever met and applies his political acumen to good candidates and good causes. Troubled about homelessness, Bill and his fellow Milwaukee Veterans for Peace (VFP) chapter members set to work to address the issue without knowing where it would lead. Their story exemplifies the power of "vets helping vets" as many Milwaukee homeless vets were eventually able to "lay it down," literally. Bill served as board president, grant writer, development chair, and even acting executive director for a few months, "because the mission of helping was too important to allow it to fail." He wrote this piece about the VFP efforts especially for this book:

Veteran Homelessness in Milwaukee, by Bill Christofferson

The Milwaukee program started on a shoestring budget, with help limited to bus passes and inexpensive cell phones, but quickly expanded to include helping veterans to get Veterans Administration benefits and other services. When VFP launched the program in 2008, it estimated 200 to 300 homeless veterans in Milwaukee, with another 5,500 veterans "at-risk." By the end of 2017, the program had furnished new apartments for 1,893 homeless veterans—six times as many the number of homeless who had been "identified" when it started. The demand for services continues unabated. More veterans are in the pipeline, on the way to homelessness. Zero homeless vets is a worthy goal, but not realistic, VFP found.

In 2008, two VFP members had begun two-hour visits twice a week to a daytime shelter and resource center for the homeless. They carried a sign saying they were looking for veterans. From interviewing vets, they immediately learned of unmet needs and began to find ways to help. Ten years later, their two-hour-a-week commitment had spawned three non-profit organizations that have helped thousands of homeless and low-income veterans to rebuild their lives.

"We learned everything the hard way," admitted Mark Foreman, president of VFP Chapter 102. "We really didn't know what we needed to address when the project began." Nevertheless, Foreman and Dennis Johnson, another VFP member who'd been an Army helicopter door gunner in Vietnam, spearheaded the effort and enlisted others: "We learned in the military that we don't leave our wounded behind. That's our guiding principle," said Johnson. "No one who has ever served the United States in uniform should end up living on the street."

Foreman was a Navy hospital corpsman assigned to the Marines in Vietnam who himself was seriously wounded and disabled. He used his decades of personal experience in dealing with the VA to personally help more than 100 veterans receive VA benefits to which they were entitled. "We'd interview them," he said. "If they were eligible for veterans benefits, because they were so fragile and knew so little about the bureaucracy, we'd literally take them by the hand to help them file a claim."

For a short time, the VFP initiative operated a transitional living house for vets who were coming off the street, but it became obvious that those veterans needed support and services way beyond a place to sleep, and the VFP initiative did not have the necessary resources. So, VFP began to collect donated furniture and household goods to help vets set up housekeeping in new living spaces.

In 2012, a new, independent non-profit, Milwaukee Homeless Veterans Initiative (MHVI) was created, separate from VFP, although many VFP members remained in key roles. The change allowed the initiative to broaden its community participation and expand its fundraising, since some traditional veterans groups and conservative foundations, while appreciating the work of the initiative, were reluctant for political reasons to donate to Veterans for Peace. Foreman was disappointed—"heartbroken," he says—that the project was no longer under the Veterans for Peace banner. But he continued to be part of the weekly outreach effort for years. Since its inception, MHVI has focused on trying to fill gaps in services, not duplicate services offered elsewhere. Its main program, home support, moves formerly homeless veterans into their new homes and provides everything they need—recycled furniture, linens, toiletries, cookware, household goods, groceries, and other necessities—to set up housekeeping and begin their new lives, with help toward regaining independence and self-respect.

Many of the veterans in the program come from a residential treatment program at the VA hospital. A federal program called HUD-VASH provides housing vouchers, but a vet is often given the keys to an apartment and little else. He or she often has no furniture—not even a bed—no household items, and no resources to purchase them. A pantry may provide food, but the vet may not even have a can opener or a saucepan. That's why it's so critically important when MHVI shows up with a truckload of furniture and essential items to make a home livable. The value of the goods, almost all donated by the community and picked up daily by MHVI's crew of two formerly homeless veterans, has reached $1.5 million.

MHVI also operates an emergency food pantry for veterans who have a short-term crisis, providing several days' worth of food; runs a Women Veterans Initiative to meet the special needs of female veterans; and offers a Bikes for Stripes program providing free, donated bicycles to homeless veterans, who frequently have no other form of transportation.

Johnson is proud and pleased that, unlike MHVI, which has a paid staff of five, his is an all-volunteer effort. "When we first moved into the church, I didn't know if there would be enough people to help us," Johnson said. "We have had so many people come forward who want to help, are happy to help, have great skills, and unlimited energy. I'm just dumbfounded and so grateful. It has changed my whole outlook on the human race." Johnson incorporated his organization and won tax exempt status from the IRS in 2016 under the name Milwaukee Homeless Veterans Services. For more information:

http://www.mkehomelessvets.org/

http://wisvetsnet.org/index.html

https://www.facebook.com/MilwaukeeHomelessVeteransServicesInc

Would that every community in America had a homeless veterans initiative like Milwaukee's. And folks like Bill Christofferson and his VFP colleagues to make it work. But why don't they, especially with so many of today's newest veterans confronting the same cold prospect? In doing the good work, and easing the pain, of countless homeless vets, the Veterans For Peace initiative in Milwaukee got caught in the crosshairs of a heavily politicized America that sees "peace" associated with Vietnam as surrender, and war as good—hence the need to create a new organization without "peace" in its name, in this case Milwaukee Homeless Veterans Initiative.

But if you ask any homeless vet in Milwaukee who it is who gives a damn about them, they might tell you that the folks who sent them off to war and forgot about them are the same ones who wouldn't support VFP's homeless initiatives in the 21st century, half a century after the end of the Vietnam war. It's time to lay that down. In song and in deed.

I first met Yvette Pino when she was brewing beverages at Dry-hootch, a coffee house for veterans in Madison. A veteran herself, she had served with the Army's 101st Airborne Division from 2002-2006 and with the 117th MP Battalion in the National Guard. Twice she'd been deployed to Iraq. What I didn't know about her then, but would discover later, was just what a remarkable artist she is.

"We feel that when people think about veteran art, they think about art therapy," she said. "This is not art therapy. This is much more than that."

Putting her art where her mouth is, Yvette is the founder of the Madison-based Veteran Print Project and the organizer of In Good Company, a community-wide event in Madison during November 2018 which coincided with the 100th anniversary of the Armistice that ended fighting in World War I. Under her leadership, veteran artwork was displayed in multiple Madison venues, often in conjunction with special events and workshops. Throughout the month, the Madison public met with artists, watched demonstrations, baked biscuits with a Navy veteran, learned a printmaking skill, or chronicled a military experience though writing workshops.

As Yvette pointed out, In Good Company was created by highly skilled and respected artists. "It is not necessarily about war, or soldiering," she admitted. "Rather, it is about connections—veteran to veteran, veteran to civilian, generation to generation."

Yvette pointed to the experience of Jesse Albrecht, a member of the Dirty Canteen, a collective of artists who served in the U.S. Armed Forces and whose exhibited work was an integral part of the In Good Company effort.

"Jesse Albrecht puts it beautifully: 'Being an artist can be a very solitary experience,'" explained Yvette. "You add a veteran experience on top of that, and it's really easy for the artist to sit and be alone with their process...and that's very detrimental."

"What I've seen and discovered," she continued, "is that many artists are doing community-based practices in an effort to not only start these conversations, but to re-engage with the community they lost when they went into the service...while being a part of the new family they gained while in service. As artists, we're constantly creatively thinking about how we can visually recreate our war experience so that people can come to a gallery and have a conversation about it. I always love creating something beautiful from an experience that was, well, not so gorgeous."

As other artistic examples, Yvette pointed to Combat Paper and the prints they make from old military uniforms they have turned into pulp, and then paper, and the raw clay and copper artworks by Joshua Zeis that "are reminiscent of what the earth does when an explosion comes up from the ground."

Although a memory of wartime, the works by Zeis, Albrecht, Pino and others are also objects of beauty.

"With In Good Company, we invited the community, and [told them] you're going to make the art with us, and we're going to talk about it,'" Pino said. "And something beautiful's going to come out of it. The experience is just as valuable a piece of art as the art itself."

Like most Vietnam veterans, Dave Flanagan has his own variation on "laying it down." With his military service and 17 years as a Dane County Circuit Court judge, Dave was the perfect person to lead the effort to establish a Veterans Treatment Court in Madison, Wisconsin. You can sense why he did in the question he posed when, as a member of the U.S. Navy's Civil Engineer Corps in the late 1960s, the native of St. Louis volunteered for Vietnam duty, asking, "Why should someone else go instead of me?" Dave's innate sense of fairness and responsibility remain manifest in who he is and what he does.

The Dane County Veterans Treatment Court literature points out that it "promotes and facilitates sobriety, recovery, and stability for veterans with a demonstrated need for treatment through options for addiction, mental health issues and regular contact with the Court." It goes on to state that "volunteer mentors, themselves veterans, are the key part of the Vets Court...each veteran is assigned a Vet Mentor who maintains contact with the vet to encourage, advise, and assist him/her." Upon successful completion of the Veterans Court treatment plan, the veteran's original charges are either dismissed, or reduced.

Surprisingly, on the day I visited the Veterans Treatment Court, the mood in the Madison courtroom was light, upbeat, and comradely, probably the result of Dave Flanagan's presiding. No audible music but a relaxing vibe that helped everyone in the courtroom to deal with tough legal issues. When I sat down later with him and Bruce Meredith, one of the court's Vet Mentors, Dave smiled at my surprise.

"It may seem kind of silly, the Subway subs and the applause for someone who declares a 'no drink anniversary' or any other achievement," he told me. "But as you saw, it actually works. The concept of a Vets Court, at least as I understand it, provides for a suspension of the normal criminal court process to permit a process of regular court appearances, in effect a court monitoring of the defendant's participation in services needed by that particular veteran. This approach, known as 'treatment courts' or 'problem-solving courts' is now being done in a range of areas, drug addiction, OWI—operating while intoxicated—domestic violence, and gambling."

Dave explained that Veterans Courts originated in 2006 when Judge Robert Russell of Buffalo, New York, noticed that a veteran in his mental health court wasn't getting positive results from his treatment. Judge Russell asked two veterans who were working at the court to intervene with the guy, and immediately Russell could tell that the veteran "looked different—his posture was different, he stood more erect, he indicated he was going to try harder to work on his problems."

Judge Russell surmised that peer support (like with Vets House) would positively impact veteran defendants in general, including the large numbers he and his colleagues were seeing in the drug and mental health courts. In 2007, he asked the Buffalo VA Medical Center and its all-veteran advisory board if they would be interested in setting aside a day each month to focus exclusively on veterans and their specific needs. The board enthusiastically volunteered to help in any way. The program spread. Here in Wisconsin, there are 16 court-connected programs covering 33 counties.

Recently retired, Dave now serves as a Veterans Court mentor because he understands the critical role they play in a veteran defendant's success. And he has high praise for the Veterans Administration (VA) and their support of the court. "The key for a Vets Court is the VA. The VA provides vital treatment at no cost to the county, or to the vet."

Even with the numerous legal and technical issues that must addressed, the heartening reality is that the Wisconsin Court System differentiates veterans and the circumstances that set them apart from typical citizens. Courts across Wisconsin are now piloting programs designed to provide better solutions for vets in the criminal justice system. To date, more than 125 veterans have applied for the Dane County (Madison) program. More than two dozen have been admitted, and half have graduated. Moreover, as Dave and his colleagues point out, the recidivism rate among Veterans Treatment Court graduates is less than 10 percent. The program helps vets resurrect independence, self-respect, and meaning in their lives. In addition, compared to incarceration, the program is cost-effective.

I tried probing Dave and Bruce about their vet mentor role, but the program is emphatic about keeping the communication between the veterans and their vet mentors confidential. "In Wisconsin, mentors have a legally recognized confidentiality privilege," Bruce explained. "We mentors cannot disclose anything except in an emergency involving harm to someone, or a criminal act."

Undeterred, I kept probing. "What is it like to be a veteran mentor?" I wondered.

"It's a commitment, all right," they both acknowledged, pointing out that the four or five hours they devote weekly as mentors must be sustained over many months.

"I was hesitant to become a mentor," Bruce admitted, explaining that he was currently mentoring an Iraq vet. "I wasn't in combat in Vietnam, and I don't know enough about the specific circumstances of the current wars. But as the managing editor of the *Deadly Writers Patrol* magazine, I've read a number of pieces by Iraq and Afghan vets and that's helped me to better understand what these younger vets have been through."

"You can't put a price tag on how valuable the veteran camaraderie is," added Dave. And of course, it takes lots of cooperation, and money, as well as time. "The VA, the Public Defender's office, the Department of Corrections—all our Vets Court people on probation are assigned to the same Department of Corrections agent—and even the Dane County district attorney—have bought into the program," he concluded. "It is essentially, however, a volunteer effort on the part of the courthouse, and a wonderful contribution of expensive resources by the VA."

Still, it often comes down to the approach and demeanor of the presiding judge, noted Bruce Meredith, emphasizing that "not every judge is a Dave Flanagan."

Thus far, we've been concerned with the creation of institutions like Vets House (evolving into today's Vet Centers), the Milwaukee Veterans Homeless Initiative, and Veterans Treatment Courts to respond to the call of veteran needs. While in each case those institutions began with a group response to a veteran's call, artistic responses to the call, including music, return us to the individual veteran trying hard to lay it down.

Like song, poetry is infused with call and response. Indeed, poets have always written in response to an earlier work that has inspired them—it's how poetic traditions develop. For example, the notable World War I poet Wilfred Owen's bitterly anti-war poem "Dulce et Decorum Est" takes its Latin title from the ancient Roman poet Horace's statement that "it is sweet and honorable to die for one's country." Confessional poems abound too, the poet's equivalent, in many instances, of laying it down. And, of course, song *is* poetry, as Adam Bradley in *The Poetry of Pop* and others have recognized.

Sending out a "call" to Vietnam vets in the early 1970s, Vietnam veteran poets Basil Paquet, Jan Barry, and Larry Rottmann founded the 1st Casualty Press and in 1972 published *Winning Hearts and Minds: War Poems by Vietnam Veterans*. The response rivaled the poems of Wilfred Owen, Siegfried Sassoon, Rupert Brooke, Joyce Kilmer, and other great World War I poets. The poems in *Winning Hearts and Minds* were at once visceral, honest, and lyrical. W.D. (Bill) Ehrhart was one of the Vietnam vets whose poetry was included in the volume, and 47 years later he's still crafting verse that takes your breath away.

Marine Bill Ehrhart, Con Thien, Vietnam, 1966. Photo courtesy Bill Ehrhart.

"My experiences in the Vietnam War, and the ongoing consequences of that war, have shaped the way I see the world," Bill confesses.
"Every poem I write is a Vietnam War poem. Sometimes it's explicit
and sometimes it's implicit. Sometimes you don't think it's there at
all. I just write poems. I write about my life and the world I live in
and the people around me. The older I am, the less inclined I am to
talk about my poetry. What I must say is in the poems. Read the poems; if they don't tell you what you need to know about my poetry,
then they're probably not very good poems." Bill responded to my
call with two recent works.

Praying at the Altar
I like pagodas.
There's something—I don't know—
secretive about them,
soul-soothing, mind-easing.
Inside, if only for a moment,
life's clutter disappears.

Once, long ago, we destroyed one:
collapsed the walls
'til the roof caved in.
Just a small one, all by itself
in the middle of nowhere,
and we were young. And bored.
Armed to the teeth.
And too much time on our hands.

Now whenever I see a pagoda,
I always go in.
I'm not a religious man,
but I light three joss sticks,
bow three times to the Buddha,
pray for my wife and daughter.
I place the burning sticks

in the vase before the altar.

In Vung Tau, I was praying
at the Temple of the Sleeping Buddha
when an old monk appeared.
He struck a large bronze bell
with a wooden mallet.
He was waking up the spirits
to receive my prayers.

Making the Children Behave
Do they think of me now
in those strange Asian villages
where nothing ever seemed
quite human
but myself
and my few grim friends
moving through them
hunched
in lines?

When they tell stories to their children
of the evil
that awaits misbehavior,
is it me they conjure?

Bill's poetry straightforwardly juxtaposes past and present to
show the past's influence on the present. In "Praying," he contrasts
his youthful behavior—bored, casually destructive of another's
culture—with his current behavior, which is respectful and participatory. The poetry itself seems a kind of prayer. In "Making the
Children Behave," he recognizes consequences that go beyond
himself—he knows that his real current self has a shadow in Vietnam. And as all of us know, you can't escape your shadow. This
poem is about acknowledging the shadow. As Bill says, "One does

not heal from the wounds of war. If one is lucky, one learns to live with the wounds."

Like Ehrhart, former Donut Dollie Bobbie Trotter (see Adagio section) has been employing poetry to help her with her own homecoming and healing. She contributed several poems to Lynda Van Devanter's book, *Visions of War: Dreams of Peace,* and read two of her poems at the dedication of the Vietnam Women's Memorial in 1993.

"After my experiences in Vietnam," she revealed in an email, "writing saved my sanity."

> *Telling*
> I was never one for secret sorrows
> gut wrenching, ulcer causing, twisted privacies,
> always had to get the poison out,
> bring it into the air and hope to find it's not so
> bad when you get it in the light...
> wear it on the sleeve, talk it to death!
> Except for some of the war stuff.
> That cannot bear the telling.
> The thing is...you've got to know going in
> that retelling it, is reliving it.
> Sometimes, that's the price of healing;
> sometimes, that's the ticket to self-destruction.
> The trick is knowing where the line is
> and whether the sharing is worth the risk.

"Is the sharing worth the risk?" Many Vietnam vets have been asking themselves that question since they've came home. Donut Dollies too. It's a calculation they shouldn't have to make, but to quote a familiar phrase from the Vietnam lexicon, "there it is."

That reluctance to share sometimes has odd, almost entertaining effects. Steve Wickland and I have been daily exercisers at UW Sports Medicine in Madison for years, talking about sports, politics, music, and the weather among other routine topics. But it wasn't until he stood up to share his poetry in one of our *We Gotta Get Out of This Place* Q&A sessions that I realized Steve was a Vietnam veteran.

Steve Wickland was an Air Force Captain adjudicating military justice for the 366th Combat Support group at Da Nang from October 1971 to October 1972. "I was an officer doing legal work—courts martial, administrative discharge hearings," he explained. "Often, I'd go off base into the city with an MP and an interpreter to interview local citizens who had claims against the Air Force. I wasn't a foot soldier carrying weapons. They had body bags there and all, it was a combat zone, but I was basically doing trial work."

In "Remembering Vietnam," a two part-poem divided into "Questions" and "Answers," Steve writes: "Memories, sometimes/ Are too much for us/Thoughts...Will there be a time for/Healing, for acknowledgment, for questions and answers that matter?" Loss and remorse are never far from the Vietnam experience, and, like so many Vietnam veterans, Steve experienced an epiphany when he saw our national memory, the Vietnam Memorial.

SOLO Steve Wickland

I love this nation. I wanted to honor America by my poetry, yet also express what it was like to return home to a nation that did not fully understand the difficulties returning veterans faced... Years rolled on, and I maintained my silence, until Maya Lin's design was chosen and the Vietnam Memorial was built. In 1984, during a visit to Washington, D.C., I arrived at the memorial with my family, not knowing that "Thomas Anthony Carter," an old Fort Lauderdale basketball opponent, and later a classmate at Tulane University, and another Tulane friend, "Rodney Chastant," were names that I would see engraved on the wall. This was my first knowledge, profoundly sad, of the early death in combat in 1967-68 of Tony and Rod—friends of such promise, now gone. To see their names on the memorial made me look back in terms of personal loss...a couple of guys, 23, 24, bright, plenty of talents—for what did they die? To see someone cut down in his youth is hard to accept...That visit closed the circle, providing a source of healing. I could now write poems, saying that those returning and those who did not serve in those circumstances could communicate, could understand each other through the efforts of many and by the emotional presence, the healing grace of the Vietnam Memorial. That wall with dignity and poignancy listed the names of the fallen, and in doing so it honored those men and women and helped heal this nation...

Over there, I kept a kind of journal, very sparse—rocket attacks, trips to Saigon, cases I was trying. I had always intended to write something, but you get to doing other things. I don't presume what I write speaks for anyone else who was over there or who is back here. It's just my personal response...but I still needed a reaction to what I wrote, as to the quality of the poems and the significance of the Vietnam War in American history, so I summoned the nerve to write to the distinguished poet Robert Penn Warren. I asked for his thoughts on the quality and whether they conveyed a sense of the unusual nature of the war. Surprisingly, the great Mr. Warren wrote back! "I am grateful for your letter and for the clippings with the poem," he wrote in his April 22, 1986 letter. "Here the poet can get emotional effect in handling abstractions in a way that would not work in ordinary poetry. Here there is nothing that provokes poetry beyond the poetry of fact." These were genuine, helpful remarks, to be sure, but Vietnam was such an ambiguous experience. It wasn't one you found yourself talking about. If it came up in conversation, people didn't pursue it. Maybe they thought you didn't want to talk about it, or that someday they'd sit down and talk about with you over a beer, but that didn't happen...In previous wars, units went over as a group and came back as a group, but in Vietnam, you went over alone and came back alone...[By] writing poetry, I'm expressing my view that we can come together by talking and listening, to better understand and move ahead with that understanding. We need, today as always, to share ideas on any topic of significance, to discuss issues with others. We can give our views and learn of theirs. We can read history. And by committing our memories to the written word, the writer can better understand and can provide a written memory for others.

Like Bill, Bobbie, and Steve, I've found that writing has helped bring me home and keep me sane. As I mentioned earlier, I've been a member of the Deadly Writers Patrol for years, and its writing rigor was crucial to my completing *DEROS Vietnam: Dispatches from the Air-Conditioned Jungle* (Warriors Publishing Group, 2012), my collection of vignettes about U.S. Army life in the rear in Vietnam presented as "story truth," a term that Tim O'Brien coined in *The Things They Carried*: "I want you to feel what I felt," he writes. "I want you to know why story-truth is truer sometimes than happening-truth."

The seeds for DWP were laid at the Madison Vet Center in the 1990s by Bob Cook and Tom Deits, two Vietnam veterans—and former Vets House staffers—who were counseling vets at the center. Vietnam vets like me were invited to join the writing sessions, and while my work and family schedule made it difficult for me to stick with the group on a regular basis, knowing that DWP existed helped keep me writing. Eventually, DWP split off from the Vet Center and a handful of us met over lunch on Fridays. Ultimately, we decided to share what we were writing more widely, and in 2006, *The Deadly Writers Patrol* magazine was born. As I write this, the magazine continues to publish biannually, on or around Memorial Day and Veterans Day. Our mission statement spoke not only to the magazine's purpose and subject matter, but also to what we expected of contributing writers: "The mission of the DWP magazine is to provide a forum for writings that originate from the Vietnam experience and to encourage greater understanding of the changes wrought by the Vietnam era...We are interested in writing that looks both outward and inward, grappling with what we were, what we became, and what we might be if we deal honestly with the things we ignored."

And we weren't done: "We believe that writing can be a mirror into the deepest corners of our spirits and our psyches, that it can reflect back what is found there. It can express the reality of suffering and explore the possibility of healing. At times writing can help us resolve problems and achieve a deeper understanding, but it can also bring us face-to-face with the parts of life that will always remain a mystery." We wanted to be explicit, direct, honest. The suffering-healing dialectic still exists in the complexities of Vietnam, and we can never explain all the mysteries of our lives. DWP also gave me the opportunity to partner with Craig Werner who became my co-author on *We Gotta Get Out of This Place*.

"The quality of the submissions and the quality of the magazine are extremely high," observed Bruce Meredith, DWP managing editor. "People care about war and its consequences—and its stories. Now that we've been at war in Afghanistan and Iraq for nearly two decades, we have another cadre of veterans and war-related issues to be explored...not to mention Vietnam, which never seems to go away."

Active duty soldiers, too, have found DWP to be a source of inspiration and support.

Take recently retired Command Sergeant Major Brian Bieniek, who joined the Army in 1990 after graduating from high school in Scottsdale, Arizona. Brian served in northern Kuwait and southern Iraq in support of Operation Iraqi Freedom with the 2nd Battalion, 128th Infantry in 2005-06 and in Baghdad, Iraq, with the 1st Squadron, 105th Cavalry in 2009 and 2010. Between tours, he earned a degree at UW-Madison where he took classes from Craig and joined DWP.

"DWP helped me put something historically and personally relevant on paper for others to read, especially my children when they're older," he said. "And it helped me focus on thinking about, and analyzing, my observations and emotions from my time overseas. Best of all, DWP motivated me to start looking at experimenting with other styles of writing besides straight, factual storytelling." (Learn more at: https://www.deadlywriterspatrol.org)

DWP-like organizations are scattered across the country. One of the best known, a meditation and writing workshop at UC-Berkeley, is Veterans Writing Group, directed by Maxine Hong Kingston, author of *The Woman Warrior* and other novels. Bill Larson and Pauline Laurent, participants in Kingston's workshop, agreed that the writing group was essential to their healing. "By joining the group, I became much more serious about healing myself," recalled Laurent. Larson was among the 80 veterans whose work appeared in the anthology *Veterans of War, Veterans of Peace* edited by Kingston. Kingston's two brothers served in Vietnam, and she told her Veterans Writing Group that the war in Vietnam "took my youth." In a 2008 interview with the *San Francisco Chronicle*, she said, "It affected my entire life. I became very interested in considering, 'How do we ever come home from that war?'"

That was a critical concern of the "Writing My Way Back Home" workshop that I attended in Iowa City in April 2013. Their mission sounded a lot like the mission statement for the *Deadly Writers Patrol* magazine: "to provide veterans space and time to write about their wartime experiences in order to heal, to be heard, and create meaningful expression." Sponsored by Midwest Military Outreach in partnership with the University of Iowa Writers' Workshop and led by faculty from the University of Iowa and Kirkwood Community College—and a few published Army veteran writers like me—the workshop featured writing exercises designed to get the veteran writing in a safe setting. There would be opportunities to discuss

our work—both as a class workshop and one-on-one with professional writers—along with a two-week, online follow-up to continue the writing and revision process. Maybe someone would write a
song, but there wasn't a session devoted to music. Rather we were
all bearing witness.

Veteran participant in Iowa's "Writing My Way Back Home"
workshop. Photo courtesy John Mikelson.

According to workshop founder Emma Rainey, a 2009 graduate of
Iowa's Nonfiction writing program, the workshop's aim "is not to
generate work of literary quality," but to "begin the powerful process for veterans to write their stories and reflect on events they
experienced in war in a way that may lead to greater insight, creativity, and healing." She and Army veteran John Mikelson, the
workshop's current convener, point out that the instructors use
writing exercises to explore wartime experiences such as fear,
boredom, anxiety, brutality, and tears.

At the welcome meet-and-greet, I was surprised to find so
many Vietnam veterans among the participants—and even more
surprised to see that half of the two dozen attendees were wom-
en, most of them post-9/11 vets. Our "marching orders," if you will,
were to draw inspiration from the words of my friend and fellow
veteran Karl Marlantes.

"This book is my song," Marlantes writes in *What is it Like to Go to War*. "Each and every one of us veterans must have a song to sing about our war before we can walk back into the community without everyone...quaking behind the walls."

I felt better already.

The next day's schedule was filled with classes, and I was scheduled to co-teach a session on blogging and online journaling with Randy Brown, aka "Charlie Sherpa," a former citizen-soldier of the Iowa Army National Guard and author of *Red Bull Rising*, a popular military-focused blog. The jam-packed day would conclude with a group dinner and then a public reading by attendees. While music seemed to be absent, it would emerge with a different lyrical accent in veteran poetry.

In fact, one of the opening sessions focused on poetry, led by a retired English professor who talked about avoiding the draft at Ann Arbor in the 1960s. Did he know who his audience was? But he spoke knowledgeably about poetry and poetic form and shared some poetry. He went on to explain *haiku*, the traditional form of Japanese poetry, three lines with the first and last containing five syllables and the middle line seven. As an old English major, I kept hearing Erza Pound's "In A Station of the Metro" repeating in my head, "The apparition of these faces in the crowd petals on a wet, black bough." But I couldn't remember where the lines broke.

And then a voice came, clear and strong, from a young woman in the back of the room: "No one heard my no," her haiku began, "all body and soul ravaged/Iraq sand in my mouth."

We were profoundly silent. Rape, military sexual trauma, was a prominent part of her war, of these current wars, and it had caught us by the throat. For some reason, I couldn't get the Rolling Stones song "Under My Thumb" out of my head. It had nothing to do directly with this female vet's pain, but then again, it had a lot to do with men in command of male-female situations. Later, after my sessions with Randy and a group of Vietnam, Desert Storm, and Iraq and Afghan vets about online journaling and blogs, I sought out and spoke with the haiku poet and a few of the other female vets. They all agreed that, while they were proud of their service, military sexual trauma was real and all too prevalent. The Air Force, for example, had begun using a play as a teaching tool to highlight sexual assault prevention. Maybe they needed to add music to make the point? Right now it seemed as if the only thing these young female vets had were one another—and workshops like this one—to provide them the sanctuary to write about their traumatic experiences, and perhaps to begin to, in their words, "heal."

"Healing" may be too optimistic a term to describe the "Writing My Way Back Home" approach because it implies a definite ending. For sure, that's part of what can start there, but, as the workshop title indicates, it's about the journey more than the destination. Too many Vietnam veterans have yet to make it home, and we can't afford to repeat the same mistake with this generation of men and women veterans. Listening to their voices, reading their stories, and helping them to express their experiences may just be the best way to bring them back, to help them lay it down.

One of the workshop participants hoping to find her voice and her story that weekend was veteran survivor Amanda Cherry. Four years later, she attended a presentation I made in Kansas City. I was surprised to see her there, to learn that she was now living in Kansas City—and that she had a guide dog with her. Therein lies a tale of writing, theater, and redemption.

SOLO   Amanda Cherry

I remember the 2013 "Writing my Way Back Home" veterans writing conference…happening at the exact right time for me and propelling me into a future I never would have imagined possible. The event itself…inspired me, connected me, and encouraged me in endeavors I probably wouldn't have tried had I not attended. So, in that sense it did change my life. At the time, I was in the process of divorcing an abusive alcoholic veteran with severe PTSD. We were still living in the same house in St.

Helens, Oregon, but living very separate lives...After speaking with the organizers of the event, I was convinced that if I attended, I would feel as though my writing was a legitimate pursuit.

Although I was studying journalism and belonged to a very supportive writers group, nearly seventeen years in an abusive marriage had convinced me I had no real talent as a writer. Even with countless articles published online and in a few local newspapers, doubt still plagued me. But I thought "if I go to the University of Iowa, the home of one of the country's best writing programs, and they tell me I'm good...well, then I've got a shot." So, I bought a plane ticket, rented a car, and booked a room at a bed and breakfast.

Saying it felt like going home would be truthful. I was born and raised in a suburb of Des Moines, Iowa, and had visited friends in Iowa City during long college weekends and breaks. I loved Iowa City, the vibe, the atmosphere; the wisdom of the place just seemed aspirational to me. So, when I arrived, my expectations were high.

As with all military veteran events I attend, I was plagued with the idea that my service and my PTSD weren't legitimate enough reasons to have a seat at the table. I was an Army medic from 1992–2000 with the Iowa Army National Guard. I had been deployed to Germany in support of Operation Joint Endeavor (Bosnia) but had not been allowed to "go down range" because I wasn't MOS qualified. I had been attached to a Public Affairs unit, and without the PA training, was required to stay behind. I suffer from PTSD, but it isn't related to my deployment or combat. My PTSD was from military sexual trauma, rape, domestic violence, and service as a civilian EMT for nearly ten years. I was not a combat veteran...I felt like a fraud coming to write about my military experience, but the "Writing My Way Back

Home" conference was also open to military family members and I was, technically, still a military spouse.

I don't remember much of what I wrote or shared with the group. I remember being inspired, welcomed, encouraged, and given that much-needed boost to my confidence. I knew a few people at the event, having served in the military with them, and left the conference with a renewed sense of inspiration...I felt like a writer for the first time. I stayed in touch with several people via social media and emails. These connections lead me to publish my first story in *Proud to Be: Writings by American Warriors, Vol. III*. I felt like I had found my calling...

Until the bottom fell out of my life.

In the two years that followed, I survived divorce, an attempt on my life by my abusive ex-husband, suicide of someone I knew, death of a close relative, unemployment, and eventually homelessness. Writing became an integral part of the healing process for me. I hadn't been in combat, but I had still experienced trauma. In June of 2015, while living in a homeless shelter for military veterans, I wrote a play called "Warriors Rising." The play focused on a story told me by a Vietnam veteran, who said the only person to welcome him home, at the height of the civil rights movement, was an African-American man. When the church shooting in Charleston, South Carolina, happened in June 2015, I realized I had a story to tell about the experiences of being a veteran and a minority living in America. Writing the play became a healing process for me. It took some time, but I went through a recovery program for domestic abuse and Dialectic Behavioral Therapy with the VA. I got a service dog, and I continued to participate in writing groups—establishing my own for women when I moved to Kansas City.

Because of the connections I made at that writing conference, I submitted a play to a playwriting competition sponsored by Arts in the Armed Forces. I told myself...IF I win, I'll donate half the money to a worthy cause. And for the life of me couldn't think of one I thought would be worthy enough to pro-pel theatre in the local community for military, veterans, and first responders. That was when I decided that if I won, I'd start my own theatre for the service community in Kansas City. That thought calmed me down.

I started looking into what it would take to start a nonprofit theatre working with military, veterans, and first responders. I didn't think I could manage it without the influx of that prize money, which I didn't win by the way, but with a lot of help from some folks who were at that "Writing my Way Back Home" conference and folks I met because of connections with others at that conference, Charlie Mike Theatre Company was born on May 1, 2018. Our first production was "Warriors Rising," the play I had written back in 2015 while living in the homeless shelter. It had nearly sold-out crowds, and every single perfor-mance had standing ovations. I gained the distinction of being the first female veteran/first responder to start a permanent theatre for military, veterans, and first responders. We've add-ed education and outreach as a part of our nonprofit, hoping to engage the community directly. Our goal is to help those who have served the community to share their stories in whatever way feels right to them. We hope to educate the public about what it is like to be of service to the community and that many of the obstacles we face...they face too." Learn more at:

http://www.charliemiketc.org

Amanda's story perfectly illustrates the call-and-response cycle. The workshop organizers heard the call of an unmet need from veterans. They responded by constructing a sanctuary in which at-tendees could write and feel validated, gathering experience and knowledge that they would use as their circumstances led them. "Warriors Rising," Amanda's play, responded to the call of another veteran's story, as did her work to establish a theater for a particu-lar audience whose calls had been ignored. She didn't necessarily "heal" at the original workshop, but she very well may have started the process there. And her theater seeks to allow others that safe place in which to make a similar start.

Another of the veteran presenters in Iowa City that weekend in 2013 was Miyoko Hijiki, whose job in Iraq in 2003–04 was to transport supplies, troops, and enemy prisoners as part of the 2133rd Transportation Company of the Iowa Army National Guard. She's written about her wartime experiences in a moving memoir, *All I Could Be: My Story as a Woman Warrior in Iraq*. Much like Amanda, she acknowledged that her participation in a writing workshop in 2010 "changed the course of my life."

As the nearly 30 of us left Iowa City that April weekend, the words of that painful haiku still echoing, we found reassurance in another reminder from Karl Marlantes and *What It is Like to Go to War*:

"Perhaps it is drawing pictures or reciting poetry about the war. Perhaps it is getting together with a small group and telling stories. Perhaps it is dreaming about it and writing the dreams down and then telling people your dreams. But it isn't enough just to do the art in solitude and sing the song alone. You must sing it to other people. Those who are afraid or uneasy must hear it. They must see the art. They must lose their fear. When the child asks, 'What is it like to go to war?' to remain silent keeps you from coming home."

But sometimes even after you literally "come home," you're not quite there. For many vets, addressing and overcoming the traumas of war involves revisiting the place where they were soldiers. Bill Christofferson and Gordon Fowler served together in Vietnam in 1967 as combat correspondents with the 1st Marine Division, based in Da Nang. While their tours overlapped, they were not identical—Bill extended and spent a total of 17 months in country.

These two self-described "ISO Snuffies" (low-ranking enlisted Marines in the Informational Service Office) shared a duet in *We Gotta Get Out of This Place*, riffing on the folk songs Gordon used to play on a beat-up Yamaha guitar he found outside the company's Thunderbird Club.

"We played everything we could remember a few words to," Gordon remembered. "Country, blues, pop, and other stuff we made up. It didn't matter if we sang the same set every night. Nobody cared…I relied on other people to come up with new songs, but they hardly ever did. So, I improvised. I even did folk music like, 'If I had a hammer, I'd kill all the folk singers.' We sang it with feeling, though."

Bill and Gordon visited our class at UW-Madison, precipitating an avalanche of laughter, tears, and applause. The singular moment occurred when they sang "There Isn't Any Jukebox in the Jungle," an original ditty written by Gordon in Vietnam. "Well, there isn't any jukebox in the jungle," the song begins, "And there are no honky tonks to pass the time/So if you're gonna write a Dear John letter/Break it to me easy, please be kind."

"I thought us Snuffies needed our own take on a "Dear John' tearjerker," Gordon recalled. "The tune just sort of came around like songs do—some of the guys helped with later verses—and we learned to sing it pretty good. I never thought it was going to be a hit with our bunch but seems it got used in a lot of their later writings.

"Bastards owe me royalties," he smiled. "But I'm not holding my breath."

But Gordon and Bill did hold their breath, and experience an epiphany, when they returned to Vietnam in 2000, travelling more than 700 miles in country with Dave Cutaia, Bill's boot camp buddy. Here's a different, acappella twist on their *We Gotta Get Out of This Place* duet.

DUET   Bill Christofferson and Gordon Fowler

Former Marine Snuffies Bill Christofferson and Gordon Fowler
greeting friendly Vietnamese during their return to Nui Loc Son,
Vietnam, 2000. Photo courtesy Bill Christofferson.

Bill: Gordon had served with me as a 1st Marine Division combat correspondent in Vietnam, while Dave had been a scout/interpreter with the 1st Battalion, 5th Marines. He'd already been back to Vietnam half a dozen times, could speak the language, and had a Vietnamese wife—it was like having our own guide. We spent three weeks exploring the country, from Hanoi to Ho Chi Minh City. It was 2000, and coincidentally we were in Vietnam at the same time as the late Senator John McCain, who was there for ceremonies marking the 25th anniversary of the end of the war. McCain had been to Hanoi before, as a prisoner for five-and-a-half years in the infamous "Hanoi Hilton" POW camp. But he, too, was on a mission of reconciliation.

Gordon: We only spent one day in an area where we had been in combat. That was not the purpose of the trip. We wanted to visit places we had never seen...but we eventually paid a visit to the Quế Sơn basin, which included Nui Loc Son, the scene of some of the bloodiest fights and hotly contested ground war for control of the rich valley. While killing thousands of NVA throughout 1967, the Marines suffered heavy casualties as well...Marine reinforcements would chopper in or force march to trap the enemy. It was sometimes critical for Marine units to get help quickly but not always possible. Many died waiting for medivacs. I was wounded here, and Bill and Dave were both involved in the Quế Sơn Valley battles.

Bill: We used to think that if we ever got to Hanoi, it would be as prisoners being paraded through the streets at gunpoint. When we finally did get there, thirty-plus years later, it was via Vietnam Airlines jet, and we were welcomed with open arms. A grim-faced customs official, dressed in a military-looking uniform and wearing a pith helmet stamped our papers, no questions asked, and we randomly chose one of a cluster of cab drivers competing for our attention to take us to a hotel. Determining that the three of us were veterans, one of the porters said, with a smile, perhaps in jest, that he had been Viet Cong. 'Congratulations,' I said, extending my hand for a handshake... that set the tone for our visit.

Gordon: The red dirt and black rocks of the Quế Sơn valley made a beautiful complementary scheme with the rich greens and the rice paddies and tree lines. The grass hooches were tucked in among the bamboo, and their cooking fire smoke mixed with the smell of nuoc mam and water buffalo dung, and the smell of Vietnamese life going on just as it had for hundreds of years.

Bill: I always used to say, back in 1966 and 1967, that Vietnam would be a beautiful country to visit if there wasn't a war on. That turned out to be a major understatement. Most of the places we went to were brand new to Gordon and me, and they were spectacular...When we were in Vietnam as Marines, we were prohibited from learning about or partaking in Vietnamese culture. Virtually everything was off limits. We never tasted Vietnamese food, and interacted, legally, at least, only with the small number of Vietnamese who had access to the base camps as barbers, laundry workers, or other functionaries. We were told that we couldn't trust any of them; your barber by day might be a VC by night. This trip was an opportunity to sample some of what we had missed—and to try to come to peace with what our country had done to the people of Vietnam. We found the people, almost universally, to be warm and welcoming. When an American talks about Vietnam, the war is usually the first thing to come to mind. But to Vietnamese, what they call "the American war" is a blip on centuries of warfare, occupation, and struggle. They genuinely seem to like Americans. It is hard to imagine us being so forgiving.

Gordon: It was strange to be back in the Quế Sơn valley. The trail seemed dry and dusty for May, worn down by foot traffic. I felt like we shouldn't be on it, but it looked well used. I knew from before that enemy troops didn't like to mine their own backyard—at least not as much as up around Da Nang and Hoi An. Still, I was uneasy. My combat instincts told me to watch for trouble—if that could even be possible with sweat running in my eyes and heat waves rising from the valley floor. I was soaking wet and my eyes stung from the salt and heat...

Bill: We had seen very little of the country as Marines, and under the worst conditions. This trip was to expand our horizons. At some point in a conversation, someone might ask if it is your first time in the country. When you say that you were there in 1967, they smile in recognition and exclaim, "Ah! Veteran!" That happened in Ho Chi Minh City, with a cyclo driver who had fought for the south, and with a former North Vietnamese Army soldier we befriended in Hanoi...In the cities, even twenty years ago, it was clear that younger people were becoming more global, and perhaps more Westernized in dress, music, and attitudes. Vietnam is a Communist country, but except for daily announcements on the loudspeakers on utility poles outside our Hanoi hotel, there was little evidence of it, and almost no public military presence. But in the villages, where farmers worked the fields with water buffalo and carried huge loads balanced on a pole on their shoulders, it could have been 1967—or 1867.

Gordon: The trail went over a small rise and veered to the right as it dropped gently to the Ly Ly River. The water was startling cobalt blue and looked as refreshing as a Pearl Beer advertisement from the "country of eleven hundred springs." I still felt the danger around me, however, and it was too quiet—like in the Western movies. Bill was out in front about ten meters and David was rear guard, behind me, but out of sight behind the rise in the trail. I hoped Dave was watching behind him for trouble and our point man was also alert. I just had to assume they knew what they were doing. After all, they were combat Marines, too...

Bill: The people we met seemed to be cheerful, industrious, and uncomplaining. But these impressions are dated, of course. When we were there in 2000, it had been only five years since the US and Vietnam had re-established diplomatic relations, and a bilateral trade agreement had just been signed. Now Americans are wearing and using products every day that were made in Vietnam. President Barack Obama visited in 2016 and ate noodles and drank beer at a street food restaurant in Hanoi with chef and TV personality Anthony Bourdain.

Gordon: Danger really? Thirty years after? The kids were caught off guard as they splashed in the Ly Ly and their naked bodies glistened in the sun. We were somewhat startled too and stopped dead in the trail to figure our next move. Would they rush us, or disappear into the jungle and fight another day? Before we could make a plan, they were out of the river, dressed and heading our way on their bikes. We took their photos, gave them Tootsie Rolls, and practiced our Vietnamese with them. They spoke some English and the less bashful ones tried it out on us. I guess the Nui Loc Son basin had finally been pacified and was no longer the killing ground it used to be. I realized that our new "invasion" was a chance to somehow connect with the country where we lived and died so long ago. Even the thoughts of dead Marines lined up for fifty yards, waiting to be picked up and sent home, didn't stop me from enjoying this place in peace, with the grandsons of our old enemies. We finished the day in nearby Mỹ Sơn, sitting in the shade, having a beer with some former Viet Cong, showing off old wounds and grooving the peace.

Bill: I don't expect to get there again. It was a once-in-a-lifetime experience—well, twice in a lifetime. As the old song says about love, Vietnam was certainly lovelier the second time around.

Gordon: Going back was emotional for us but enlightening. There was finally peace in the valley.

Vietnamese children swimming at Nui Loc Son, Vietnam,
2000. Photo courtesy Bill Christofferson.

One of the many interesting postscripts from that visit is the friendship that developed between Gordon, an accomplished artist, and ex-NVA fighter Dinh Luc, a well-known wood block artist from Hanoi. Bill, Dave, and Gordon found Dinh after paying a visit to the Vietnam Museum of Ethnology, where a book of his work was on sale. Later, the three of them visited Dinh's studio, saw his work, met his family—and made a lasting connection. The next year, Dinh visited Gordon at his home in Austin and participated in a printmaking show at the University of Texas. Today, the former combatants remain in touch, and Dinh Luc's son is attending college in the U.S.

Vietnam kept calling, and these Vietnam vets responded. And on a hot May afternoon in 2000, Bill, Gordon, and Dave finally laid Vietnam down, not at the Vietnam Veterans Memorial in D. C. where the bitter Vietnam vet in Olin Murrell's song decides it's "time to lay it down," but in the country where they waged war.

Women veterans' modes for laying it down differ from those of male veterans because their roles in Vietnam and their gender roles in the U.S. differed. First, they were volunteers, all roughly 11,000 of them stationed in Vietnam during the war. Second, 90 percent were nurses. Others served as physicians, physical therapists, and other personnel in the medical field; air traffic control, military intelligence, administration, and in many other capacities. An unknown number of civilian women also served in Vietnam as news correspondents and humanitarian workers. Third, there was no public memory of women's service in Vietnam. None.

I know from my many conversations and email exchanges with nurses like Mary Reynolds Powell, Sue O'Neill, and Kay Bauer; donut dollies like Bobbie Trotter and Jeannie Christie; and fellow REMFs like Linda McClenahan and Karen Psimadis that many of them, too, have struggled mightily, often in isolation or obscurity. Diane Carlson Evans and other female Vietnam veterans created a Vietnam Women's Memorial on the grounds of the Vietnam Veterans Memorial in Washington, D.C. to lessen their isolation and insist that their experiences be publicly recognized.

A native of Minnesota, Diane Carlson Evans graduated as a registered nurse from St. Barnabas Hospital School in Minneapolis. She later spent six years in the military, including a year in Vietnam in 1968–69 as trauma nurse in the surgical and burn wards at Vũng Tàu and later as a head nurse (captain) in a surgical unit at Pleiku.

Her mantra during the ten years it took to have the Vietnam Women's Memorial established was "Women are also soldiers. Women also need to heal. Their service is worthy of honor and recognition."

Diane intuited that millions of visitors would come to the Vietnam Veterans Memorial in D.C., so she dedicated years of her life to the Vietnam Women's Memorial's formation. "The debate that was raging then," Diane recalled, "was whether to put up another statue of men who'd fought since not everyone was sold on Maya Lin's design. 'If they put up another statue to men, they'll completely forget about the women,' I told my husband. 'Who's going to do that?' he asked, and I knew in my heart that it had to be me."

But she couldn't do it alone, and other female veterans like Kay Bauer, whom you met in the Overture, were watching, admiring, and pitching in. Kay shared her thoughts with the Minnesota Historical Society's Minnesota Women Vietnam Veterans Oral History Project.

SOLO   Kay Bauer

Vietnam Women's Memorial, Washington, D. C. Photo courtesy Diane Carlson Evans.

The Vietnam Women's Memorial was the first time, the very first time, that this nation had said, "Yes!" Women have been involved in war, had to put up with the same things. We didn't shoot people. That wasn't our job. But we had to be there and take care of the aftermath of what went on. Women have been involved forever. I mean, how could we not be? We didn't always wear uniforms. Not everybody wore a military uniform that was there, but some of us obviously did...We started doing more research on women who served in the continental wars, the women who served in these other wars, and, in order to serve, yes, the nurses were there, but they weren't actually part of the military. The other women, in order to get involved, dressed up as men. Usually, no one ever found that they were men until they'd been injured. One woman got two purple hearts before anybody realized she was a woman. The nation as a whole never recognized that we were there or that we did anything or that we were part of any effort, so it was the first time...

One of the things that we did here in Minnesota—because this is where Diane Carlson Evans was—was to reach out to all the women veterans, saying, "This may be a Vietnam women's memorial, but we need all of the women involved. None of you have ever been recognized." My sister's mother-in-law was a World War II vet. She was in the Philippines...The first state Diane went to, of course, was Wisconsin, her home state. Then she started going to other states. We helped her write letters and compose letters...Once she got more women in the nation involved, then she had groups in each state. Diane set up, with Donna-Marie Boulay, the Vietnam Women's Memorial Project, so that we could accept donations...We did various things to raise funds for that, like sell the little statues. I tried to get the Army, Navy, and Air Force Reserves involved in that, too. We had to get at least two Acts of Congress passed to authorize the building of the memorial—and to build it where it is on the grounds near the Wall.

The dedication in 1993 was part of a three-day Celebration of Patriotism and Courage, from November 10 to 12 in Washington, D.C. A bunch of us from here got into a SUV and drove to Washington and were there for that. We all were so excited. I still have all the stuff from there. We had a little candle. I took that to the ten-year reunion. The Navy had bandolier kind of things that we wore with our buttons and that on it. It was a wonderful, wonderful, wonderful weekend...and while we all tried to help Diane it was her vision. It was her dream. There's no doubt about that. It always was.

Vietnam veterans Kay Bauer (far right) and Doug Bradley at the "End of the Tour" concert, Twin Cities Public TV studios, November 2017. Photo courtesy Twin Cities Public TV.

Thanks to Diane Carlson Evans and the thousands of supporters like Kay Bauer, the Vietnam Women's Memorial was the first tangible symbol of honor for American women's wartime service. Designed by New Mexico sculptor Glenna Goodacre, the multi-figure bronze monument stands 6 feet 8 inches tall and weighs one ton. It portrays three Vietnam-era women, one of whom is caring for a wounded male soldier. "It wasn't easy," Diane wrote on her website. "I didn't accomplish this monumental effort alone. I am grateful to all and can never thank enough each and every person who made a difference. In the end, was it worth the anguish of the never-ending trials and tribulations—the loss of ten years in the hours given to accomplishing every step, every feat? I see the answer every time I visit the Vietnam Women's Memorial" (http://www.dianecarlsonevans.com).

Mary Reynolds Powell and Bobbie Trotter were there that November 1993 afternoon for the Monument's dedication. Mary's teenage son and daughter joined her and her husband Doug, an Army doctor who served with MEDCAPS (Medical Civic Action Program) in Vietnam.

"It was a perfect autumn day, with brilliant sunlight and brightly colored leaves," she wrote me, "The crowd was festive; the celebration was female from start to finish! It was fabulous to be part of an emotional experience that affirmed what we had been through in Vietnam, where it had not been possible to acknowledge emotion...We filled the grounds near the Wall, and shouts of joy could be heard as people reunited. I hugged two of my supervisors from the 24th Evac Hospital—something I would never have believed could happen—and when they pulled the drape off Glenna Goodacre's statue, I sobbed as the crowd roared.

"After the ceremony," Mary continued, "we walked to the statue and, again, tears flowed. Notes and flowers had been left at its base. I remember looking at each of the three women closely, but the woman on her knees with her hands outstretched in a gesture of helplessness brought me to my knees, and I shed the tears I could not in Vietnam."

Bobbie Trotter, who shared two of her poems at the Memorial's dedication, offered this reflection: "Personally, standing on that stage to read my poems, looking out at thousands of candles lighting the darkness, made all the struggle and pain worthwhile. I hold it in my heart as one of the greatest moments of my life."

But Bobbie recalls that "it was a horrific battle" to get the monument built. "In this age of the #MeToo movement," Bobbie continued, "some might like to know how hard it was. What stands in D.C. is NOT the original design. The original was of a nurse in fatigues, stethoscope around her neck holding her steel pot helmet. This is the statue I traveled around with, trying to raise money until there was a great protest against it, including the director of the D.C. art commission, who said, 'If we give it to the women, we'll have to give it to the dogs.' Needless to say, this not only pissed off the women but many of our Vietnam brothers who then camped out on the capitol steps on our behalf...Then there was the whole process of 'We have to have an open contest.' It took over ten years to get that statue dedicated."

"Finally, the strength of women was on display," Mary Reynolds Powell noted. "Our strength! I visit those women in the sculpture whenever I am in D.C. We are one." When Mary spoke to our class in Madison, she shared a story about dancing and singing along to "We Gotta Get Out of This Place" on New Year's Eve 1970 in Vietnam. The song was playing in her head that day in Washington, too. She and her fellow nurses did get out of that place, and now their war, their pain, would become part of our Vietnam truth.

So too may "Women at War: Warrior Songs," which won Album of the Year at the 2019 Wisconsin Area Music Awards. It's the second release from the Story to Song program, one that matches women veterans with artists who are talented in storytelling and music. Designed to transform buried experiences and feelings into a song that heals and entertains while also educating, motivating, and inspiring, Story to Song demonstrates how women veterans are using music as a part of the process of homecoming. You can imagine Amanda Cherry, Kay Bauer, Diane Carlson Evans, Mary Reynolds Powell, and the other women who served all having a song of their own. A tapestry of service and song, now a part of our Vietnam public memory.

Both the Vietnam Veterans Memorial and Vietnam Women's Memorial brought comfort, and in many instances, healing, to veterans. They are outside, public spaces. But what of the interiors that veterans spend considerable time in? What if the rudiments of recovery were brought to bear on the design of these spaces? A response to that call returns us to Iowa, specifically the Cedar Rapids Iowa Veterans Memorial Building, whose renovation incorporated evidence-based research on healing environments with the goal of creating a welcoming and therapeutic environment for traumatized vets. Army veteran John Mikelson is vice president of Midwest Military Outreach, which is housed in the building.

SOLO John Mikelson

U.S. Army veteran John Mikelson, vice president of Iowa's Midwest Military Outreach. Photo courtesy John Mikelson.

In the period after deployment and service, the relationship between the veteran and his or her family, friends, and society changes profoundly. The health issues faced by veterans are different from those of the general civilian population. Many of those who have served in the military have been exposed to dangerous, life-threatening events. Those who have served in direct combat and support roles have experienced the loss of comrades, wounds of the body, mind, and spirit, and other life-altering traumas. It is the unique responsibility of the VA to treat all wounds after military service—physical, mental, and emotional. Because a person's emotions are often at the center of their suffering, these emotions must be addressed in order for healing to take place. Unlike civilian healing settings, VA healing settings must take into account the fact that veterans are wounded within the context of service.

The purpose of the VA Healing Environment Design Guidelines is to establish a holistic "Healing Environment" framework. The guidelines describe ways to plan and design the key public elements of a healthcare facility and include "healing design principles" to provide a therapeutic environment, connect to nature, create a veteran-embracing environment, reflect region and community, and be patient-centered.

"Healing design" elements of Cedar Rapids Iowa Veterans Memorial Building, Photo courtesy John Mikelson.

The "Writing My Way Back Home Workshop" was one of the first activities in the Veterans Memorial Building, followed by music, arts, gardening, and other workshops. One of the things we seek to do is provide dedicated display areas and art-making spaces to support integration of the arts into the VA environment and into therapy regimens. The arts validate emotions and contribute to healing. They assist in creating bonds among veterans of different generations and service units...There's historical precedent—Greek theater originated for the purposes of veteran healing and public catharsis. The Greek comedies and tragedies were created by veterans and performed by veterans for veteran audiences.

Many, but not all of our veterans are faced with mental health challenges. The common denominator is loss: of ideals, of brethren, and of a sense of connection to their families and to the civilian community. As veterans re-enter the civilian sector, they are still coping with trauma and loss.

The Cedar Rapids Iowa Veterans Memorial Building seeks to empower veterans by encouraging their artistic expression. That effort follows on the veterans' freelance artistic creations, particularly songs that speak to their trauma and loss.

The urgency to heal, lay it down, like in *Next Stop is Vietnam: The War on Record, 1961–2008* compilation, has persisted among many Vietnam veteran musicians. Three whose music was entirely interwoven with their personal stories and artistic healing are William Vincent Walker, otherwise known as Billy Bang, Jim Wachtendonk, and James "Kimo" Williams. They literally kept themselves alive by giving musical expression to their Vietnam and post-Vietnam experiences.

Billy Bang was one of the vet musicians we most wanted to interview for *We Gotta Get Out of This Place*. His was a singular talent and a unique sound—in his hands, a violin can burn and squeal, sending shivers up your spine, but it can also weep and sing. Listening to his music, I was transported back to Vietnam. I was convinced that the power of his music had as much to do with his Vietnam experience as his enormous talent.

William Vincent Walker, aka Billy Bang. Public domain.

Regrettably, Billy Bang died in 2011 before we had a chance to connect with him. My hunch is that maybe the lung cancer that caused his untimely demise at 63 had something to do with Vietnam. He'd spent most of his 365 days in Vietnam in the field where the Army sprayed abundant amounts of Agent Orange as a defoliant. The VA itself has stated it "must grant service connection on a presumptive basis for lung cancers associated with exposure to Agent Orange to veterans who served in Vietnam between 1962 and 1975."

As a child growing up in Harlem and the Bronx during the '50s and '60s, Billy played bongos and danced in the subways of New York City. His musical passion eventually led to a brief obsession with classical violin, but, by 1967 he'd dropped out of school. Now 18, he was quickly drafted. After several months of infantry training, Billy was sent to Vietnam. Barely three days in-country, he was dropped by helicopter into a firefight near the Cambodian border. Soon, Billy Bang was a squad leader, then sergeant. He went on ambushes, "humped the boonies," and became an expert rifleman.

He returned from the war angry. In an extensive interview with Thomas Conrad in *Jazz Times* in 2005, Billy bared his soul.

"When I came home, I felt really abused. I felt kidnapped, to be honest, and I was very angry. I felt I was tricked into doing something that I should never have done, and the reasons that were laid out for why I did it never made sense to me. I just felt like somebody took a period of my life—a very precious period, 19 to 21—and destroyed it."

While in the Army, Billy had gotten his G.E.D., and after his discharge attended Queens College on the G.I. Bill, studying pre-law. But, much like me and my own flirtation with a law career prior to being drafted, Billy became aware that the law was there to protect the status quo, not to change it. He dropped out of Queens College and, like a good many disillusioned African-American vets, gravitated to the radical left, which embraced his prodigious skills in weaponry.

And then there came a moment that changed his life, and the face of creative music, forever. Billy was sent to a pawn shop in Baltimore to purchase handguns for use in a "revolutionary action" but became enamored of a violin hanging on the wall. He bought the violin, not the guns, and buried himself in music.

Yet Vietnam continued to haunt Billy Bang. "I made one big mistake in my life—fighting against the Vietnamese, a people who had done absolutely nothing to me," Bang said on numerous occasions. "I went all the way to their land to fight them, for no reason 'cept I was told to. I felt very badly about that. I lived in Vietnam, totally, all the time. I couldn't get on with my life. I couldn't even handle the Fourth of July."

As music became his escape, Billy practiced all day and night to develop his emotive violin voice. He moved to New York City's East Village and became a student with jazz guru Leroy Jenkins, who introduced him to the up-and-coming New York free music-loft scene. It was where he belonged. From the mid-'70s on, he collaborated with most of the major players in avant-garde jazz, led or co-led several respected ensembles, and eventually made more than 30 recordings.

His nights were plagued by nightmares, however. Like many Vietnam vets, he treated his PTSD with drugs and booze. He spent the late '90s in Berlin, and returned to New York in 2000, broke. That's when his friend Jean-Pierre Leduc suggested that Billy do an album about his Vietnam experience.

"Wait a fucking minute," Bang reportedly said. "I don't talk about that.'" Still, in his apartment for weeks afterwards, he wrote and played music. "That's when I started reliving it and crying again and going through the nightmares. Everything came back to me."

Vietnam: The Aftermath was released on Justin Time Records in 2001. The cover of the album depicts jazz violinist Billy as the grunt he was in Vietnam. He's facing the camera, bare-chested, with a look Vietnam vets refer to as "the thousand-yard stare," cigar in his mouth, machine gun slung over his shoulder, dog tags dangling on his chest, the trees of the triple canopy Vietnam jungle surround-

ing him. On the back, inlaid against the jungle setting, is a track listing with titles like "Tunnel Rat (Flashlight and a 45)," "Tet Offensive," "Bien Hoa Blues," "Fire in the Hole," and "Saigon Phunk." With the opening track, "Yo! Ho Chi Minh Is in the House," we're introduced to the danger and tension that encompasses Vietnam. Even the song's Vietnamese modulations and timbres portend a place that won't be kind to strangers.

Billy had hoped to have every instrument on *Vietnam: The Aftermath* played by a Vietnam veteran. As it turned out, six of the nine musicians who appear on the recording, including conductor Butch Morris, served in Vietnam. The musician-veterans list their ranks and serial numbers under their names in the album's liner notes.

"We had been carrying around a lot of baggage," Bang said of the effort, riffing on the "lay it down" mantra. "It was only in the writing and performing of this music that I remembered things I'd absolutely been trying to forget. To write this music honestly, I had to face what I'd been through. Then I finally started feeling lighter. I started to deal with my drug and alcohol issues. It was like coming out of a coma."

Yes, much like laying it down. Listening to *Vietnam: The Aftermath* put me right back in Vietnam. The fear, panic, chaos and insanity of the war stream out of Ted Daniel's trumpet and Frank Lowe's tenor sax, as well as Sonny Fortune's flute and John Hicks's piano. But it's Billy's bowed and bent and soaring, and sometimes weeping, violin that fashions the actual feel of Vietnam.

Vietnam: The Aftermath let Billy Bang tell his Vietnam story, but was only a step on his path to healing. Four years later he released *Vietnam: Reflections*, also on the Justin Time label. Most of the musicians from the first album were back, plus another Vietnam vet, Henry Threadgill, on reeds. *Reflections* is not a repetition of *Aftermath*, but rather another step in Billy's healing. Incorporating the Vietnamese dulcimer and vocals, he interwove traditional Vietnamese songs with his own originals. Billy's synthesis of cultures and traditions ultimately speaks to reconciliation. The album's most moving piece, "Doi Moi," finds a solitary Billy and his jazz violin alongside the rhythm section. He told *Jazz Times* that "'Doi Moi' is my imagining of what Vietnam might be like today."

Imagination eventually gave way to reality when Billy and German artist Markus Hansen collaborated to produce *Billy Bang's Redemption Song*, a documentary following Billy's return to Vietnam and his travel there. The project originated in the men's shared interest in memory and the power of creativity to heal.

"As a German, I've always had an interest in how one transcends trauma," Hansen told Bang. Like so many other Vietnam veterans, Billy went back to Vietnam to confront the past in the present. *Billy Bang's Redemption Song* is a physical journey, a musical journey, and a trip into Bang's memory.

Billy introduces himself almost regretfully at the opening of the film: "They call me Bang, Billy Bang...The experience in Vietnam was traumatic and terribly frightening. When I returned home, I eventually turned to drugs, alcohol, and music to forget the devastation and destruction of human life we left in Vietnam."

With the documentary crew following him, Billy visits many of Vietnam's war-era sites that have since become tourist attractions, Often, he has to pause and regroup, having to explain his visceral reactions to his tour guides and translator, all of whom are too young to have any experience of the war.

"She got killed in the American War?" Billy asks a Vietnamese man who tells him his grandmother was killed by a U.S. bomb. "Shit, man, I'm sorry. Now I'm really sorry," Billy grimaces. "I shattered these people, and I'm back here right now saying I love them. It doesn't make sense."

During his visit, Bang creates some truly remarkable collaborations by sitting in with Vietnamese musicians working in many genres. He plays along with famous singer Siu Black in her home among the Montagnards in the Central Highlands. He jams with jazz musicians at a Ho Chi Minh (formely Saigon) club, sits in with traditional folk performers, performs along with the Hanoi Symphony Orchestra, and has an unforgettable improvisational session with a player on the danda, a giant stone xylophone played with wooden hammers, reputed to be the oldest form of musical instrument in the world.

The film testifies to emotional processing: "Some thoughts I couldn't verbalize," Billy says at one point. "It wasn't about verbalizing it. It was like...it was a profound feeling. It might take me weeks to really consider what I felt." The place, the opportunities to remember and consider, the artistic creation and collaborations, all combined to show us Billy Bang's process of healing.

Just before his death in 2011, Billy completed another album about war-related issues entitled *Prayer for Peace*. There are thematic threads from the two Vietnam albums, but Billy seems to be in a very different place here, personally and musically. It's jazzier than the Vietnam albums and includes a lot of riffs to his jazz idols like Snuff Smith, Sun Ra, and John Coltrane.

What I found most striking about *Prayer for Peace* were Billy's comments in the liner notes: "When I was thinking in terms of the war, it brought me to a more serene place in my mind [so I could] speak more about peace. We do not need war, any kind of war...We should listen to each other and be good to each other."

So, be good to one another. Seek alternatives to conflict and war. And keep on listening to Billy Bang and appreciate the honesty and expressivity—and spirituality—of his Vietnam music.

Still, the lingering question, the one I wanted to ask Billy Bang in person, was whether the two Vietnam albums and the film brought closure to his Vietnam, whether he considered himself healed by the time he recorded *Prayer for Peace*. But I never got to ask him because he died unexpectedly in April 2011. His passing left a hole, not just in avant-garde jazz circles, but in the hearts of Vietnam vets like me. Now that he's gone, we'll never know. All we can do is listen to his testimony and ask ourselves whether he only escaped from Vietnam, or whether he finally came home.

More than two years of presentations, a whirlwind of music and witness and honesty, had blurred some of my recollections. But I knew that there'd never been this many wheelchairs before. On Monday, March 29, 2016—National Vietnam Veterans Day—I was presenting solo at the William S. Middleton Memorial Veterans Hospital in Madison, Wisconsin. Lt. Col. Tim Donovan, chief of public affairs at the Hospital, had scheduled my appearance over the noon hour, and the hospital staff were busy ushering scores of veterans into the auditorium in wheelchairs. They'd even opened the large double doors at the back of the auditorium to allow several veterans in their hospital beds to join the festivities. I had yet to play a single song, and I was already overcome by the Vietnam War damage in front of me. But I knew in my heart that the call, the music I'd be playing, and the response by these veterans would get me, and them, through.

Just before he introduced me, Tim handed me a copy of the afternoon's program with a familiar name listed beside the Veterans Art presentation—Jim Wachtendonk. And nearly 40 years of songs and art and struggle and sorrow came cascading back...

'Nam choppers painting by Jim Wachtendonk. Photo courtesy Doug Bradley.

I first met Jim and his wife Sukie in the late 1970s when I was preparing an article about dioxin, the chemical agent known as Agent Orange, that was used extensively as a defoliant in Vietnam. My fellow Vietnam veterans and I were becoming more and more aware of the perils of Agent Orange exposure as large numbers of our veteran peers, many of whom had been exposed to Agent Orange in Vietnam, were dying young. One of the nation's premier researchers on the dangers of dioxin at that time was Dr. James Allen of the University of Wisconsin-Madison. I was trying to wrap up my article when Dr. Allen mentioned that there were a few Vietnam vets in the Madison area who were complaining to the Veterans Administration about skin rashes, fatigue, dizziness, and stomach and liver problems. Some of their children were being born with birth defects. One of those families was the Wachtendonks.

Jim was exposed to Agent Orange while serving as an Army K-9 handler in 1970–71 with the 212th Military Police Unit at Long Binh and the 595th MPS at Cam Ranh Bay. Recalling the spraying and its effect on the Vietnamese vegetation, he wondered at the time "If this is what it does to plants, what's it doing to us?"

In 1976 Sukie gave birth to their daughter, Ree Anne, who was diagnosed with health issues so severe—aqueductal stenosis resulting in hydrocephalus—that she was not expected to live. She underwent experimental brain surgery. Around the same time, Jim and Sukie saw a TV news segment on veterans and Agent Orange. In it, reporter Bill Kurtis spoke with Maude DeVictor, a veterans' benefits counselor who had raised the alarm about Agent Orange and its long-term effects on Vietnam veterans. A phone call from Sukie began a friendship with DeVictor. It also began the battle waged by the Wachtendonks and other Vietnam veterans to have veterans and their families compensated by the VA for Agent Orange poisoning. In 1978 the Wachtendonks became the first Wisconsin vet family to join the class-action suit against Dow Chemical, the producer of dioxin.

The long, sorry history of industry lies and delays, its harass-
ment of academic researchers like Dr. Allen, and its indifference to
the suffering of individual veterans and their families is now well
known. When Sukie testified in court, "Dow and Monsanto reps
followed and openly attacked my credibility, my life experiences,
my research, and my Agent Orange and VVAW [Vietnam Veterans
Against War] work," she remembered. "Dr. Allen testified about research that he'd begun in 1958, and Dow worked to discredit him
too. All research on Agent Orange at UW's Waisman Center, including Dr. Allen's, ended because Dow threatened to cut all of its research funding at the University of Wisconsin."

But if the history of the fight over Agent Orange that eventually
finished with a class action settlement is known and documented,
the nature of the pain the veterans, their families, and the Vietnamese suffered and suffer is less known, and the specifics of that
pain should always matter. Ree Anne Wachtendonk needed long
hours of care. She was unable to roll over or lift her head. Sukie
worked with her daily for hours. Two years after Ree Anne's birth,
Sukie found herself working just as hard with her new son, Zachary. Both Wachtendonk children had eye and muscle disorders, epilepsy, autism, brain deformities, bone deformities, and other serious health problems. The children suffered so many seizures that
the Wachtendonks stopped calling for ambulances. "We just stayed
with them until the seizures ended," Jim told me.

"I had to teach Zack how to raise his head, walk, and crawl,"
Sukie said. "They told me he would be a vegetable, but he wasn't
a vegetable. He was a successful human being. He was sweet, and
he was my hero." Sadly, Zachary James Wachtendonk, passed away
in March 2009 from health complications caused by Agent Orange.

For years during his family's struggle, Jim Wachtendonk found
strength and solace in music. Having played guitar as a young
boy, and as a soldier in Vietnam, he persevered after his return to
the U.S. He performed wherever he could—hotels, coffee houses,
churches—anywhere folks would listen. His original songs were

blunt, stark and personal. "Hurting More" is about his family's grim experience with the aftereffects of Agent Orange: "Who holds the answers to this Agent Orange?" he asks in the song, "Who takes the blame for us? It might have been better if we died."

In its sneeringly hilarious desire to rig a bomb in the toilets of the men in charge, his "Claymore Polka," is one of the true classics of Vietnam veteran music: "The Army taught me well," he sings to the brass who put him and others at risk, "and I hope you to go hell. And maybe I can hurry things along?"

The consequences of Agent Orange made guitar playing increasingly difficult for Jim. Seeing a small set of watercolors one day, Sukie suggested that he try painting. He has been painting ever since, eventually branching out to three-dimensional art. That progression led to our joint appearance on that March 2017 afternoon at the VA Hospital in Madison.

"This never would have happened if Sukie hadn't put that thought in my head," he told me. "It was so important. She's in many of my paintings. She's the keeper of the light."

Jim Wachtendonk's studio, Richland Center, Wisconsin. Photo courtesy Doug Bradley.

Jim added that he wants to create public art with a purpose. One such piece struck a chord with his local community. He spray-painted a 30-gallon drum white, then added a 10-inch orange ring around it. He displayed it in the Richland County Bank for a week. A sign attracted the attention of bank customers: "Do You Know Someone Touched by Agent Orange? If you know someone touched by Agent Orange, please write down their name on my art barrel as we remember. Perhaps so shall others."

"There's a couple of pens there, and folks have been going in and writing down the names of loved ones," Jim said. "My goal as an artist is to have folks fill that thing full of names, and then I'll paint another. That's action, right?"

If Agent Orange were only in a book and not a real chemical weapon, it might symbolize the ongoing, generational suffering of the Vietnam war. Jim suffered aftereffects, his son Zack suffered,

Zachary James Wachtendonk funeral photo, 2009. Photo courtesy Sukie Wachtendonk.

and the whole family lost Zack so early. Yes, Ree Anne is married and the mother of two children, but how much did she suffer along the way, and how did her parents manage to care for her, educate themselves, and participate actively in the fight to establish the truth about Agent Orange? And even though Vietnam veterans and their families were awarded a $180 million class action settlement, the chemical companies and the government did not have to admit liability. In this "successful" class action suit, individual veterans and their families received less than $15,000 each for their pain and suffering.

I wrapped up my music presentation that cold March afternoon at the VA Hospital by playing "We Gotta Get Out of This Place." The whole audience—veterans, nurses, attendants, doctors, and staff—

sang along lustily. I stayed for Jim's presentation, and when he was done, he presented me with one of his exquisite acrylic paintings that now sits above my work space where I do my writing. And his piece entitled "Guitars for Vets" graces the cover of this book.

Still, I double-check the local obituaries every day for fear that Jim or his daughter or one of his grandchildren will have succumbed to the toxic legacy of Agent Orange.

James "Kimo" Williams is one of those special people who is easy to like, and admire. He and his Vietnam band "The Soul Coordinators" featured prominently in *We Gotta Get Out of This Place*, and he visited Madison several times to present to our UW class and to the public at the Wisconsin Veterans Museum. A classical composer—Kimo has written five pieces for string quartets, five symphonies, and array of jazz-themed large ensemble works—he is the recipient of numerous awards, including the Vietnam Veterans of America's Excellence in the Arts Award, the People-To-People International's Presidents Award, and the League of Black Women's Black Rose Award. He is also a Fulbright Specialist and Encore Purpose Prize Fellow.

Kimo is also known for his participation in the Lt. Dan Band which he founded in the mid 1990s. He invited actor Gary Sinise, who played the character Lieutenant Dan Taylor in the film Forrest Gump, to be a part of his jam group, The G&K Classic Rock Band, which they then renamed the Lt. Dan Band. In everything, Kimo is committed to utilizing the arts to help veterans. His organization, the United States Veterans Art Program (USVAP), provides artistic resources such as musical instruments, photography equipment, painting, graphics, and ceramics supplies to state and federal veterans facilities for use by veterans, inpatient or outpatient, with the support of therapists. As Kimo says "these tools not only provide resources that facilities might not be able to buy, but they also bring public attention to the power of art and art therapy."

One of the more powerful moments every semester in our Vietnam class occurs when our students listen to Kimo's extraordinary and moving piece, *Symphony For The Sons of Nam*, which was praised by the late, great Studs Terkel: "The opening passage to *Symphony For The Sons of Nam* is such a stirring one with its touch of American Jazz, folk melodies, country music, and Asiatic themes."

Reminiscent of Mussorgsky's celebrated *Pictures at an Exhibition*, Kimo's *Symphony For The Sons of Nam* is presented in eleven "events" with titles like "March of the Sons," "In Country," "Leaving the Jungle," and "Flying Home." Much like Billy Bang's *Vietnam: The Aftermath*—but with an encompassing orchestral sound—Kimo's piece transports you to Vietnam and into the real experience of a U.S. soldier. It is at times exhilarating, harrowing, anxious, and peaceful. For the last "event," entitled "Flying Home," Kimo notes that "a peaceful happiness overtakes me as I vow to keep in my heart the realization of the fragility of life and the importance of cherishing every moment."

Kimo and USVAP are indeed helping veterans to "lay it down" when it comes to Vietnam and art, be it via music or photography or film or painting, as it helps to bring these men and women home. And maybe, in a way, Kimo Williams, too.

> SOLO   James "Kimo" Williams
>
> As a country since World War II, we have portrayed the military soldier from a John Wayne-the-hero perspective. As a young boy, I grew up wanting to experience the type of heroism that I saw in so many movies in the '60s...As a composer, I have used music as a way to tell what I call "my story" of serving in Vietnam and my perspective of those who have served throughout history, especially the African-American Veteran. When I was commissioned by West Point and wrote my score "Buffalo Soldiers," my research provided a clear understanding of what the African-American service members then, and since, have had

to endure in serving this country. These black service members—some who were former slaves—enlisted into the Army to fight the battles out west and were subjected to a relentless barrage of hatred in all forms not only from the perceived enemy but from fellow soldiers and from America.

Since I returned from Vietnam and found my voice with music, I have always wanted to speak to my military service experiences and to my thoughts on what it means to serve. In 1990 I composed and produced a Jazz-rock CD called "War Stories" to cathartically address my service in Vietnam through music. During the recording of this CD, I utilized thirty musicians along with other recording personnel. Of those thirty, only one person asked me anything about my experience in Vietnam. The rest were evidently not connected or interested in the purpose of the music product. Their lack of inquisitiveness is indicative of society's disinterest in those who served in the military since the Vietnam War, other than those with personal connections to the War experience...What has worked for me to cope with this sense of unease, was composing music. Through music, I have been able to highlight events that were personally relevant to me while serving in Vietnam. I did not and do not feel a need to engage in the one-upmanship with other veterans, nor feel the guilt associated with not actually killing the enemy on the battlefield. With music, I can express my personal experiences as a veteran, comment on veterans throughout history, and at the same time communicate aspects of my life that impact on my values. The syntax associated with the spoken language has never been enough to fully speak to the emotions that are reflected in my music.

I truly believe art, utilized expressively, can be a nucleus that might bring about the beginnings of a dialog between a veteran, his experiences, and his external world, and in the long run impact on his well-being. It is well documented that expressive arts therapies have had a positive effect on Veterans health. In fact, music therapy had its beginnings with the U.S. Army back in 1945 where it was used to address the recuperation of military service members in Army hospitals. Once we begin to look at veterans as individuals with individual experiences, we can get away from the hero-warrior syndrome and tear down the frame of reference as prescribed by society and the media.

USVAP seeks to do its part by providing art resources to Veteran Medical Facilities through our Artistic Tools initiative. The VA has been at the forefront of understanding the power of art and providing quality, expressive therapies as a tool for addressing a Veterans well-being.

As a soldier in Vietnam, I would come in from the jungle and play guitar at the service club. This was my main way of coping. My soldier band, The Soul Coordinators, played throughout Vietnam, at remote firebases and in hospital wards. Through this, I realized the power of music not only for entertainment but also for soothing the stress of combat. After the war, I was always asked about my experiences as a combat soldier in Vietnam but could never find the right words to express my thoughts. So, in 1986 I confronted the emotions from my time in Vietnam and began work on a symphony. In 1994, my second symphony, "Fanfare for Life," was commissioned by AT&T, and in 1997, "Buffalo Soldiers" was commissioned by the West Point Academy.

In 1998, I returned to Vietnam, hoping to complete my unfinished symphony, but instead, I discovered truths about myself that I had long avoided. I knew I could not be the only veteran to experience these feelings, so I created a nonprofit to develop collaborative arts projects with Vietnamese and American artists. By 2008, that work evolved, as had our mission. We were renamed the United States Veterans Art Program (USVAP), and our mission is to provide art resources—musical instruments, photography equipment, painting, graphics and ceramics supplies—to state and federal veterans facilities, to be used by veterans, inpatient or outpatient, with the support of therapists. These tools not only provide resources that facilities might not be able to buy, but also bring public attention to the power of art and art therapy. Art therapy can be tailored to the individual patient. It can be used by family members to get around veterans' communication barriers. It can build social and motor skills, increase coping mechanisms and reinforce memory and expressive ability. I have experienced this, and seen it happen, many times over. Creative art activities are now recognized as an important component of healthcare.

As crucial as the Vietnam War was to my generation, it is more important for me, as the great-grandson of a slave, to contribute to humanity in my time here on this earth. Writing music is my second tour of duty, but helping veterans express and understand their experiences through art is my true calling.

Fast forward to September of 2017, and Hugo Keesing and I are presenting at Penn State University, helping WPSU, the campus's PBS station, launch their own Vietnam-centered programming to coincide with the national broadcast of the Burns-Novick "The Vietnam War" series. WPSU's Frank Christopher and Jerry Zolten had interviewed the two of us for their two-hour radio documentary. Its title? *Time to Lay It Down.*

Perhaps it's appropriate that we leave the last word on this topic to one of those who had to lay down the most—her home, her family, her career, her county—and much, much more. I'm speaking of the South Vietnamese, specifically Nguyen Thi Mai, or "Miss Mai" as she was affectionately called by me and innumerable U.S. soldiers who "adopted" her as their little sister during their year at the U.S. Army's Command Information Headquarters in Vietnam. My closest Army friend, George Moriarty, and I had the good fortune of being stationed together both stateside and in Vietnam in 1970 and 1971. As 23-year-old college-educated draftees, we were not your average GIs, and George's added responsibilities of a wife and a baby daughter made him seem much older and more mature. Despite our different circumstances, we became close friends at the Army Hometown News Center in Kansas City, Missouri, and even closer at the Information Office (IO) with the U. S. Army Republic of Vietnam Headquarters (USARV) in Long Binh, South Vietnam in 1970 and 1971.

The first time I entered the USARV IO premises, I encountered a pretty, petite young Vietnamese woman who worked as a secretary-receptionist in the office. She smiled at me, said good morning, and introduced herself as "Co Mai" ("Miss Mai" in English). Thus, began our yearlong friendship. Mai was more than just window dressing in a drab Army office in the heart of Southeast Asia. She was sunshine and hope and promise to us scared, homesick GIs. During the most difficult days of our 365-day Vietnam tour, Miss Mai was often the only light in an otherwise very long and dark tunnel.

Miss Mai at her typewriter in the USARV IO office, Long Binh, Vietnam, 1971. Photo courtesy Nguyen Thi Mai.

Given our different personalities, George and I interacted differently with Miss Mai. I joked and kidded her relentlessly, as if she were my baby sister, and she'd call me "Bradley" or "Numbah Ten

GI" in response. George, on the other hand, was "Uncle George" or simply George, the only one Miss Mai called by his first name.

Among the many happy moments George and I spent with Miss Mai in Vietnam, two stand out: celebrating her birthday in July 1971 (she didn't reveal her age at the time, but I only recently discovered she is two years our senior!) and having dinner at her family home in Saigon just before our tour was up later that year. Of the former I remember giving her a large stuffed dog that I thought suited her childlike personality. Of the latter, I recall that George and I got lost trying to find her address at 80/115 Tran Quang Dieu Street in bustling, unpredictable—and often precarious—Saigon. When we finally arrived, Mai was a little put out by our being late, but ushered her large, extended family out of the living room of their tiny home and presented us with a bountiful feast of steak and spaghetti! To this day, I don't know how she was able to find food like that to serve us, but it was, hands down, the best meal I ate during my 365 days in Vietnam.

As "Uncle George" and I sat there, dining by candlelight in Miss Mai's home, it was hard to think of ourselves as soldiers from a foreign country who'd been sent here to fight in a war. It felt more like we were hanging out with an old, dear friend. Even though the war was ubiquitous and all-consuming, we never talked to Miss Mai about it. The war was our link, it was what had connected us and brought us together, but we would never, ever, discuss it.

George and I departed Vietnam within hours of each other in November 1971. When I visited him and his family later that year, and the next and the next, we reminisced about that meal at Miss Mai's house and her infectious enthusiasm and good will. Not knowing what would transpire in Vietnam in a few years, we feared for her and her safety.

"She'll never get out of Vietnam alive," was our quiet consensus. But she did.

Music isn't at the center of Mai's story, but like so many "veterans" of the Vietnam experience there is a song that's stayed with her. Strangely, it's "White Christmas," Irving Berlin's 1942 paean to an old-fashioned Christmas sung by Bing Crosby. It was broadcast on AFVN in April 1975 as a signal to Miss Mai and other South Vietnamese to hurry to the U.S. embassy in Saigon if they wanted to get out of Vietnam before the North Vietnamese arrived.

SOLO   Miss Mai

In early April 1975, I and other South Vietnamese who worked for the Army were given "top secret" briefings about the Americans' evacuation plans as the enemy came closer to our base. I knew I was a marked woman because of my many years of service to the U.S. military, but our commanding officer promise us that we would be able to get out of the country with spouses and children when the time came to leave. But as single mother—I recently adopt my cousin two-year-old daughter—I want my whole family—mommy and daddy and nine brother and sister—be able to leave. The Army tell me that since I have no husband, I have to evacuate with just my young child.

I was so sad...but I also know that if my family to be safe, I have to act. So, at next office briefing, I get up nerve to tell Colonel his offer not fair to single people like me. He seem upset by my question. He look at me and ask "Mai, what do *you* think is fair?" I tell him I have five brothers and four sisters, a daughter, and my parents, and I want to take all of them with me. I broke down, telling him if I had to leave home without them, I not going.

The Army make good on its promise. On April 22, 1975, I leave Vietnam with my three younger brothers, two younger sisters, and my two-year-old adopted daughter. The rest of my family stay behind. We arrive at Camp Pendleton, California, on May 1, 1975. Only then I realize me and my family now "refugees." We live in crowded military camp with hundreds of other airlifted Vietnamese, without any money, food, or hope.

One of the Red Cross volunteers to assist us Vietnamese refugees was Larry Lee, the brother-in-law of Dennis Murrell, a Vietnam vet who'd been stationed in my office at USARV-IO! He told his brother-in-law wants to come in Camp Pendleton to looking for me...At that time I was in the camp only one week, in the morning after we have breakfast around 9 a.m. I was in the tent with my daughter and my sisters I heard a loud speaker voice "attention-attention whose name is Nguyen Thi Mai worked for USARV-IO? Please come to the Command Post you have visitors!"

Miss Mai (second from right) and her family, California. Left to right: Mai's son David, Mai's "daddy," Mai, and her daughter Christina.

I know that is only for me, I rushed ran to the Command Post. Dennis Murrell was there waiting, he looks at me and smiled, at that time my tears flowing down, I can only say "Dennis, Dennis" and I crying, crying again and again. Dennis still looks at me and smiled, he waited for a few seconds then he put his hands on my shoulders and say, "Thank God, Mai; I found you." Standing next to him was a young man, he looked at him and said, "Mai this is Larry Lee my brother-in-law." A week later another former USARV-IO soldier, David Lewis, come see me and contact colonel who our former boss in Vietnam. The colonel agree to sponsor me and my family! I was so happy because I love the Colonel just like my daddy. So, we all leave Camp Pendleton in early June 1975.

My American sponsor wife—the Colonel away on assignment—took us to their home in Florida, but she treat us like domestic servants. We only live in sponsor's house for forty-two days, and then I move us out to be more independent. We live in Miami for thirteen months and then move back to California in hope of a better life and because my younger sister marry Larry Lee, and I don't want her to be alone in California...

There I have a home, a job, a husband, but he die in 1992, and a son. My son only eight-year-old when my husband die, and it very difficult for a single person like me but I make it. I sponsor my parents and sister to the U. S. in 1990. My daddy still with us. I've even return to Vietnam several times. I have sincere gratitude to the United States government and American people who has opened their arms to my family in particular and other Vietnamese people in general to come to this country. I love United States because this country became my second country. Thanks United States again and again.

I knew I would see my good friends Bradley and Uncle George again. Uncle Bradley, did you remember why I now call Uncle Bradley and Uncle George? Because we have agreed that with each other we are brothers and sister so ever I am married and have children my children have to call both of you are "uncle"...call you "uncle" just for my children.

Raised as Buddhist, I have a strong belief in cause and effect. You and George are part of that, part of the good that came out of the war...We always owe another person something, even if it just understanding and appreciate what they been through... There an old Buddhist saying that sum this up, everything we been through—"Reconciliation is to understand both sides; to go to one side and describe the suffering being endured by the other side, and then go to the other side and describe the suffering being endured by the first side."

Former USARV IO colleagues George Moriarty (left), Nguyen Thi Mai, and Doug Bradley, reunited in Chocorua, New Hampshire, 2007.

Mai's song, if you will, is one of forgiveness and reconciliation. Because of her, George and I have been able to better appreciate the suffering of her "side"—she and the other South Vietnamese who stood by us in Vietnam, day in and day out. It's fair to say we've reconciled with Mai, as she has with America, and, in a way, with Vietnam. Not sure we can say the same for all Vietnamese, all Vietnam veterans, or all of America for that matter. That hard work still needs to be done and won't happen until all of us "lay it down."

The artistic impulse was always alive and well in our classroom at UW-Madison, thanks in large part to Anthony Black. A native of New York and a veteran of both the U.S. Army and the Marine Corps, Anthony was one of two Teaching Assistants (TAs) for our course on music and Vietnam. Beyond his music chops, Anthony helped our students to embrace Vietnam and the 1960s in highly visual ways. He's been focused on education since leaving military service, pursing a Ph.D. from UW-Madison after an MA (UW-Madison) and MFA (Temple University). He is an accomplished visual artist and has a strong interest in visual rhetoric and visual culture. Besides our course, Anthony's teaching ranges from studio art practices to African-American literature to art history.

SOLO   Anthony Black

I've been an artist since I was a child. Like most young boys, I found inspiration in comic books. Jack Kirby set the example for me, and my muses were outrageously muscled heroes who'd taken up the responsibility to protect the weak and helpless. My obsession was with the Marvel universe and its grittier representation of Spiderman's New York, as compared to Superman's Metropolis or Batman's Gotham City, and the X-Men universe's plot parallel between mutant hatred and racial intolerance. I would have been too young to articulate the appeal besides saying something along the lines of it feels real. Real meant that Marvel's settings seemed to match my Brooklyn home: there were villains, monsters, ne'er do wells preying on the helpless. Real, however, did not conjure up heroes with "powers and abilities far beyond those of mortal men."

That is where art came in. I copied them from the pages of comics, then created my own, and at each step imagined what it would be like to be a powerful, benevolent force in the world. Fast forward: at age 17, I found myself in 2002 running around Marine Corps Recruit Depot, Parris Island. My primary duties, it seemed, were to keep sand fleas hydrated with the sweat of my labor...and to labor. A lot. We were informed, in word and deed, that enduring the torments of the quarterdeck, performing manual of arms with a footlocker, and mastering a thousand yard stare were just a few of the many trials to be endured if one were to become a hero. Another ability—which a recruit learned early if he was wise—was invisibility. You did your damnedest to not draw Drill Instructor Staff Sergeant Turmoil's attention. But I failed at invisibility. I pinged on his radar be-

cause he'd heard that I was an AHR-teest and my talent was required for the platoon 2002's guidon.

The platoon guidon was a flag atop a pole designed and produced by a hapless artistic recruit. It was to be a singular em-
blem, distinct and representative of your platoon. Sequestered
in the Drill Instructor's house adjacent to the quarterdeck, I
was given paint, a laundry bag ironed and Magic-sized flat. I
chose to render an Iron Mike character in the center of a blood
red flag. Behind him was my interpretation of a spectral devil
dog. DI Turmoil sniffed his critique of my work, damning my
lack of compositional foresight: why would I paint the devil dog
red on a red background? I tried to tell him that creative vision imagined the beast as an apparition and hence ephemeral.
My protestations, hampered as they were by the prohibition of
the use personal pronouns, went unheeded. Instead, I was re-
warded with supplemental super-hero training. The guidon
flew nonetheless.

I didn't paint many heroes after that. My artistic output
consisted primarily of portraits of love interests. After leaving
active duty, I enrolled in college and studied fine art where my
tenure in the USMC made me a curiosity to others. A jarhead
practicing art and devoted to literary studies? It was total incon-
gruity to many. The public imagination cannot reconcile the
Marine Corps mythos with its idea of an artistic soul. Marines,
however, understand the ever-present flickering in and out of
mortality implicit in the oath, and service summons up a mit-
igating yearning to create, to make. For some of us, having in
our young minds imagined ourselves rendered heroes, the gen-
erative, protective, and healing potential of art grounded us as
we later served in the armed forces. Afterwards, art sustained
us and allowed us to say what heroes aren't expected to say.

DA CAPO

"Who'll Stop the Rain"

Good men through the ages, trying to find the sun;
And I wonder, still I wonder, who'll stop the rain?
—John Fogerty, "Who'll Stop the Rain"

Hearing that song, I feel as if I'm back in church, or back at the Stax Museum of American Soul Music, or any of the many places where Craig and I heard testimony, bore witness, called to an audience who responded. But more often than not, "Who'll Stop the Rain" returns me to a classroom at UW-Madison because it is the last song we play for our students after 15 weeks of teaching a course on the music of the Vietnam War. By that time, many of our students—as young as 18 or 19—feel as if they've been in Vietnam. Each and every time the song finishes, there's a peaceful silence in the classroom as most of the students file toward us to thank us, often with a hug, for what some of them claim has been "a life-altering experience."

"And I wonder, still I wonder," I ask as the rain continues to fall...in Detroit and Da Nang, in Madison and the Mekong Delta, in Seattle and Saigon...why can't we stop the rain? Why haven't we as a nation and a people been able to completely move on?

Maybe it has something to do with having lost more than a war in Vietnam. We also lost our moral standing with many of our post-WWII allies, our sense of our own moral surety, our sense of justice...and perhaps our heart and soul in the process. We lost a good portion of a generation and its idealism and energy, too. As the late Michael Herr points out in his pitch-perfect Vietnam memoir *Dis-*

patches, "Out on the street, I couldn't tell the Vietnam veterans from the rock and roll veterans. The Sixties had made so many casualties, its war and its music had run power off the same circuit for so long they didn't have the fuse" Earlier in *Dispatches* Herr rues the war's waste: "There was such a dense concentration of American energy there, American and essentially adolescent, if that energy could have been channeled into anything more than noise, waste, and pain, it would have lighted up Indochina for a thousand years."

Alas, the lights went out in Indochina, and in America too. And we still ask why, perhaps not expecting an answer but still sending a call, hoping for a response to Creedence Clearwater Revival's poignant musical query, "Who'll Stop the Rain?"

Craig and I kept searching for answers out on the road, mile after mile, community after community, conversation after conversation. Along the way, many exceptional people responded. Their comments ranged from calls to bring back the draft (Dave Flanagan) to connecting the dots for a public that doesn't know the history or have the proper context for Vietnam (Mary Reynolds Powell); from stopping corruption and war profiteering in the military and intelligence services (John Ketwig) to establishing a national museum for the Vietnam veteran (Jim Laverty). Rap groups, paper-boat making, a National Day of Reconciliation, prayer, education, tribal canoe journeys, poetry, monuments, documentaries, guitars and guitar lessons, welcome home celebrations, art, protest, Memorial Day writers projects, and more were among the recommended antidotes.

And, of course, music. Always music...

If there was any sort of consensus after our presentations, interviews, and conversations, it was that we as a nation need to find a way move on from Vietnam, finally. In some ways that's as challenging to America as moving on from the Civil War, which in too many ways we haven't. Vietnam closure requires a fuller awareness, understanding, and reconciliation of the soldier/veteran experience that, from my experience, is best facilitated by the music of the Vietnam era and the music-based memories of Vietnam veterans. That's what audiences responded to, it's why the veterans opened up, and it's how we, and the nation, can best come together.

The song that inspires this chapter, the band that recorded it, and the artist who wrote it know something about that. In the 1990s, Craig spent many hours with John Fogerty, Doug Clifford, and Stu Cook of CCR. He brought his understanding and appreciation for what CCR had achieved, and what they and their music meant to Vietnam veterans, to those interviews. As he points out in *Up Around the Bend: The Oral History of Creedence Clearwater Revival*: "At its peak, CCR reached an audience that encompassed hippies, bikers, counterculture intellectuals, rock-and-roll traditionalists, grunts trying to relax in the hooches and PXs of Vietnam, and a whole bunch of kids who couldn't have cared less about anything other than a good tune and a rockin' beat." Or as CCR drummer Doug Clifford claimed, "Creedence is a feel, man. It starts in the rhythm section and goes up to the great voice this guy [John F.] had."

CCR's "feel" has deep roots in the blues and a blues emphasis on call and response. African American novelist Ralph Ellison, best

Craig Werner

known for the classic novel *Invisible Man*, defines the blues as "an impulse to keep the painful details and episodes of a brutal experience alive in one's aching consciousness, to finger its jagged grain, and to transcend it, not by the consolation of philosophy but by squeezing from it a near-tragic, near-comic lyricism. As a form, the blues is an autobiographical chronicle of personal catastrophe expressed lyrically."

Craig often quoted verbatim these lines and others from Ellison and other memorable African American writers. He expanded on that definition by pointing out "Ellison's explanation testifies to the fact that all of us—you, me, John Fogerty, CCR, veterans—have our own brutal experiences to deal with.

"The blues speak to our dilemmas," Craig continued. "Not just as a specific music but as a way of confronting the human condition...The idea of the blues impulse helps us hear the shared conversation between Bob Dylan's 'Desolation Row' and Bessie Smith's 'Downhearted Blues;' between Bruce Springsteen's 'Backstreets ' and Howlin' Wolf's 'Down in the Bottom.'"

This was all part of my own education and was helping me appreciate what it was about the veteran experience I had possibly missed or misunderstood. The veterans' own expressions—in what they shared with us in the conversations after our presentations and what they were hearing in the songs they remembered—were parts of the greater whole. Their "personal catastrophes" connected them, and us, not just to the music, but to one another, veteran and non-veteran alike, in ways we hadn't known. As we all "fingered the jagged grain" of our own brutal experiences, and listened to its lyrical expression, we could better appreciate, respond, and understand.

John Fogerty and CCR were on to this, getting at the heart of Vietnam specifically while, either consciously or unconsciously, finding unity, or at least connections, in their unique lyrical expression. "I wrote that ('Who'll Stop the Rain') in the midst of the Vietnam era," he told Craig. "It was kind of a fatalistic view. I was a person who felt powerless. I realized a split in me. I'd grown up as an American, and I was proud to be an American, yet I realized these people in Washington weren't my country; they were representatives of the government. And with a great sense of powerlessness, I was asking questions I had no answer to, meaning, why does this have to be this way? Why are these people in charge, and yet they don't seem to be listening to us, the people they say they are representing?"

CCR's Doug Clifford echoed similar themes: "'Who'll Stop the Rain' was about the Nixon administration, basically the reign of terror he was putting the youth of America [through] having to go fight this war that was a corrupt war. A lot of people were making millions of dollars off that war basically on young blood."

The power and resonance of "Who'll Stop the Rain" give a rock response to the folk music of Phil Ochs and early Bob Dylan. The song has an acoustic, folk-rock feel, opening with an instantly recognizable acoustic guitar riff. Fogerty characterizes the song as just this amalgam: "I wrote that on my electric guitar, but un-plugged so it sounded very acoustical...which means we're talking a kind of folk-rock"

Music historian Richie Unterberger saw "Who'll Stop the Rain" as "one of John Fogerty's most gentle melodies, yet a singable and memorable one that he invests with passion—particularly in the latter part of the verses—and one with yet another rousing, hooky, almost spiritual harmonized chorus. It's also sprinkled with nice touches like a moody chord progression in the instrumental break that appears nowhere else in the song; the way the harmonized chorus briefly becomes a cappella the last time it's sung; and the half-minute fadeout, reinforcing the central motif of a rain that goes on and on and on."

The prominent rock historian Dave Marsh, a strong supporter of Vietnam vets, ranked "Who'll Stop the Rain" number 26 in his book *The Heart Of Rock & Soul—The 1001 Greatest Singles Ever Made*, in part because of its themes: "Fogerty is rock and roll's version of an Old Testament prophet, preaching pessimism rather than dam-nation," he writes. "And this voice is as far from the assurance of Elvis or Aretha as you can get...The idea that rock and roll is light-hearted good time music stops here, at the gateway to its heart of darkness."

CCR was one of the first bands to openly criticize the war while unambiguously supporting the soldier. Because it captures, simply and lyrically, the never-ending distress and discontent contemplated by "good men through the ages," who have offered "Five Year Plans and New Deals/wrapped in golden chains" as well as the Woodstock generation. "Who'll Stop the Rain" is prescient, because it calls out from the unease that as yet the nation seems unwilling to acknowledge, let alone resolve. Fifty years later, the song still rings true, and it still inspires response.

Fogerty deliberately made the song invitational: "When I would write a song like 'Who'll Stop the Rain,' I made it general and epochal. I tried to stretch it and make it bigger so that it wasn't just a song about me, so that lots of other people could look into the song and see themselves in it too." Indeed, they have, in the best sense of call and response, as Craig and I witnessed across the chorus of voices who responded to *We Gotta Get Out of This Place* at various volumes and in varying tones of anger, pride, guilt, and sadness. Everybody seemed to comprehend the conundrum spelled out in "Who'll Stop the Rain."

CCR band members had to confront the same decisions as other young American men, to participate or protest, to stay or serve. John Fogerty and Doug Clifford both avoided Vietnam by, in Fogerty's words, "finagling" their way into reserve units. "I managed to get in the reserves because I had contacted them before I got drafted," recalled Fogerty. "Luckily for me, I didn't have to go overseas or serve the full three years in the hard-core army, the regular army."

Missouri-native and former Dane County (Wisconsin) Judge Dave Flanagan, whom you met in the Rondo section, took a different path. And while "Who'll Stop the Rain" isn't his Vietnam song—he has a soft spot for "Ruby, Don't Take Your Love to Town" by Kenny Rogers and the First Edition—Dave voices the complexities of his choice in nearly all the tones of anger, pride, guilt, and sadness that Craig and I heard in the vet responses after our presentations.

SOLO   Dave Flanagan

When it comes to the war, I have always been, and remain, somewhat conflicted. I worked for Gene McCarthy and Bobby Kennedy. Back then I'd read enough of the works by the war correspondent Bernard Fall to know there was no good side in the [Vietnam] 1954 truce and its aftermath, and that this all was wasteful, cruel, and unlikely to end well.

Despite all that, I "dodged the draft" by enlisting in Navy OCS rather than by heading to Canada or saying I had bone spurs. I did not ask to be, nor even wanted to be, in the CEC, Navy Civil Engineer Corps. I had hoped to be floating on some "tin can" destroyer. Being in CEC posed the possibility of my having to go to Vietnam in support of the Marines. Once I got to a San Diego unit in 1969, I liked the work and the people. Also, it was a unit that did not normally rotate to Vietnam, as did most Seabee battalions.

Nevertheless, when a Vietnam project came up, I volunteered and off I went. I did not go on any jungle patrol or even shoot a gun toward anyone. I simply told myself, "Why should someone else have to go instead of me?" I probably could have ducked it. At bottom, however, I thought the work would be interesting and challenging. It was.

Did any of us go over there thinking we were stopping an attack on San Francisco? Boy, I sure didn't. I was mostly seeking to prove to myself that my anti-war sentiments were not primarily grounded in cowardice. Not smart but true. I was hoping, even more after I got there, that what we could achieve was a sort of Laos/Cambodia neutrality deal. I understood that Marlboro-smoking Uncle Ho was a charismatic, dedicated nationalist, but I also understood there were mean, vindictive guys on his team.

I did not get to know any Vietnamese well, indeed if at all, but those I did meet and work with I liked a lot—I briefly taught English in a little Village "outside the wire" composed of Catholics who had fled south in '54...Beautiful country [with] energetic, resourceful people.

When I came back to the States I continued to vote and, in law school, work against the war. I thought the war ending in 1975, was, on balance, probably a good thing for the Vietnamese in the long run, but was extremely ashamed of the people we left behind.

So, what's my conflict? Well, unlike some folks, when I chose to go there, I knew at least something about the history of Indochina. I knew that in 1969 the war was not any contest between good and evil. I knew it probably involved no significant national interest. Perhaps I should have avoided going over there but, to be honest, I still think I made the right choice at the moment. I really don't regret it. No doubt, some discomfort comes from the fact that "my war" was "interesting and challenging" indeed somewhat formative, while for many Vietnamese and Americans it was a terrible, scarring experience.

Moreover, I do not share the gleeful pride of some long-time antiwar activists because, in my view, all their effort and noise did not do anything but elevate Richard Nixon and end the draft. As far as I was concerned, ending the draft was/is a cornerstone of the "I got mine!" ethic and was, I deeply believe, a terribly destructive turn for society. We still have wars. They are still easy to get into and hard to get out of. Today they are somewhat easier to get into because the politicians are sending other people's kids, many of them who are, I'm sorry to say, essentially being exploited because they have few or no other choices in their lives and futures...There are not a lot of vets in Congress today. They are voting funds for things they think they understand through watching war movies. Ironically, today's surest path to election by a progressive politician is a military record!

I hold no ill will toward guys who went to Canada, but I doubt that I will ever forgive Jane Fonda. On balance, I am not eager to associate with old line antiwar types who seem to think they nobly won something. The war would have ended, maybe even sooner, without them, and I think they hurt our society by killing the draft.

So many voices like Flanagan's were emerging from the chorus of responders that Craig and I sometimes felt like choir directors, trying to arrange the "singers," hearing voices that excelled in a particular region or on a specific topic. As the earlier chapters here show, many responses to Vietnam are artistic, and I want to include one more here, from Anh-Hoa Thi Nguyen, *Waves Unfolding: A Paper Memorial*.

A first-generation Vietnamese-American, Nguyen is a poet, community activist, and educator. Her parents were among the 800,000 "boat people"—refugees who fled Vietnam between 1976 and 1992 to avoid imprisonment or persecution. That Vietnamese diaspora gave her the impetus for *Waves Unfolding*: "There were so many lives lost during the many 'waves' of Vietnamese refugees," she explained when I first met her, at the closing event for *Minnesota Remembers Vietnam* (See the Overture section). She pointed out that in addition to the 800,000 boat people, nearly one million Vietnamese had fled North Vietnam for the South from 1954 to 1955, a previous diaspora.

Nguyen mourned and commemorated, and invited the public to participate: "Many lives were lost...too many...Boats are symbols of freedom and survival and life, so I invited the public to help fold a collection of 1,000 paper boats to commemorate the lives lost during the Vietnamese refugee waves of 1954 and the end of the Vietnam War in Vietnam from 1975–1992.

"By sitting and folding paper together," Anh-Hoa continued, "we create a representation of a person that was unaccounted for—a father, mother, sister, or brother—while prompting a consideration of the refugee crisis that is currently taking place on other waters in other boats." A simple act, a powerful metaphor. Amid thousands of Minnesota lakes, Anh-Hoa's paper boats have plenty of open water.

Some boats could eventually come to shore at The Museum of the Vietnam Veteran, the brainchild of Bill Brewster, curator of collections with the First Division Museum in Cantigny, Illinois. In Bill's vision, such a museum would "focus on the stories of the veterans who fought in the war. The visitor will find objects, photos,

 and media that relate the history of the conflict as told through the voices of the veterans," Brewster told me. "Beyond all the U.S. service branches, the museum will be unique in that it will present the history and stories of all veterans from the conflict, including our South Vietnamese, Hmong, and Montagnard allies. There will be no sanitation of the facts," he added emphatically. "All of the horror and trauma will remain, as will the good."

Brewster's dream has great appeal for Jim Laverty, who served as an Army interpreter in Vietnam with the 101st Airborne Division from 1968 to 1969: "I think the Museum for Vietnam Veterans would be a great thing for Vietnam Vets and for the country." He was especially pleased that the Vietnamese soldiers he served with in Vietnam would have their stories and experiences included in the museum. "We need to have room for them in the Vietnam story. Those who are here are Americans, too. And they're so patriotic."

Brewster, Laverty, and others involved with the Museum of the Vietnam Veteran see it as both a way into Vietnam for many Americans and also a way out for veterans and the public. "People couldn't separate politicians from warriors back then," Laverty mused. "We all need to understand more of all sides so we can heal."

As the Museum of the Vietnam Veteran seeks to help stop, or at least lighten, the rain, the music of CCR and others will be integral, added Brewster, underscoring that music specific to each phase of the war will be featured prominently and incorporated into the respective gallery space. If it ever happens, of course.

On the other hand—and there's always an "on the other hand" where Vietnam is concerned—veterans like John Ketwig don't harbor such lofty illusions for some of the legacies of Vietnam. John was a wheel and track-vehicle mechanic, welder, and body repairman in Vietnam in 1967–68 where he witnessed the Battle of Dak To and the Tet Offensive. A lifetime member of Vietnam Veterans Against the War, as well as a member of Veterans for Peace and Vietnam Veterans of America, he is the author of ...*and a hard rain fell: A G.I.'s True Story of the War in Vietnam* and *Vietnam Reconsidered: The War, the Times, and Why They Matter*. In his latest book, Ketwig exposes the corruption and profiteering which are at the heart of the U.S. mission in Southeast Asia. It's yet another part of the Vietnam story that was missed by most Americans.

SOLO John Ketwig

During my two years in the war zone, I saw some unusual things and thought they were just one-of-a-kind anomalies. Only in later years have I learned about the rampant corruption and profiteering practiced at the highest levels of our military, intelligence, and contracted forces throughout Southeast Asia.

The "intelligence" function in Southeast Asia was supplied by the CIA who were simultaneously supplying opium and heroin from the Laotian village of Lon Thien to the Corsican mafia and ultimately the world. Their reports of enemy activities back to Saigon and Washington were in fact "moonlighting" after they'd lined their own pockets by day. Many of our military officers were just as corrupt, and we, the powerless enlisted men stuck on the other side of the planet and in great danger, often saw these strange things but thought we were seeing an anomaly, a small screw-up or minor little peccadillo in search of a few illicit dollars, or a ticket to a Pentagon office. We really weren't sure just what we were seeing, but some of us knew it stunk, and we became cynical and disillusioned....

The corporations made lots of money in Vietnam. The decision makers in Washington were receiving input from big business, the top military officials, defense contractors, and the CIA intelligence community. Every transaction was a squeeze play with the parameters dictated by greed. The business of death and destruction was booming. Very few of the profiteers were ever held to account or challenged in any way. Millions of innocent people died. A few got rich and powerful.

If the American military operations in Southeast Asia were low-hanging fruit to crooks, we can only wonder what new schemes are sucking the blood out of current American efforts in the long wars in the Middle East. We do know that in May of 2004 something in the neighborhood of $6.6 to over $18 billion in American $100 bills were unloaded in Iraq. Loaded onto pallets, this was so much American cash that it required 21 flights by C-130 cargo planes to deliver it to Baghdad. Every penny of that money simply disappeared! The loss was reported by a few news services, but the money has never been located, let alone recovered! As an American taxpayer, if you wonder how we could accumulate a national debt of more than $20 trillion, the government's indifference to this theft is a glaring clue...And today we are seeing reports that the opium business in Afghanistan, once nearly eradicated, is thriving since the U.S. invaded that country 17 years ago...Perhaps today's wrongdoers were emboldened by the history of corruption in Vietnam?

I often wish my father-in-law, Ted Shannon, was here to give me guidance, support, and a heavy dose of his unbridled optimism. He passed away in late 2016 after a full, and fulfilling, 98 years. Having served with distinction as a U.S. Army military governor in Sicily and Italy during World War II, Ted had an extraordinary career as a professor and higher education administrator with the University of Wisconsin. He was one of the chief stewards of UW's heralded "Wisconsin Idea" which asserts that the "boundaries of the campus are the boundaries of the state." Ted was a committed and engaged democrat and Democrat. He and I talked frequently about our wars and our service and the pursuit of peace. Ted contended, more than once, that the opposite of militarism was not pacifism, but feminism.

World War II Army Captain Ted Shannon. Photo courtesy Doug Bradley.

To find whatever the opposite of militarism is, we have to at least agree on the nature of what militarism inevitably brings: war. In that vein, and in tribute to Ted, here are the conclusions of experience from veteran Mary Reynolds Powell, who served as a U.S. Army nurse at the 24th Evacuation Hospital at Long Binh, South Vietnam in 1970–71.

SOLO   Mary Reynolds Powell

Vietnam veteran Mary Reynolds Powell. Photo courtesy Mary Reynolds Powell.

I've got a deep commitment to "connecting the dots" for the audiences I address. They don't know the history, have no sense of the context, for Vietnam. I want them to know that, and I want them to connect it to the guys who had to do the fighting. That way, I'm able to connect the history of the Vietnam war to the individual who has had to bear the burden of that war, even today. They still carry that burden internally. And it's hell...

We didn't learn anything [from Vietnam]—we were too wrapped up in our myths about what America was after World War II. We'd won, we were the victors, we were the most powerful nation on earth, and we let our arrogance and hubris and racism get the better of us...They called us Vietnam vets crybabies, but we're not. If you're carrying pain, have PTSD, and you can't get it out in a safe setting, get help from someone who'll listen and understand, seek something that's stuck in the 18 or 19-year-old version of you, you're not an immature whiner, you're wounded...It's never too late to unpack the Vietnam experience. In fact, you should do it before you leave this earth. Find someone who will listen. It isn't too late. But our current toxic environment makes it harder, that's for sure.

Here's the root of the matter. War is damaging. Let me say that again. War is damaging. It's always going to be the burden of the combat soldier to carry the war.

Our parents tell us it is wrong to kill; our churches preach it is wrong to kill; our teachers teach us it is wrong to kill; our government forbids us to kill. And then one day the leaders of our country declare war and tell us it is OK to send our young people to kill on our behalf; it is OK to rain destruction on mothers, fathers, and children in a foreign land; it is OK to do whatever it takes to win, for win we must.

It is all so simple.

From its rationale, to its language, to its execution, the selling of war is simple. It is slogans and flags, music and gold stars, abstract principles, clean uniforms, smart bombs, and enemies who are less than human. We are good and the enemy is bad.

But war is not simple.

It is vaporized and burned men, women, and babies, people just like us. It is homes turned to rubble and weddings turned to bloodbaths. It is the cries of a hungry infant in its dead mother's arms, and a wife carried in the arms of a keening husband. It is the end of faith for old people and the destruction of hope for the young. It is a young soldier who dies calling for his mother and a surviving soldier with a "thousand-yard stare" who is condemned to a lifetime of hell no one understands. It is a medic who can't wash the blood off his hands.

It is a theft from those who are hungry and will never be fed, those who are homeless who will never be housed, and those in need of care who will never receive it. It is the theft of a family's future generations and a society's future leaders. It is the loss of a country's soul. It is misery and pain, destruction and degradation that sow the seeds for more of the same. It is evil, and there are no winners. This, then, is the human cost of war.

Mary, and her fellow Army nurse Sue O'Neill, visited our class and overwhelmed our students with their honesty and courage. They, along with Bill Ehrhart, John Ketwig, and Kimo Williams, are among the scores of Vietnam veterans who've joined us and shared their war experiences. Another kind of sharing occurred when the members of the Vets On Frets musical group, an offshoot of Guitars for Vets, serenaded the class with songs and stories. "Who'll Stop the Rain" is among their selections, as are "For What It's Worth," "Detroit City," and some original compositions. Our students were always moved, as were the vet musicians, according to Rick Larson, a Vets on Frets organizer. Rick was a hospital corpsman aboard the USS Repose off the coast of South Vietnam from 1968–69. Playing the guitar, privately and publicly, has been important and thera-peutic for him, and he is quick to credit Guitars for Vets for helping him learn his craft.

"Vets on Frets didn't leave Guitars for Vets," he explained. "One of the instructors in Guitars for Vets wanted to form a group where veterans who'd learned the rudiments of the guitar could continue playing."

Neil O'Connor, the group's 12-string guitar player and an Army veteran, added: "Think of Vets on Frets more as a spin-off from the national guitar instruction program, a sort of 'independent study' group, if you will."

Whatever you want to call it, the prevailing notion of using music as therapy—in this instance guitar playing—has proven extremely popular. Today, Guitars for Vets (G4V), which originated in Milwaukee in 2007, now has more than 40 chapters in 20 states and has served more than 2,000 veterans. According to co-founder Patrick Nettesheim, G4V provides veterans with 10 free private guitar lessons. "Just giving somebody a guitar is like giving somebody a plane and them not knowing how to fly; that's where the teaching element comes in," he explained. Upon completion, the vet gets a free Yamaha FG700S guitar with a gig bag that includes an extra set of strings, picks, an electric guitar tuner, a peg winder, a strap, and a guitar stand.

Craig and I met Pat and his G4V co-founder Dan Van Buskirk at LZ Lambeau in 2010 where they gave a dynamic presentation. And we've shared the stage with our Vets on Frets friends here in Madison on several occasions because we all believe in the power of music to soothe and to heal. G4V's Nettesheim said it best when he told Milwaukee's Shepherd Express that Guitars for Vets is "healing the world through music. What better utilization of the talent that I have and all the volunteers have than to bring those who are in pain some windows of serenity once again and help them find their joy? Guitars for Vets can help soften the heart. It's an actual practice of loving kindness. And we're building community with our guitars, and I believe that peace eventually will come to this world via the experience of our warriors because their understanding of the brutality of war is very deep and very troubling."

And so, the music continues to play. In our heads and in our hearts. And it may be just what helps to get us through this last wall of Vietnam.

On the final day of our UW class about music and Vietnam—just before we play "Who'll Stop the Rain"—Craig and our two TAs, William Schuth and Anthony Black, both post 9/11 Marine veterans, give their final thoughts on the semester-long journey. Over 15 weeks, we've read, written, talked, listened, and absorbed Vietnam through visits from vets like Mary Reynolds Powell, Sue O'Neill, Moses Mora, Native drum circle leader Tom Holm, Jay Maloney, spiritual activist and caretaker Sister Sarge, poet Bill Ehrhart, and cyber griot Art Flowers. Ultimately, our students struggle with the same dilemmas as Vietnam vets, seeking answers to the same questions. Because I am the teaching team's Vietnam veteran, they let me play the final chorus, have the last word. I look out over the room, take a deep breath, and share a story from my 365 days at war in Vietnam. I repeat it here to close this chapter, this book, this odyssey, with the knowledge that it isn't the last word on Vietnam. But with the hope it sends a call to a wounded America, and that America can finally lay it down, ultimately respond to Vietnam veterans with understanding and harmony.

SOLO Doug Bradley

During my tour in Vietnam, many GIs embellished their traditional Army outfits with everything from love beads, necklaces, and in some cases, peace symbols, none of which the military brass approved of. One of the more striking accoutrements a soldier could wear was a Montagnard bracelet. Handcrafted by tribesmen from the Central Highlands, the customary bracelets were made from old brass shells beaten down, filed, etched, and polished with sandstones. The gift of one of these bracelets is considered a high honor and bestows upon the receiver a lifelong commitment of friendship from the giver. And therein lies my story.

One of my more interesting assignments as a U.S. Army information specialist in Vietnam was to prepare an article for *Uptight,* an in-country Army magazine, on the basic training of young South Vietnamese soldiers. At that time, the ARVN, as we called them—the initials stood for Army of the Republic of Vietnam—were taking on more of the ground war while we began sending our combat units home. I spent a few days at a basic training site near Long Thanh, interviewing ARVN drill instructors, U.S. Army advisors, and young recruits. I also met a Montagnard soldier, and as I prepared to leave, he presented me with a bracelet, asking that I, in return, promise to bring peace to Vietnam. Taken aback, I apologetically told him "I'm afraid I'm not able to do that."

He shook his head and then shared this universal tale, which, curiously, I've heard echoes of in Toni Morrison's speech accepting the Nobel prize for literature. She introduced the tale by saying, "I have heard this story, or one exactly like it, in the lore of several cultures." One of those is the Montagnard culture.

"In our village," my new Montagnard friend began, "there is one elder who commands the most respect and authority. He's able to predict the future and possesses the wisdom to solve every problem, answer every question. One of the young newcomers in the village brags to his friends and neighbors that he knows how to baffle the village elder and, eventually, the day of reckoning arrives. The young man, holding a lizard behind his back, approaches the elder, and poses a question.

"Tell me, all-knowing one," he asks, "if the lizard I'm holding behind my back is alive or dead."

The elder pauses, listening intently. The young man repeats his question. "Is the lizard I'm holding alive or dead?" The young questioner is confident in the knowledge that if the elder says the lizard is alive, he'll squeeze and kill it. If the elder says it's dead, he'll show him that the lizard is alive.

The young man must repeat the question a third time, and, as everyone in the village watches, the tribal elder looks at the young man and says: 'The answer to that, my friend, is in your hands.'"

Let's all open our hands and see what we hold.

About the Author

Doug Bradley has written extensively about his Vietnam, and post-Vietnam, experiences. Drafted into the U.S. Army in March 1970, he served as an information specialist (journalist) for the U.S. Army Republic of Vietnam headquarters at Long Binh, South Vietnam, from November 1970 to November 1971. Doug relocated to Madison, Wisconsin, in 1974 where he helped establish Vets House, a storefront, community-based service center for Vietnam-era veterans. He is the author of *DEROS Vietnam: Dispatches from the Air-Conditioned Jungle* and co-author, with Craig Werner, of *We Gotta Get Out of This Place: The Soundtrack of the Vietnam War* (UMass Press, 2015), which was named BEST MUSIC BOOK of 2015 by *Rolling Stone* magazine.

ACKNOWLEDGMENTS

"Acknowledging" can't begin to express the extent of my gratitude and gratefulness to the many wonderful people who have sustained me every mile of this journey.

My family is first and foremost. Loving thanks to my wife, Pam Shannon, my daughter Summer, and my son Ian, and their spouses Brandon Strand and Mary Bradley. There's also an extended family of Shannons, Bradleys, and Strands who have never wavered in their support, and I can't thank them enough. Perhaps best of all, my young grandsons, Jack and Bo Strand, have brightened my world each and every day. A writer couldn't have two better muses than Bo and Jack. And while I lost my beloved father-in-law, Ted Shannon, and number one fan, my mom Lucy Bradley, during the writing of Who'll Stop the Rain, they hovered over my shoulder every day.

My dear friend, and *We Gotta Get Out of This Place* co-author Craig Werner, has been a most dependable ally throughout. He's a one-of-a-kind teacher, scholar, writer, and music aficionado. Craig's insights, edits, and contributions have enhanced this book greatly.

Others, too, have helped, in ways large and small, among them Missy Dehn Kubitschek, Gretchen Poston, and my Vietnam brother Jim Wachtendonk's art and music. My industrious editor, Julia Dye, has been instrumental in molding *Who'll Stop the Rain* into its final shape.

My deepest thanks go to the men and women whose voices and experiences fill these pages—and to the musicians and artists whose music has helped them, and me, to get home from the war. Too many to spell out, but essential shout outs to Chuck and Tom Hagel, Karl Marlantes, Sue O'Neill, Bill Ehrhart, Mary Reynolds Powell, Dan Naylor, Bill Christofferson, Moses Mora, Mai Nguyen, John Mikelson, Shad Meshad, and Bob Fraser. Special thanks to Dave Boocker at the University of Nebraska at Omaha for the invitation to their exceptional 2016 Vietnam symposium and to Jeff Kollath of the Stax Museum of American Soul Music for his support.

Last, but not least, profound thanks to all the women and men, veterans and non-veterans, who joined me and Craig in honest conversation about war, music, and memory. They openly shared their experiences, pain, guilt, redemption—and hope. Their optimism gives me hope and makes me think we just might stop the rain.

—Doug Bradley, Madison, WI, Fall 2019

FINALE

To listen to a playlist of the songs that inspired this book, go to : warbooks.pub/playlist

"Who'll Stop the Rain"—CCR. Written by John Fogerty. Performed by Creedence Clearwater Revival. Produced by John Fogerty. Released by Fantasy Records in January 1970.

"Can I Get a Witness"—Marvin Gaye. Written by Brian Holland, Eddie Holland, and Lamont Dozier. Performed by Marvin Gaye. Produced by Brian Holland and Lamont Dozier. Released by UNI/Motown in September, 1964.

"Fortunate Son"—CCR. Written by John Fogerty. Performed by Creedence Clearwater Revival. Produced by John Fogerty. Released by Fantasy Records in November 1969.

"Run Through the Jungle"—CCR. Written by John Fogerty. Performed by Creedence Clearwater Revival. Produced by John Fogerty. Released by Fantasy Records in April 1970.

"Bad Moon Rising"—CCR. Written by John Fogerty. Performed by Creedence Clearwater Revival. Produced by John Fogerty. Released by Fantasy Records in April 1969.

"Proud Mary"—CCR. Written by John Fogerty. Performed by Creedence Clearwater Revival. Produced by John Fogerty. Released by Fantasy Records in January 1969.

"Green River"—CCR. Written by John Fogerty. Performed by Creedence Clearwater Revival. Produced by John Fogerty. Released by Fantasy Records in August 1969.

"Hey Tonight"—CCR. Written by John Fogerty. Performed by Creedence Clearwater Revival. Produced by John Fogerty. Released by Fantasy Records in January 1970.

"We Gotta Get Out of This Place"—the Animals. "We Gotta Get Out of This Place." Written by Barry Mann and Cynthia Weil. Performed by The Animals. Produced by Released in the U.S., MGM, August 1965.

"I'll Take You There"—Staple Singers. Written by Alvertis Isbell. Performed by The Staple Singers. Produced by Al Bell. Released by Stax in February 1972.

"Love Letters in the Sand"—Pat Boone. Written by Charles F. Kenny, J. Fred Coots, and Nick A. Kenny. Performed by Pat Boone and Billy Vaughn. Produced by Randy Wood. Released by Geffen in 1957.

"Heartbreak Hotel"—Elvis Presley. Written by Elvis Presley, Mae Boren Axton, and Tommy Durden. Performed Elvis Presley. Produced by Steve Sholes. Released by RCA Records Label in January 1956.

"Blue Suede Shoes"—Carl Perkins. Written by Carl Perkins. Performed by Elvis Presley. Released by RCA Victor in September 1956.

"Marching off to War"—William Bell. Written by Eddie Floyd. Performed by William Bell. Released by Stax in 1966.

"I Stand Accused"—Isaac Hayes. Written by Billy Butler and Jerry Butler. Performed by Isaac Hayes. Released by Stax in April 1970.

"Angel of the Morning"—Merilee Rush. Written by Chip Taylor. Performed by Merrilee Rush & the Turnabouts. Released by Arista/Legacy in February 1968.

"Fire"—Crazy World of Arthur Brown. Written by Arthur Brown, Vincent Krane, Mike Finesilver, and Peter Ker. Performed by the Crazy world of Arthur Brown. Released by Esoteric Recordings in 1968.

"Reflections of My Life"—Marmalade. Written by William Campbell and Thomas McAleese. Performed by Marmalade. Released by Decca in November 1969.

"Rainbow"—Marmalade. Written by William Campbell and Thomas McAleese. Performed by Marmalade. Released by Decca in 1970.

"Waist Deep in the Big Muddy"—Pete Seeger. Written by Pete Seeger. Performed by Pete Seeger. Produced by John Hammond. Released by Columbia Records in 1967.

"Houston"—Dean Martin. Written by L. Hazelwood. Performed by Dean Martin. Produced by Jimmy Brown. Released by Legacy Recordings in the Summer of 1965.

"Soldier Boy"—the Shirelles. Written Florence Greenburg and Luther Dixon. Performed by the Shirelles. Released by Bell Sound Studios in 1962.

"Mr. Lonely"—Bobby Vinton. Written by Bobby Vinton and Gene Allan. Performed by Bobby Vinton. Produced by Bob Morgan. Released by Epic/Legacy in 1964.

"Stand By Me"—Ben E. King. Written by Ben E. King, Jerry Leiber, and Mike Stoller. Produced by Jerry Leiber, and Mike Stoller. Released by Atco in April 1961.

"Bring the Boys Home"—Freda Payne. Written by Angelo Bond, General Johnson, and Greg Perry. Performed by Freda Payne. Released by Invictus Is 9092 in May 1971.

"Blame It on My Youth"—Fred Astaire

"Rainy Night in Georgia"—Brooke Benton. Written by Tony Joe White. Performed by Brook Benton. Released by Cotillion/Atlantic in 1969.

"Ring of Fire"—Johnny Cash. Written by J Carter and M. Kilgore Performed by Johnny Cash. Produced by Don Law and Frank Jones. Released by Columbia Nashville Records in April 1963.

"San Francisco Bay Blues"—Jesse Fuller. Written by Jesse Fuller. Performed by Jesse Fuller. Released by World Song in 1955.

"Ventura Highway"—America. Written by Dewey Bunnell. Performed by America. Produced by America. Released by Warner Records in September 1972.

"I Get Around"—Beach Boys. Written by Brian Wilson and Mike Love. Performed by The Beach Boys. Produced by Brian Wilson. Released by Capital Records in May 1964.

"Good Vibrations"—Beach Boys. Written by Brian Wilson and Mike Love. Performed by The Beach Boys. Produced by Brian Wilson. Released by Capital Records in October 1966.

"Fun, Fun, Fun"—the Beach Boys. Written by Brian Wilson and Mike Love. Performed by The Beach Boys. Produced by Brian Wilson. Released by Capital Records in January 1964.

"Sloop John B"—Beach Boys. Written by Brian Wilson and Mike Love. Performed by The Beach Boys. Produced by Brian Wilson. Released by Capital Records in December 1966.

"Johnny B Goode"—Chuck Berry. Written by Chuck Berry. Performed by Chuck Berry. Produced by Leonard Chess and Phil Cares. Released by Chess in March 1958.

"Okie from Muskogee"—Merle Haggard. Written by Roy Edward Burris and Merle Haggard. Performed by Merle Haggard. Produced by Fuzzy Owen. Released by Capital in September 1969.

"Fighting Side of Me"—Merle Haggard. Written by Merle Haggard. Performed by Merle Haggard. Produced by Ken Nelson. Released by Capital in January 1970.

"Ballad of the Green Berets"—Barry Sadler. Written by Robin Moore and Sgt. Berry Sadler. Performed by Sgt. Berry Sadler and Sid Bass. Produced by Andy Wiswell. Released by RCA Victor in January 1966.

"I Ain't a Marchin Anymore"—Phil Ochs. Written by Phil Ochs. Performed by Phil Ochs. Produced by Jac Holzman and Paul A. Rothchild. Released by Elektra in 1965.

"Draft Dodger Rag"—Phil Ochs. Written by Phil Ochs. Performed by Phil Ochs. Produced by Jac Holzman. Released by Elektra in 1965.

"Lyndon Johnson Told the Nation"—Tom Paxton. Written by Tom Paxton. Performed by Tom Paxton. Produced by Paul A. Rothchild. Released by Rhino/Elektra in 1965.

"Don't Think Twice It's Alright"—Bob Dylan. Written by Bob Dylan. Performed by Bob Dylan. Produced by John Hammond. Released by Columbia in August 1963.

"Blowin in the Wind"—Bob Dylan. Written by Bob Dylan. Performed by Bob Dylan. Produced by John Hammond. Released by Columbia Studios in August 1963.

"The Times They Are A' Changin"—Bob Dylan. Written by Bob Dylan. Performed by Bob Dylan. Produced by John Wilson. Released by Columbia Studios in January 1964.

"With God On Our Side"—Bob Dylan. Written by Bob Dylan. Performed by Bob Dylan. Produced by Tom Wilson. Released by Columbia Studios in January 1964

"Masters of War"—Bob Dylan. Written by Bob Dylan. Performed by Bob Dylan. Produced by Tom Wilson. Released by Columbia Records in May 1963.

"Like a Rolling Stone"—Bob Dylan. Written by Bob Dylan. Performed by Bob Dylan. Produced by Tom Wilson. Released by Columbia Studios in July 1964.

"Desolation Row"—Bob Dylan. Written by Bob Dylan. Performed by Bob Dylan. Produced by Bob Johnston. Released by Columbia Studios in August 1965.

"War"—Edwin Starr. Written by Barrett Strong and Norman Whitfield. Performed by Edwin Starr. Produced by Edwin Starr. Released by UNI/Motown in June 1970.

"Summer Soldier"—Stewart Francke. Written by Stewart Francke. Performed by Stewart Francke and Bruce Springsteen. Released by Blue Boundary Records in May 2011.

"A Change is Gonna Come"—Sam Cooke. Written by Sam Cooke. Performed by Sam Cooke. Released by RCA Victor in February 1964.

"While My Guitar Gently Weeps"—Beatles. Written by George Harrison. Performed by the Beatles. Produced by George Martin. Released by Apple/EMI Studios in November 1968.

"I Want to Hold Your Hand"—the Beatles. Written by John Lennon and Paul McCartney. Performed by the Beatles. Produced by George Martin and Giles Martin. Released by Parlophone/EMI Studios in November 1963.

"Sgt. Pepper's Lonely Hearts Club Band"—Beatles. Written by John Lennon and Paul McCartney. Performed by The Beatles. Produced by George Martin. Released by Parlophone/EMI Studios in May 1967.

Sgt. Pepper (album)—the Beatles. Performed by The Beatles. Produced by George Martin. Released by Parlophone/EMI Studios in May 1967.

"Hey Jude"—the Beatles, Written by John Lennon and Paul McCartney. Performed by the Beatles. Produced by George Martin and Giles Martin. Released by Apple in August 1968.

The White Album—the Beatles. Performed by The Beatles. Produced by George Martin. Released by Apple/EMI Studios in November 1968.

"Say it Loud, I'm Black and I'm Proud"—James Brown. Written by James Brown and Alfred Ellis. Performed by James Brown. Produced by James Brown. Released by King in August 1968.

"Papa's Got a Brand New Bag"—James Brown. Written by James Brown. Performed by James Brown. Produced by James Brown. Released by King in June 1965.

"Come See About Me"—the Supremes. Written by Brian Holland, Eddie Holland, and Lamont Dozier. Performed by The Supremes. Produced by Brian Holland and Lamont Dozier. Released by Motown in October 1964.

"Where Did Our Love Go"—the Supremes. Written by Brian Holland, Edward Holland Jr., and Lamont Dozier. Performed by the Supremes. Produced by Brian Holland and Lamont Dozier. Released by Motown in June 1964.

"You Can't Hurry Love"—the Supremes. Written by Brian Holland, Eddie Holland, and Lamont Dozier. Performed by the Supremes. Produced by Brian Holland and Lamont Dozier. Released by Motown in July 1966.

"My Girl"—the Temptations. Written by Ronald White and Smokey Robinson. Performed by the Temptations. Produced by Smokey Robinson and Ronald White. Released by Motown in December 1964.

"Gimme Shelter"—The Rolling Stones. Written by Keith Richards and Mick Jagger. Performed by the Rolling Stones. Produced by Jimmy Miller. Released by ABKCO in December 1968.

"Under My Thumb"—Rolling Stones. Written by Keith Richards and Mick Jagger. Performed by the Rolling Stones. Produced by Andrew Loog Oldham. Released by ABKCO in April 1966.

"Satisfaction"—the Rolling Stones. Written by Keith Richards and Mick Jagger. Performed by the Rolling Stones. Produced by Andrew Loog Oldham. Released by ABKCO in June 1965.

"Feel Like I'm Fixin' to Die Rag"—Country Joe and the Fish. Written by Joe McDonald. Performed by Country Joe and the Fish. Released by Vanguard Records in 1967.

"California Dreaming"—the Mamas and the Papas. Written by John Phillis and Michelle Phillips. Performed by the Mamas and the Papas. Produced by Lou Adler. Released by Dunhill Records in December 1965.

"Monday Monday"—the Mamas and the Papas. Written by John Phillips. Performed by The Mamas and the Papas. Produced by Lou Adler. Released Dunhill Records in March 1966.

"Hold On I'm Coming"—Sam and Dave. Written by David Porter and Isaac Hayes. Performed by Sam and Dave. Released by Stax/ Atlantic in March 1966.

"Soul Man"—Sam and Dave. Written by David Porter and Isaac Hayes. Performed by Sam and Dave. Produced by Dave Porter and Isaac Hayes. Released by Stax/Atlantic in September 1967.

"Chain of Fools"—Aretha Franklin. Written by Don Covay. Performed by Aretha Franklin. Produced by Jerry Wexler. Released by Atlantic in November 1967.

"Time Has Come Today"—Chambers Brothers. Written by Joseph Chambers and Willie Chambers. Performed by The Chamber Brothers. Produced by Al Quaglieri, Steve Berkowitz, and David Rubinson. Released by Columbia in December 1967.

"Down in the Bottom"—Howlin Wolf. Written by Willie Dixon. Performed by Howlin Wolf. Produced by Willie Dixon, Leonard Chess, and Phil Chess. Released by Chess in January 1962.

"Jimmy Mack"—Martha and the Vandellas. Written by Brian Holland, Eddie Holland, and Lamont Dozier. Performed by Martha Reeves and the Vendellas. Produced by Brian Holland and Lamont Dozier. Released by UNI/Motown in February 1967.

"Homeward Bound"—Simon and Garfunkel. Written by Paul Simon. Performed by Simon and Garfunkel. Produced by Bob Johnson. Released by Columbia/Legacy in January 1966.

"Bridge Over Troubled Water"—Simon and Garfunkel. Written by Paul Simon. Performed by Simon and Garfunkel. Produced by Paul Simon, Art Garfunkel, and Roy Halee. Released by Columbia in January 1970.

"Scarborough Fair"—Simon and Garfunkel. Performed by Simon and Garfunkel. Produced by Bob Johnson. Released by Columbia/Legacy in 1966.

"Sounds of Silence"—Simon and Garfunkel. Written by Paul Simon. Performed by Simon and Garfunkel. Produced by Tom Wilson. Released by Columbia/Legacy in September 1965.

"Detroit City"—Bobby Bare. Written by Danny Dill and Mel Tillis. Performed by Bobby Bare. Produced by Chet Atkins. Released by RCA Victor in May 1963.

"Wolverton Mountain"—Claude King. Written by Carole King and M. Kilgore. Performed by Claude King. Produced by Don Law and Frank Jones. Released by Columbia in March 1962.

"Sittin on the Dock of the Bay"—Otis Redding. Written by Otis Redding and Steve Cropper. Performed by Otis Redding. Produced by Steve Cropper. Released by Rhino Atlantic in January 1968.

"And When I Die"—Blood, Sweat and Tears. Written by Laura Nyro. Performed by Blood, Sweat, and Tears. Produced by James William Guercio. Released by Columbia in September 1969.

"In-a-Gadda-da-vida"—Iron Butterfly. Written by Doug Ingle. Performed by Iron Butterfly. Produced by Jim Hilton. Released by Rhino/Elektra in June 1968.

"The Letter"—the Box Tops. Written by Wayne Carson. Performed by the Box Tops. Produced by Dan Penn. Released by Arista/Legacy in August 1967.

"Purple Haze"—Jimi Hendrix. Written by Jimi Hendrix. Performed by Jimi Hendrix. Produced by Chas Chandler and Dave Siddle. Released by Legacy Recordings in March 1967.

"Machine Gun"–Jimi Hendrix. Written by Jimi Hendrix. Produced by Jimi Hendrix. Produced by Heaven Research. Released by Capital Records in March 1970.

"Star-Spangled Banner"–Jimi Hendrix. Written by Francis Scott Key. Performed by Jimi Hendrix. Released by Legacy Recordings in 1970.

"All Along the Watchtower"–Jimi Hendrix. Written by Bob Dylan. Performed by Jimi Hendrix. Produced by Jimi Hendrix. Released by Legacy Recordings in January 1968.

"These Boots Are Made for Walkin'"–Nancy Sinatra. Written by Lee Hazlewood. Performed by Nancy Sinatra. Produced by Lee Hazlewood. Released by Reprise in December 1965.

"Last Train to Clarksville"–the Monkees. Written by Bobby Hart and Tommy Boyce. Performed by The Monkees. Produced by Bobby Hart and Tommy Boyce. Released by Colgems/Rhino in August 1966.

"For What It's Worth"–Buffalo Springfield. Written by Stephen Stills. Performed by Buffalo Springfield. Produced by Brian Stone and Charles Green. Released by Rhino/Elektra in December 1966.

"Piece of My Heart"–Big Brother/Janis Joplin. Written by Bert Berns and Jerry Ragovoy. Performed by Big Brother & Janis Joplin. Produced by John Simon. Released by Columbia/Legacy in 1968.

"Leaving on a Jet Plane"–Peter, Paul and Mary. Written by John Denver. Performed by Peter, Paul, and Mary. Produced by Albert B. Grossman. Released by Warner Records in October 1969.

"Where Have All the Flowers Gone"–Peter, Paul and Mary. Written by Pete Seeger. Performed by Peter, Paul, and Mary. Produced by Albert B. Grossman. Released by Rhino/Warner Records in March 1965.

"Riders on the Storm"–the Doors. Written by Jim Morrison, John Densmore, and Ray Manzarek. Performed by The Doors. Produced by Bruce Botnick, Jim Morrison, John Densmore, Ray Manzarek, and Bobby Krieger. Released by Rhino/Elektra in June 1971.

"White Rabbit"—Jefferson Airplane. Written by Grace Slick. Performed by Jefferson Airplane. Produced by Rick Jarrad. Released by RCA Victor in June 1967.

"Ohio"—Crosby Stills Nash and Young. Written by Neil Young. Performed by Crosby, Stills, Nash, and Young. Produced by Crosby, Stills, Nash, and Young. Released by Rhino Atlantic in June 1970.

"Vietnam Veterano"—Al Reyes. Written by Al Reyes. Performed Al Reyes. Released by Smithsonian Folkways Recordings in September 2005.

"What's Going On"—Marvin Gaye. Written by Al Cleveland, Marvin Gaye, and Renaldo Benson. Performed by Marvin Gaye. Produced by Marvin Gaye. Released by Motown in May 1971.

"Back Streets"—Bruce Springsteen. Written by Bruce Springsteen. Performed by Bruce Springsteen. Produced by Bruce Springsteen, Jon Landau, and Mike Appel. Released by Columbia Records in August in 1975.

"Lost in the Flood"—Bruce Springsteen. Written by Bruce Springsteen. Performed by Bruce Springsteen. Produced by Mike Appel and Jim Cretecos. Released by Columbia Records in January 1973.

"Brothers Under the Bridge"—Bruce Springsteen. Written by Bruce Springsteen. Performed by Bruce Springsteen. Produced by Bruce Springsteen and Chuck Plotkin. Released by Columbia Legacy in 1998.

"Born in the USA"—Bruce Springsteen. Written by Bruce Springsteen. Performed by Bruce Springsteen. Produced by Bruce Springsteen, Stevie Van Zandt, Jon Landau, and Chuck Plotkin. Released by Columbia in June 1984.

"Tunnel Rat (flashlight and .45)"—Billy Bang. Written by Billy Bang. Performed by Billy Bang. Produced by Justin Time Records in 2001.

"Tet Offensive"—Billy Bang. Written by Billy Bang. Performed by Billy Bang. Produced by Justin Time Records in 2001.

"Saigon Phunk"—Billy Bang. Written by Billy Bang. Performed by Billy Bang. Produced by Justin Time Records in 2001.

"Fire in the Hole"—Billy Bang. Written by Billy Bang. Performed by Billy Bang. Produced by Justin Time Records in 2001.

"Bien Hoa Blues"—Billy Bang. Written by Billy Bang. Performed by Billy Bang. Produced by Justin Time Records in 1998.

"Doi Moi"—Billy Bang. Written by Billy Bang. Performed by Billy Bang. Produced by Justin Time Records in 2005.

"White Christmas"—Bing Crosby. Written by Irving Berlin. Performed by Bing Crosby, John Scott Trotter & His Orchestra, and Ken Darby Singers. Produced by John Scott Trotter. Released Decca/Geffen in 1942.

"Symphony for the Sons of Nam"—Kimo Williams. Written by Kimo Williams. Performed by Kimo Williams. Released by Little Beck Music in 2007.

"Vietnam Vet"—Dick Jonas. Written by Dick Jonas. Performed by Dick Jonas. Released by Coldpix in 1997.

Shellshock PTSD—Blind Albert

"Veterans Lament"—Jim Cook and Taylor McKinnon. Written by Jim Cook and Taylor McKinnon. Performed by Jim Cook and Taylor McKinnon. Released by Holly Records in 2002.

"This Shirt of Mine"—Sarge Lincecum

VA Shuffle—Martin and Holiday

Who Are the Names on the Wall—Martin and Holiday

Time to Lay it Down—Martin and Holiday

Claymore Polka—Jim Wachtendonk

Hurting More—Jim Wachtendonk

A Love Supreme—John Coltrane. Written by John Coltrane. Performed by John Coltrane. Produced by Bob Thiele. Released by Impulse! in January 1965.

"Woodstock"—Joni Mitchell. Written by Joni Mitchell. Performed by Joni Mitchell. Produced by Joni Mitchell. Released by Reprise/Rhino in April 1970.

"There's a Kind of Hush"—Herman's Hermits. Written by Geoff Stephens and Les Reed. Performed by Herman's Hermits. Produced by Mickie Most. Released by Abko Music & Records, Inc. in January 1967.

"San Francisco (Be Sure to Wear Flowers in Your Hair)"—Scott McKenzie. Written by John Phillips. Performed by Scott McKenzie. Produced by John Philips and Lou Adler. Released by Columbia/Legacy in May 1967.

"Ruby Don't Take Your Love to Town"—Kenny Rogers and the First Edition. Written by Mel Tillis. Performed by Kenny Rogers & The First Edition. Produced by Jimmy Bowen. Released by Universal Music Enterprises in 1969.

"Brown Eyed Girl"—Van Morrison. Written by Van Morrison. Performed by Van Morrison. Produced by Bert Burns. Released by Columbia/Legacy in June 1967.

"There Isn't Any Jukebox in the Jungle"—Gordon Fowler

"Down Hearted Blues"—Bessie Smith. Written by Alberta Hunter and Lovie Austin. Performed by Bessie Smith. Released by Columbia/Legacy in February 1923.

FOR FURTHER READING

Several of the contributors to *Who'll Stop the Rain* have written about their Vietnam and post-Vietnam experiences, and I've highlighted some prominent examples here. In addition, a handful of books and articles have greatly influenced my thinking and perspective, likewise noted. Finally, while books about the music of the Vietnam War are a rarity, there are a few that either emphasize the music per se, allude to its significance, or highlight its consumer aspects.

Bradley, Doug and Werner, Craig. *We Gotta Get Out of This Place: The Soundtrack of the Vietnam War*. University of Massachusetts Press, 2015.

Werner, Craig. *A Change Is Gonna Come: Music, Race, and the Soul of America*. University of Michigan Press; Revised edition, 2006; *Up Around the Bend: An Oral History of Creedence Clearwater Revival*. Avon Books, 1999; and *Higher Ground: Stevie Wonder, Aretha Franklin, Curtis Mayfield, and the Rise and Fall of American Soul*. Crown, 2004.

Reporting Vietnam: American Journalism 1959–1975. Library of America, 1998.

Fitzgerald, Frances. *Fire in the Lake: The Vietnamese and the Americans in Vietnam*. Little Brown, 1972.

Karnow, Stanley, *Vietnam: A History*. Random House, 1983.

Young, Marilyn. *Vietnam Wars 1945–1990*. Harper Perennial, Reprint edition 1991.

Bear Family Records. *Next Stop Is Vietnam: The War On Record, 1961–2008*. 13 CDs and a 304-page book. Hambergen, Germany, 2010.

Powell, Mary Reynolds. *A World of Hurt: Between Innocence and Arrogance in Vietnam*. Greenleaf Book Group, 2000.

Sheehan, Neil. *A Bright Shining Lie*. Vintage Books, 1989.

Emerson, Gloria. *Winners and Losers: Battles, Retreats, Gains, Losses and Ruins from the Vietnam War*. Random House, 1977.

Vea, Alfredo. *Gods Go Begging*. Penguin Group, 1999.

Marlantes, Karl. *Matterhorn: A Novel of the Vietnam War*. Grove Press, 2010; and *What it is Like to Go to War*. Atlantic Monthly Press, 2011.

O'Neil, Susan. *Don't Mean Nothing*. Serving House Books, 2010.

Hemingway, Ernest. *In Our Time*. Scribner, 1925.

Maraniss, David. *They Marched Into Sunlight*. Simon & Schuster, 2003.

Appy, Christian G. *Working-Class War: American Combat Soldiers and Vietnam*. University of North Carolina Press, 1993; and Patriots, The Vietnam War Remembered from All Sides. Penguin, 2003.

Houdek, Matthew and Phillips, Kendall R. "Public Memory" in *Oxford Research Encyclopedia of Communication*. January 2017.

Schonfeld, Zach. "How Creedence Clearwater Revival Became the Soundtrack to Every Vietnam Movie." *Pitchfork*. February 20, 2018.

Ketwig, John. *...and a hard rain fell: A G.I.'s True Story of the War in Vietnam*. Macmillan, 1985; and *Vietnam Reconsidered: The War, the Times, and Why They Matter*. Trine Day Publishing, 2019.

Bolger, Daniel P. *Our Year of War: Two Brothers, Vietnam, and a Nation Divided*. Da Capo Press, 2017.

Hagopian, Patrick. *The Vietnam War in American Memory: Veterans, Memorials, and the Politics of Healing*. University of Massachusetts Press, 2009.

Kieran, David. *Forever Vietnam: How a Divisive War Changed American Public Memory.* University of Massachusetts Press, 2014.

Lin, Maya, "Making the Memorial." *New York Review of Books.* November 2, 2000.

Komunyakaa, Yusef. *Dien Cai Dau.* Wesleyan University Press, 1988.

Lembcke, Jerry. *The Spitting Image: Myth, Memory, and the Legacy of Vietnam.* NYU Press, 2000.

Van Devanter, Lynda. *Home Before Morning: The Story of an Army Nurse in Vietnam.* University of Massachusetts Press. Reprint edition, 2001.

Hasford, Gustav. *The Short-Timers.* Harper & Row, 1979.

Deadly Writers Patrol magazine: https://www.deadlywriterspatrol.org

Meshad, Shad. *Captain for Dark Mornings: A True Story.* Creative Image Associates, 1982.

Linehan, Adam. "Sebastian Junger: Over-Valorizing Vets Does More Harm Than Good." *Task & Purpose,* May, 2016.

Lair, Meredith H. *Armed with Abundance: Consumerism and Soldiering in the Vietnam War.* University of North Carolina Press, 2011.

Rottman, Larry; Barry, Jan; and Paquet, Basil (editors). *Winning Hearts and Minds: War Poems by Vietnam Veterans.* First Casualty Press, 1972.

O'Brien, Tim. *The Things They Carried.* Houghton Mifflin, 1990.

Herr, Michael. *Dispatches.* Knopf, 1977.

Terry, Wallace. *Bloods: Black Veterans of the Vietnam War: An Oral History.* Ballantine, 1985.

Marsh, Dave. *The Heart Of Rock & Soul: The 1001 Greatest Singles Ever Made.* Da Capo Press, 1999.

Kingston, Maxine Hong (editor). *Veterans of War, Veterans of Peace*. Koa Books, 2006.

Ninh, Bao. *The Sorrow of War*. Riverhead Books, 1999.

Wilcox, Fred A. *Waiting for an Army to Die: The Tragedy of Agent Orange*. Seven Stories Press, September 2011.

Conrad, Thomas. "Billy Bang: Separate Peace." *Jazz Times*, December 2005.

Ehrhart, W.D. *Vietnam-Perkasie: A Combat Marine Memoir*. McFarland and Company, 1983.

Kovic, Ron. *Born on the Fourth of July*. Pocket, 1976.

Sack, John. *M*. New American Library, 1966.

Rabe, David. *The Basic Training of Pavlo Hummel*; *Sticks and Bones*; *Streamers* (plays).